TO/ ALFR

WHAT A GREAT MACHINT BUGGER ME I STILL COR SPELL

Peter Hill

BEER, THERE AND
EVERYWHERE

A twenty-six year pub crawl
(The early years 1984-1990)

I was born in 1956, in West Bromwich, Staffordshire and educated at Greets Green School, until 1967, then Manor High School, Wednesbury, until 1972. Starting as a Trainee Draughtsman at Stelwyn Construction, Oldbury, then leaving to become an apprentice with Delta Rods in Greets Green. A year was spent at the Training Centre, Dartmouth Street, Birmingham (1973 to 1974). Returning to be a maintenance engineer and receiving 25 years of service award in 1998. My hobbies include darts, cartoon drawing, dialect poems and watching West Bromwich Albion (Up the Baggies).

I've made two model metal plaques of pubs, one in 1990, which hangs in the pub in the Black Country museum. The other, in 1993, hangs in the pub at Blists Hill Museum. I've self-published three booklets: *A Black Country pub-crawl of West Bromwich*, *101 pubs in the Black Country* and *Family pubs in the Black Country*. The Black Country Ale Tairsters make the 1991, 92 and 93 Guinness Book of Records, and are currently in the Ripley's book of amazing facts. I've been with my partner Dawn, since our 1500th pub and have a son Wade, 19 and a daughter Jodee, 17.

BEER, THERE AND EVERYWHERE

A twenty-six year pub crawl
(The early years 1984-1990)

Peter Hill

BEER, THERE AND EVERYWHERE

A twenty-six year pub crawl
(The early years 1984-1990)

Olympia Publishers
London

www.olympiapublishers.com
OLYMPIA PAPERBACK EDITION

Copyright © Peter Hill 2011

The right of Peter Hill to be identified as author of
this work has been asserted in accordance with sections 77 and 78 of the
Copyright, Designs and Patents Act 1988.

All Rights Reserved

No reproduction, copy or transmission of this publication
may be made without written permission.
No paragraph of this publication may be reproduced,
copied or transmitted save with the written permission of the publisher, or in
accordance with the provisions
of the Copyright Act 1956 (as amended).

Any person who commits any unauthorised act in relation to
this publication may be liable to criminal
prosecution and civil claims for damage.

A CIP catalogue record for this title is
available from the British Library.

ISBN: 978-1-84897-104-2

This is a work of fact and all the names, characters, places and incidents are
from the travels of the author.

First Published in 2011

Olympia Publishers
60 Cannon Street
London
EC4N 6NP

Printed in Great Britain

Dedication

Mom and Dad, March 1955

Love you both. Thanks for everything you've helped me achieve in life.

In memory of my dear mother who sadly passed away while this book was being published.

Love you forever and you'll always be in my thoughts.

Acknowledgments

I would like to thank the following people, who, without their help, my stories and tales would have remained in my cupboard and my adventures untold.

Without the help of my proof-reader and fellow drinker, Neil Jones (Council Neil), I doubt this book would have ever made it into print. Without Bank's Mild ale, the adventures would never have begun and without Banks's Brewery, sponsoring my book it wouldn't have seen the light-of-day. Special thanks to Sarah Deeming and Joanne Wyke, for all the help and organisation needed in promoting this book. I best mention my darling daughter Jodee too, or I'll be in for it, for the numerous times she read through many of my chapters.

What can I say about all the past and present Black Country Ale Tairsters and the numerous guests that were invited on our special occasions?

"Gerra pint dahn ya wazzin!"

Who, without their aid and friendship, my adventures would have been unaffordable. They are:

Joe Hill (Oggy), John Drew (Drewy), Karl Bradley (Doc), Rob Jones (Leo), Wayne Hill, Lionel Randall, John and Tony Blundell (the Bungle brothers), Tim Hill, Rob Hill (Cuzz), Gavin Pace (Gav), Steve Edwards (Fast Eddy), Jeff Lawler (the Yidd), Graham Reeder (Gray), Jason Aston (Jase), Mark Abrahams, Joe Billingham, Den (Billy Boy) Billingham, John Jones (Jazza), Dennis Foundling, John Fox (Foxy), Tony Lowe (Lowey), Doug Shakespeare, Mick Billingham, Dave Price (Little Derv), Malcolm Maynard (Mac), Nathan Ellis, Neale Corns (Nibs), Paul Henwood, Neil Henwood, John Oakes (Trigga), Lee Tromans, Wayne Hill (Junior), Jeff Drew, Wade Hill, Paul Green,

Darren Merrick, Gary Hill, Steve Hall, Les Massey, Steve Evitts, Alan Gibbs, Neil Maskell, Roy Powell, Mike Ball, Allan Halloran, Paul Burford, John Bunce, Bob Shaw, John Callaghan, Geoff Summers and Dudley/South Staffs Camra, especially Tony Hitchmough.

A special thanks and not forgetting the superb patience and skill of our drivers, Kelvin Price (Kel), Gary Mountain (Glitta) and Richard Hill (Rich). CHEERS LADS!

Not forgetting a great lad who is sadly missed, you will always be in our memories, Alan Wyke (Algy). **R**est **In P**ubs my old pal.

Last of all, thanks to the numerous licensees we have met over the years, past and present, for your generosity and friendship, we shall be eternally grateful. To those that are long gone, God Bless you all, especially Les Carter, what a great bloke. If you are looking down on us from above Les, I hope I've helped in retaining your memory throughout my book.

CHAPTERS

INTRODUCTION 15

CHAPTER 1
IT'S MILD FOR THIS TIME OF YEAR 19

CHAPTER 2
GUNTHER, GUNTHER GIVE US A WAVE 42

CHAPTER 3
A THOUSAND MEMORIES 54

CHAPTER 4
BATS GO BANKS'S 76

CHAPTER 5
THE PINT NORTH 92

CHAPTER 6
HIGHER, LOWER! LOWER!! 112

CHAPTER 7
BONSOIR MONSIEUR 125

CHAPTER 8
WHEN THE CHIPS ARE DOWN 135

CHAPTER 9
VIVA ROSS VEGAS 159

CHAPTER 10
UNDER THE MOON OF LOVE 173

CHAPTER 11
THE SUP SOUTH SESSION 183

CHAPTER 12
2,000 NOT OUT 199

CHAPTER 13
THE FINAL FLAGON					211

CHAPTER 14
OFFSPRING OF OFFA				219

CHAPTER 15
WE ARE EMMETS					231

CHAPTER 16
3,000 CHEERS!					253

INTRODUCTION

Many pub books and guides are written solely about the pubs and just details where to find them, what beers they sell and the facilities on offer. My book, however, charts the early years of the Black Country Ale Tairsters, from the inception in 1984 all the way to 1990 and pub number 3,000 situated in the Black Country Living Museum, Dudley. This book sets out to be a warts-and-all tale, setting out the trials and tribulations of drinking (mostly irresponsibly), eating (mostly steak), sleeping (mostly rough) and travelling (mostly too far) in the cause of charity and enjoyment.

Our trips have not just been restricted to the British Isles and my book deals with several eventful forays to continental Europe. It shows how the over-exuberance and excesses of youth were gradually replaced by a more mature, albeit not entirely sensible attitude towards the noble quest. It shows how the pubs, the people we met on the way and the places, gradually became more important to us than the headache that inevitably followed. It also gives the reader a glimpse into the lives of several extremely amusing and world-class drinkers.

My story charts the events, incidents and social times had by all and prove that even in these modern times, an expedition to unknown parts can still provide excitement and adventure for anyone prepared to give it a bash. Included in my book are photographs of some of the fabulous licensees we have met, (sadly a few have passed away). Many pubs I've recorded have undoubtedly disappeared too.

I have used the grammar and words of the Black Country dialect where I considered it appropriate to do so. I have not always been word-for-word accurate with the dialogue because the colourful use of our day-to-day language would probably offend Gordon Ramsey. People may be offended by our apparent lack of social skills but we are what we are. Or as they say in the Black Country, we am what we am!

It's about pubs, people and places.

Our adventure is still continuing and we have now had a drink in over 15,000 pubs.

So, tell me a better hobby than this!

CHAPTER 1

IT'S MILD FOR THIS TIME OF YEAR

Dipsomania? Yes, I don't know what it means either, where's that dictionary?

'A craving for alcohol'. We'll work on this, as we sample another frothing beverage of mild ale (our favourite tipple) in *The Yew Tree* (West Bromwich). A gang of us, all with hops for brains, decides that as part of a small charity stunt we will visit every 'Pint and Platter' pub Banks's and Hansons are promoting. Pint and Platter is quite a unique idea dreamt up by Wolverhampton & Dudley Brewery to offer decent pub grub between noon and 2.00 p.m. instead of the usual cobs, pickled eggs and other snacks. There are about 300 pubs taking part in the promotion and we have a map listing all the pub names and their locations. Our trip is going to take us to into Wales and many English counties. Most of us have never been to these parts of Great Britain and the thought of hitting the road makes us feel like explorers. Our gang consists of sixteen lads and the growing excitement only leads to larger quantities of creamy mild ale being quaffed. Abandoning the *Yew Tree* will not amuse its gaffer, Fat Larry. I'm pretty sure he'll miss our humour, but even more so he will miss our money and the ring of his till. It's Friday November 3rd 1984 and the lads are all dressed in Banks's T-shirts, purchased off the brewery for £3.45 each. Tonight we stay local; a gentle session to warm us up and get us into the right frame of mind for tomorrow's epic maiden voyage. The lads are heading for Wales, with a map and a mission. Let's start the barrel rolling, happy days ahead.

After a sound night's kip we're ready for today's tour, but first to warm our bellies up and wet our wazzins (an old Black Country word for throat) why not start in a typical locals' drinking den, the *Oliver Cromwell* (West Bromwich). Spending three hours on our dinnertime binge indulged in fermented ales, our four cars depart late afternoon on what we expect to be a long drive. Suddenly, our journey comes to an abrupt stop no more than four miles away in Bilston, when the lead car stops at the pelican crossing, only to find two rastafarians stubbornly refusing to move from in front of the car. They then hurl insults and the usual gestures, until the lads in the cars behind all jump out – this must have come as a great surprise to them as they leg it down the high street with the fittest of us making sure they don't return in a hurry. The road is now clear for us to continue on our long drive to our first pub, the *White Lion Hotel* (Welshpool). Unfortunately it's not yet open, but with a gentle knocking of the doors and windows our thirst is satisfied. With the night as dark as Guinness we set off on another decent drive reaching our next port of call, the *Garthangharad* (Llwyngwril) near the Welsh coast. The traditional supping liquid in this establishment has travelled about as well as we have, shook up and exhausted."Form a line to the bog," said Billy-boy-Den. This is the order of the day, as everyone proceeds in smuggling their drink in single file down the plughole. This is the first drink I've ever seen with a seaweed head and a salty palate, no wonder this is a coastal pub, I'd rather drink seawater. Mind you it is somewhere to stretch the old joints.

Leaving now for a short stop at Machynlleth before a longer stop in Aberystwyth where at one of the pubs, the residents from the local loony bin are on a night out. Actually, it's the students from the nearby college who have made the lounge into a bouncy castle, jumping up and down on the seats and tonight's entertainment is the dying fly, nice to see them enjoying themselves though. Headed now to our last pub of the day, *The Black Lion* (Llanbadarn Fawr), what a lovely time we're having in here.

"Time for a bender," says Leo, one of our main beer suppers.

"Yoe'm right!" comes the reply, as if we weren't all ready on one.

Pints, bottles and shorts are happily swallowed until the early hours. Some of the regulars ask us to go to their all night bonfire party but by now, one chap has become three or four, depending on how fast the room is spinning and my words are coming out all backwards. Well it is 1.30 a.m., schow we shay our goodbyes to everyone and stumble outside to the cars. Here we get our sleeping stuff out, which consists of sleeping bags, extra jumpers, 'Benny' hats and each one of us has a six feet open-ended plastic bag. These we shall crawl into just in case the heavens dispose of some unwanted water sometime during the night, when we're comfortably bedded down. Now all we have to do is find a nice quiet spot in the adjacent graveyard. Some decide a wiser move is to crash out in the motors, whilst the majority agree to kip where we shouldn't get disturbed. Although sleeping with one eye open might be a good idea! It's fairly warm for this time of year as I journey off into cuckoo land.

We awake early in the morning to an amusing event that happened during the night, told by the lads who were woken by this whilst asleep in the cars. It seems two courting couples intent on their own ideas for the use of the graveyard, were casually walking through at about 3.30 a.m. when, suddenly, one of us must have sat up in our plastic bag for a good stretch and a yawn, with the glare of the moon and the rustling of the plastic appearing from the back of a grave stone, panic set in. All you could hear then, we're told, were screams and four teenagers running for their lives through the church gates, past the cars and home.

"Hey Hilly, that's the closest yoe've slept with a woman in years," said Lionel the littlest of our mob, who weighs in at seven stone dripping wet. "An' her (she) had the worms." laughed Doc, the ginger-haired git.

"Her (she) would have," I said, "she died in 1896."

After the jokes and sarcasm, it's time for breakfast. Out come the gas bottles and cookers. In with the bacon and eggs and down comes the rain. So quickly, Jazza and Dennis get our utility plastic bags and shut them in the top of the car doors from one to another. This makes a perfect shelter to continue cooking. What a great first trip this is as we eat our sandwiches on a rainy November morning in a graveyard. A worker's welly in a nearby hut comes in handy for the ones who need a piddle in private. After a wholesome breakfast and relieved bladders, we head homeward but not before stopping for a top up at the *Six Ashes* (near Bobbington) Staffordshire, to mark off another of the pubs on our map.

My gran's got my dinner waiting for me, so I hurriedly dash home and polish it off, having a quick brush up and off out again at 6.30 p.m. to resume our refreshment trail. Meeting up with the lads and after a steady drive to Rugeley we arrive at the *Eaton Lodge Hotel*. Outside here, one young chap shouts over to Oggy, my dad, and asks, "Got a penny for the guy, mister?"

"Here's a couple of bob son," replied Oggy.

On handing over a few coppers, the Guy Fawkes, sitting next to the young chap, suddenly reaches out for the money.

At this, Oggy's legs wobble and if it wasn't for his blood pressure tablets, we'd have had to wheel him in the pub in a barrow. We all had a good laugh at this, because it sure took us all by surprise. The young lad's mate had stuffed paper in his coat, up his trousers, in his sleeves and with a mask and hat on certainly fooled everyone. I'm just glad my old man donated first. With pubs in Rugeley happily sampled in, tonight's run is over.

During the next couple of weeks we've continued knocking our pub total up visiting pubs in Kidderminster and our local Black Country area. Whilst touring these I've been asking the licensees if they would care to donate anything towards equipment for Russell's Hall Hospital in Dudley and most have donated £1 or £2. We've also settled on Sunday nights being the main pub run night of the week. This makes our visits simpler to get our book signed, ask for our charity money and park easier in the towns, due to fewer people going out.

It's now December and we're off on another weekend pub-crawl. This time it's in Leicestershire and our rendezvous point on this excursion is *The Black Dog* (Oadby). Arriving here at 1.45 p.m. pints all round was the order of the day and we downed these in no time. Best order a few more, it shuts at 2.30 p.m. due to the draconian licensing hours in England. Well, what a stroke of luck. The gaffer being a jovial chap tells us not to rush, we'll be okay for a few more.

"A lock-in. Great!" said Doc.

"Ar, let's make the best of it, my old pal," I replied.

"Yoe get the beer in then Hilly!" came his reply.

This is not really what I had in mind, but I succumbed to the pressure of a democratic vote.

How right the gaffer was. After eight pints each and four hours later we stroll out of this boozer. We succeed in visiting five more alehouses before closing time. I have a vague memory of the establishments toured tonight, but all I can remember is having my book signed as proof of our visits. Our appetite needs fulfilling, so off now for a 'Chinkie' curry, before venturing out into the wilds. Out back yonder we find an excellent spot to encamp on a slope of a hill. Now it's the same procedure as our last run, inside our plastic bags. Tonight, with the pitter-patter of the raindrops and the effects of today's drink, I lapse into unconsciousness.

On waking up on a cold damp freezing morning we find we're half submerged in a quagmire of a bog. We've actually slid down the bank during the night and ended up in this muddy mess.

"Wake up lads, we're drowning!" shouted John, one of the Bungle brothers, known for his comical chat-up lines with the girls and usually he bungles everything. (A favourite one-liner of his is asking a girl if she's got an aspirin for his headache).

"Bloody Hell!" yelled a terrified Lionel. "All my socks are wet."

"Doe (don't) blame me lads, I day (didn't) see the swamp last night. It was too dark and I was too bladdered to notice a thing," I said defensively.

Anyway, I feel groggy to say the least this morning and after packing all our gear away, we drive until we find a café. The drive takes us into Derby where down the road from the railway station we find an ideal place to eat. I'm still in a bit of a stupor as I stagger inside, sit myself down and proceed to put my head on my arms laid out across the table.

"Excuse me," said the lady owner, "I don't allow druggies in here."

"Please give me a menu and a couple of headache tablets," I said as I explained our challenge and the reason for feeling as I do. This she accepted and I'm allowed to stay. It's only now I recall sampling a curry last night as half of it is down my shirt. No matter, after a little bite to eat and a cup of tea I don't feel like a pickled gherkin anymore. After paying our bill, we set off for the *Grandstand* pub in Derby, arriving a little too early at 11 a.m. As it doesn't open until noon we all buy a newspaper, except John who's trying to get his windscreen clean to no avail.

"What's up John?" said Oggy.

"I cor (can't) get my windscreen clean," he replied. "Wheer's (where's) that bottle of whisky," said Oggy.

John says, "Yoe'm starting on the drink early, ay ya?"

So Oggy comes up with a brilliant idea and pours the contents of the whisky bottle all over his windscreen. "Ogggyyyy!" Screams John, who's now gone a little potty. "What a waste of good spirit."

But the experiment certainly does the trick.

On opening time in we go. It's a massive pub with lots of snooker tables and its own outdoor cricket pitch. The gaffer tells us that there was a racecourse at the back of the pub hence the name. We stop here, swigging ale for a while then drive home, arriving early afternoon. All in all an eventful trip to say the least. Again no time is wasted our next destination is Stourbridge undertaking 6 pubs. On completion of these, we disband until further notice, because with the Christmas period approaching, it's going to be impossible to get all the lads together.

With 1984 out of the way, it's February 1985 before meeting up

...d during this month we only manage three pubs. Things start... now it's March and we're all back together as one unit. ...task relentlessly' is now our motto, with pubs in ...nster and Stourbridge having our seal of approval ...nbark on a journey into Hereford and Worcester. ...nsumption around Worcester we bump into 3 ...nd Andy, who hand out calling cards with ...them, as they are all West Bromwich ...ut to be from our area and are not just ...but every pub owned by Bank's and ...t or two with these lads we say our ...to do: *The Portobello*, close to ...b in hysterics. He's drunk too ...s way in the lounge room.

...continues walking round the room... find the hole in the wall where the door fits. ......exit, falls down the step throws up and leaves the shape of m...... equally spaced mounds along the ground, until flaking out on the back seat of his motor. Back in the pub we finish off our beers and jokes with the locals and leave quietly and drive a few hundred yards down the road to the entrance of the golf course. Having had enough booze today to fill a goldfish pond, out comes our kipping clobber (sleeping clothes) and we jump over the wall onto the golf course, leaving Lionel to sleep it off in the car.

"Number two green will do, we'll settle here for the night," I said to Tony, the other Bungle brother.

We all congregate on the perfectly flat green, for what we hope is going to be a relaxing night, but bright flashing blue lights and torches very quickly disturb us. It's the local police force and we're told they've been watching us and if we had driven any further we would have had it. After giving our names and addresses and explaining that we're on a charity pub-crawl, they noticed one of us was missing, Lionel. The police then open the car door and find him out of his noggen [head], with bits of today's food and drink all down him. They try questioning him and get nothing back but grunts and moans.

"If you keep quiet, we will allow you back on number two green," said the officer.

"Okay, we'll be no problem," Tony replies.

Fair play to the coppers and we can now get some well-deserved shuteye. What a day!

Sunday morning I'm woken by a nasty little wammel [dog] yapping at my feet. You'd think the woman walking her mutt would have some consideration wouldn't you? It's too early to get up so I nod off again. By the time it's ready to rise, the sun is out and with all my extra clobber on, I'm hot. Up we get and back to the car, to check on Hercules, a.k.a Lionel.

"How am ya mate?" I said, as Lionel admired his designer shirt of carrots and beer stains.

"Yoe was in a right state last night, especially when the coppers had ya."

"I wor [wasn't] that bad, I'd have remembered if they had," said Lionel, in a slow drawl.

With last night's escapades out the way and after a bite to eat we head off home. Lionel still refuses to believe a word of what had happened.

During the next few weeks we continue knocking back the beers in Droitwich, Telford and various other towns. We have now passed our first milestone of over 100 pubs and have a couple of hundred pounds in the charity kitty. It's May 4th 1985. What will today's tour bring? As we resolutely undertake another expedition into Tenbury Wells and Cleobury Mortimer before finally finishing at *The Bridge* (Stanford). This is a country pub, by the river with its own caravan and camping site. Inside here we have more than the weekly-recommended health units allow you in one session. I fancy a go on the fruit machine and put 10p in. Nothing happens.

"Excuse me gaffer, I've put 10p in this machine and it's not working," I said.

I get my 10p back off him and I try the fruit machine again. It works this time. Sadly, I win nothing so I give it another go and again it wouldn't work.

"Hey gaffer, it's not working again!" I say again.

At this, the gaffer comes over and says, "Do you realise it's 20p a go on this machine?"

Ah, what a prize Willy Wonka and everybody bursts out laughing. With closing time upon us, we leave to nod off outside by some dustbins, all settled down nicely in our plastic bags.

"Nighty night everyone," yawns Oggy.

I'm first to rise at 7.30 a.m. The small shop nearby is open so I trot over to buy me a pint of milk and a Marathon chocolate bar. My wazzin's as dry as a boon [bone].

"Morning," I say to an old lady in the shop.

She then gestures outside. "The rubbish some people leave behind is disgusting, just look at that pile of old plastic bags someone's left.

"No, no you've got it all wrong!" I explained but a quick reply comes back off the shopkeeper: "It won't be there long, I've phoned for the bin-men to take it away."

"Blimey! They cor do that, my dad and my mates are in theer [there]," I reply with a shocked look on my face.

From the shop I could see the dustbin wagon arrive, so I promptly run over to wake them up before they end up in little square cubes and dumped on the tip for seagull fodder. The lads couldn't believe what nearly happened to them, so in the future a safer dossing down place is recommended. To see the expression on their faces was quite hilarious though and in the end, was well worth the panic. Later we converge on the shop, where they enjoy a good-humoured banter about it with the old lady. We begin our journey home, stopping to sample a few beers in a couple of pubs on the way until dinner-time closing.

Through the week a dozen more pubs are visited before our normal Sunday run, taking in Royal Leamington Spa and Warwick. In *The Racehorse* (Warwick) the gaffer asks us if we are in the area again to pop in to have a longer drink together. Six days pass and, surprisingly, there's a horse race meeting on at Warwick racecourse, yet another excuse for a beer run is under way. It's an evening meeting, there's no need to rush around; the sun is out, so all we need is our horses to come in. There's a good crowd here tonight, I think most of them have come to see 'A Match' between Lester Piggott and John Francome. A really enjoyable time is had by all, with most of the lads breaking even, except for the 'Templegate' of our party, my dad, Oggy. As normal, all we can hear him say is, "Where's my oss (horse) gone?" Mind you, I could have done with winning a bit more than I have – I've actually won enough money to fill a thimbleful of coconuts! Warwick races is well worth a visit and the presence of licensed establishments, not far away, makes it that much better. By the way, Lester won the big showdown.

Now for that pub we visited last week, *The Racehorse*. This is very near the racecourse, so in we go. While sitting in the lounge, the gaffer recognises our drinking clan and asks us to stop over later for a late night drink after time. But first he asked if we had ever had a tour of a pub cellar.

Amazingly, none of us have, so down the steps we go. In the cellar we find a young chap filtering beer, back into the barrel.

"Is that a normal practice?" I ask the gaffer.

"This I use for the tourists in the lounge bar, my best beer we'll have later in the bar room." he replied.

How right he is, as we make merriment until 2 a.m. to be precise and by now everyone's either out of his tree or Dutch Elm has set in. We call time ourselves. What hospitality, and it's farewell and thanks to a sound gaffer. Glad we weren't tourists though.

We stagger back to the cars, which are parked nearby on Warwick racecourse. Out come our accommodation bags and we nip under the rails separating the car-park from the final furlong and we bed down for the night. To the astonishment of us all, the groundsman on his tractor chugging and ripping up the fences, abruptly wakes us early Sunday morning 19th May. He's amazed to find us all lying under the last hurdle in the straight and said, in a not too pleasant tone of voice,

"You're lucky this morning. Usually the horses have a canter and a practice training jump around the course, so can you get up now and bugger off!"

So, yet again, it seems we found another not-so-safe haven to lay down our spinning brain buckets. Will we ever learn?

Drove into Rugby now and had a walkabout while waiting for the *William Webb Ellis* pub, named after the founder of Rugby football, to open. Suffering with the effects of the extended boozing binge in *The Racehorse* until the early hours, one pint is enough for me. Another pub completed and another journey home. Sleep recovery takes a couple of hours, then out again tonight to Stafford. The following week sees us in Wolverhampton.

Our next consumption of ales takes our adventurers into Shropshire. It's June 1st and John Bungle decides to drink pint for pint with Oggy. Last one today we finish off in the *New Inn* (Chirk), at 8 p.m. By the time 9.30 p.m. arrives John has passed out and he's lying across the table. Didn't get 'overs' in this place, so left – and outside there's a field that looks like it will come in very handy indeed. The 'Bungle Brothers' and myself settle down in the long grass, while the others use the car-park and the cars. I'm having a deep sleep, until John suddenly screams, "Wake up Hilly, Tony. Run!"

Half dozed and not focusing too well just yet, through the early morning rays of sunshine, I work out a terrifying sight of about a dozen cows running towards us. There's no time to waste, these cows from ground level look like the size of zeppelins, so John and me leave our shoes and sleeping bags and run for it. John climbs over the gate and I dive over it, scraping all the skin off my shins. Tony's still asleep, surrounded by this angry mob of cows whose territory we've invaded, so we throw some bibbles [pebbles] at him. This seems to do the trick and, on opening his eyes, he's quite shocked to see so many large nostrils dripping snot down on him. Calmly, to our surprise he takes it all in his stride, he stands up, collects everyone's gear and confidently walks slowly away.

Strutting his stuff across the field, saying, "They'm only cows, they woe hurt ya."

Mind you, he did move a little quicker when we mentioned the appearance of a bull. Tony, on handing over my sleeping bag and with a cocky smirk on his face said, "Yoer fust [first] job today Hilly, is to remove that large dollop of cow dung out of it."

One day we might by some remote chance, find a place where for once, we might get a decent few hours shut eye without any disturbance whatsoever. Soon we're all wide-eyed; cooking our breakfast with our camping stoves on the car-park and then driving home.

Enough beer towels have been collected now for all of us to be measured up for a beer towel coat apiece. These we have obtained from the numerous pubs we have visited to date. Nine are used for each coat and my mom sews mine together, with an inside pocket, for a well-earned fiver. On our next gathering we make a grand sight. Colourful and totally different, this is to be our general attire from this day forth. The weekly Sunday night runs continue to take place until a second beer run to Leicestershire gets under way. This is a steady, quiet affair, compared to our usual travels, completing the remaining pubs missed on our last ale trail around here. With the day's drinking complete, we travel and encamp for the night on a field near where the battle of Bosworth took place in 1485. This is where Richard III lost his crown and his life to Henry Tudor's army. The reign of the Tudors had begun and Henry VII was King. The quietness of this run is now somewhat loud, as we're all having a bit of a singsong and telling jokes. This annoys and upsets a few of the nearby weekend gypsies, who are on a short break in their caravans. After half-an-hour of raising the noise level, one by one we all drop off to sleep, to the delight of the local residents. Our travel route back home, after a nice night out under the stars, sees us take in two newly built Banks's pubs; the *Galley Gap* (Nuneaton) and the last one of our dinnertime session the *Leg 'n' Cramp* (Walsgrove). Local Tipton and Dudley pubs during the week take us up to Sunday dinnertime June 23rd, when just for the fun of it we drive all the way down to Bristol to visit two pubs, the *Bristol Bridge Inn* and *The Stanshaws Court Hotel* (Yate). Yet we stop off first at the army barracks near Tewkesbury. The reason for this is another of our members, Tim, who is in the army, is stationed here, and he loves flying pigeons. He's brought them down with him in the back of his car and lets them loose inside the army base. Somehow I think they'll make it home long before we do, if they're not shot for trespassing on British territory and invading our air space. We've done quite a distance today just for two pubs, but worth the effort. Fast Eddy, yet another member, who's got his nickname due to the small motorbike he rides, lives up to his name today as he hammers his Mini motorcar at a speed of 105 m.p.h. back to base.

The following Sunday dinnertime sees us venture southwards again to the recently built *The Basket Maker* (Quedgley), Gloucestershire. While here the landlord asks us to all come back again and have a proper drink together. Lionel thanked him and said we might do so. Well, six days later we take up the offer and arrive back for our promised session. We turn up on the Saturday night in our beer towel coats and on entry the gaffer takes one look at us and we never set eyes on him again during our whole nights stay in this establishment. Never mind, a good time and a good drink is had here. As usual, we're last out the pub and decide to sleep outside on the grass. Graham, a recent recruit, who is now a bit of a 'Basket Case' himself, finds a kid's bike in the adjacent supermarket car-park.

"Here lads, I'll race you," he said. "Yoe lot in the supermarket trolleys and me on the bike."

"Goo on then," was the reply.

In no time there are trolleys everywhere, making a right racket. It's Monte Carlo or bust.

With this exhausting escapade at an end, albeit a little rowdy we settle down on the grass. Not for long though. It seems we've upset the local residents and the police turn up. We're warned about the din we've been making and they tell us to behave ourselves. Like any large group of chaps who have had a few, you'll always get a boisterous noisy period, then a singsong before passing out. This follows very quickly. The night goes by with regular checking up periods by the local constabulary, which wakes me up on each visit, but we're obeying orders, as vegetation is well under way. On reviving the dead early this Sunday morning, and with most of us looking like we've been through a state of metamorphosis and resembling ruptured gargoyles, we slowly load the cars with our gear and hangovers and steadily drive home. I have two hours shut eye, then a succulent beef dinner and off out again on tonight's run to Stoke and Leek.

Monday evening we visit a newly built pub called the *Village Inn* (Wednesbury). This pub is near where we live and is to have a big impact on our charity pub crawl. Here we discuss the possibility of visiting all the Banks's and Hansons' pubs, a total of 748. It's going to be impossible without a list of their pubs. I've already enquired at their brewery, but there's no list available. To our astonishment on overhearing our conversation the landlord said, "I have a full list of every one lads, on photostat copies. You're welcome to have them if it will further your cause."

"Just what we need. Thanks gaffer," I said.

This is a stroke of luck. We're all gleefully smiling over our pint pots, looking forward to the unknown adventures awaiting us. Another worthwhile cause can benefit from our added liquid consumption, agreeing on collecting donations for Heath Lane Hospital, West Bromwich. The landlord shouts over that a liver transplant unit would probably come in quite handy.

The silly craze amongst us at the moment is tying a few strands of white nylon string, about two foot long together by a knot at one end. This is then melted at the end using a match and stuck on the backside of some unfortunate chap's trousers, making a wonderful bushy tail. On our arrival at the *Hilly House Inn* near Dudley, a gentleman parks his Rolls Royce and on entering the pub leans on the bar to order his drink. 'Operation Molten Knot' gets under way, with him walking around the lounge swishing his tail to everyone's amusement. Departing before he suspects anything, leaving the pub in a much jollier atmosphere than when we arrived. Travelling home in my ever-reliable Vauxhall Victor, it conks out at the traffic lights on top of King's Hill, Dudley.

"Lionel, my old pal, take over the steering," I said.

"No problem," he says as the Bungle Brothers and myself give it a push. With the car now moving increasingly faster down the hill and the three of us now sitting on the boot, we shout to Lionel, "Put ya foot on the brake, mate... NOW!"

A problem now occurs. Lionel's only a little chap and he's unable to reach the pedal.

Clinging on for dear life, a sharp right turn towards Burnt Tree Island sees the departure of John and myself as we gambol into the road. This leaves Tony howling as the car speeds through red lights, with him holding on for dear life looking more like a squashed gnat on the back of the rear windscreen, as it continues its journey around the island and disappears from view. After a walk that seems like we've been on a trek with Hannibal and his elephants and with feet throbbing like a thumb hit with an ommer [hammer], we eventually catch up with Lionel and Tony. They are now scoffing fish and chips and are chuffed that we've had to walk and they haven't. It turns out that the car gradually came to a halt and Tony took over the controls and the thing started up, no trouble. What a relief to get home. It's a good job all this happened after midnight because I dread to think of the chaos and commotion we'd have caused at a busier time of the day. Relaxing with a nice cup of tay [tea], I go to bed to round off an eventful if somewhat perilous night out. Throughout the next few weeks we take in more Black Country pubs, plus a first trip into Cheshire. Our grand total of licensed premises now stands at 300. With the longest time spent sleeping rough while on a pub trail being one night. The forthcoming trip will be six! The reason our travels haven't extended to more than one night out before always has been the crazy opening hours of all pubs. These being in general 11 a.m. to 2.30 p.m. and 6 p.m. to 10.30 p.m. Which means we would have to find things to do for about three hours until the evening opening session. So this trip is going to be rather different from any others in the past.

The day has arrived, Sunday July 28th 1985. Enthusiasm is high as we tour our local pubs before setting off towards Bridgnorth. Completing the Banks's boozers available here, we venture off to the last belly filler of the day the *Kings Arms* (Sutton Chelmarsh). It's pitch black on coming out of this excellent country pub and our expedition now takes us into narrow secluded lanes even further into the countryside. In one of these isolated lanes we park up for the night. We decide on sleeping in the cars as we've checked the field opposite and there are loads of little bugs jumping about, in whatever crops are growing in it.

On rising early in the morning a pint of milk wouldn't go amiss and would go down very nicely with my Kelloggs's variety pack. But, out in the wilds with nothing for miles there's not much hope of this. All of a sudden, believe it or not, a milk float pulls up at the farmer's gate and leaves two pints. One goes missing and an instant breakfast is had by all. Soberly we slowly journey on, arriving a little too early at 10 a.m. for opening time in Much Wenlock. Here we view the old Priory ruins and a very interesting local museum, broadening our intelligence and understanding in the society and environment of bygone days in rural areas of old England. Opening time and let's get in the *Wheatland Fox*, a nice place to start today's trail and a nice pint of mild before leaving and sampling beers in Madeley and Dawley. Then entering into the delightful little riverside town of Ironbridge, with its many interesting museums and an old Victorian post-box is still in use. It's here Abraham Darby assembled the world's first awe-inspiring bridge of iron that has spanned the river since 1779. Let's not forget its selection of watering holes too. Unfortunately on arriving at the *Boat* (Jackfield), we've just missed the dinnertime session. With, as I've said earlier, approximately three hours to kill, why not pay a trip to nearby Blist's Hill Museum? This turns out to be an ingenious idea, as it's now tipping down of rain. We take shelter in an old cottage at the far end of the museum, lived in as recently as 1977, which we find totally fascinating as it's been brought in brick by brick from its original site. There are also many more delightful buildings including a pub, which was moved here in 1983 – you've guessed it, closed for the anti-social afternoon drinking hours. A sweet shop and bread shop, a bank, where soon you'll be able to change your money into the equivalent pre-decimal coinage (real British money) in exchange for goods. Tony reminds me of the day we went decimal, in February 1971. When one day he was getting 240 Black Jacks or Hobo Chews for a £1 and the very next day he only got 200. What a fiddle, he said.

"What a pisser Tony." I said sympathetically.

The rain eases off now, and with many more attractions to see, this takes us quite a while. A visit here is certainly recommended.

Anyway, time is getting on and we leave for *The Boat* pub. Most locals get to this pub by walking across the wooden footbridge high above the River Severn that was built in 1922 as a war memorial. *The Boat* is an early nineteenth century building and its first official licence was in 1841. In here we're told when the river bursts its banks the place is usually submerged in a few feet of water and there's actually flood level markers from different years shown on the wall. We're all enjoying a lovely session on the beer today and we finish our exploits at the *Butchers Arms* (Weston Rhyn) near Oswestry. We couldn't have dropped on a better pub with us enjoying our beers late into the night and the licensee's kindly letting us sleep in their beer garden.

In the morning, we get up and are treated to toast and tea by our hosts before saying goodbye. Today we taste ales in Wales, Cheshire, Birkenhead then back into Wales at Flint. Stopping for a pint in the *Three Pigeons* and fish and chips from the local chip shop, which we eat in the castle ruins on the sea front. Now we drive into Towyn near Rhyl, where Tony's family have hired a caravan for a week. There are no Banks's pubs to do around here, so we buy some cans of beer and get a small fire going on the beach, swapping stories and tales with Tony's sister Tina and her friend Derry. Slept outside the caravan tonight as it's full up inside it. Breakfast the following morning is courtesy of Tony's mom and dad, then it's off towards Aberystwyth.

Travelling on our way here we pass through a remarkable area with slate everywhere, a very bewitching site, near Blaenau Ffestiniog. With slate hills, slate houses, slate ground, it's a slate I'll never forget. Unsurprisingly our first stop of the day is called the *Slaters Arms* (Upper Corris), which is just off the main road, with a sharp turn left and down a steep hill to get to this village. Our thirst quenched, appetite satisfied, we exit the pub, entered the car, putt-putt, ding-ding, yes, my good old Vauxhall Victor the vibrating piece of junk I call a car refuses to start. Some hard pushing and crash starting eventually wins the day and a rest is required to level off the beer in our bellies. After one more pub stop we arrive in Aberystwyth and have a walk about and play on the games in the amusement arcade. Yes we've time to kill, since the pubs are not open again until later.

"Tony have yoe brought those old 10p brass tokens of mine with ya out of my car?" I said.

"Yes," says Tony, "Wheer did yoe get this bag of tokens from?"

"They'm from work. Loads of them came in a skip for melting down in the furnaces and the quicker they were coming off the skip, the quicker all my workmates were bagging them up to play on the fruit machines."

We put dozens in the fruit machines, making it a profitable afternoon. The only reason we stop was that the machines started paying us back in the same tokens we put in!

Gluttons? No not us surely, but we do go for something else to eat again. In tonight's final tipsy tavern, we meet two couples from Dudley, which is not far away from where we live. They end up joining our merriment and invite us back to their caravan. With the bell ringing last orders we leave and follow them to their site. Outside their caravan we get a barbecue under way, with steak sandwiches, followed by a cup of tay [tea]. Now we're ready for boozeland or should that be snoozeland? I end up on a comfortable mattress where, dreaming about tomorrow's session, I drop off into a sound sleep. What a hospitable foursome I think as we're woken up with a full English breakfast. Devouring this we say our thanks and leave.

"Hilly yoe'd never believe that would ya mate?" said a full-up Tony.

"It's got to be fate my old pal," I reply.

It's Thursday August 1st and again our journey to the first pub is a long one, the *Vaga Tavern* (Hunderton) in Hereford. There are a few alehouses to sample the mild in today, so after a quiet day yesterday and a decent drink to open with, we swallow on regardless, stopping at pubs in Great Malvern and Worcester. Having had a few ales this afternoon and with it now being dinner-time closing, we sleep the effects of the beer off under the sun's rays on Worcester racecourse, for a cracking couple of well earned two hours' rest. Can't waste opening time so it's back into Worcester city, then it's off into the country, completing today's fifteenth pub in the *The Crown Inn* (Martley). On arriving quite late for what we thought would be our *final* tipple, we get chatting to a chap at the bar who turns out to be the local police constable, off duty. "Lads," he says, "no need to rush your last drink as more is available if required, nudge, nudge."

As if we haven't had enough, we manage somehow to last until 1 a.m. With a belly full of beers, the licensee, to our relief said, "Lads you all look knackered, you might as well sleep in my adjoining field."

It's off to bed, with us all totally whacked out. Little did he tell us we'd be pecked up as early as 6 a.m. by ducks and chickens; it seems we're interfering with their passage to the pond and hen house. Undeterred at this we cover our heads for another couple of hours' snooze, before rising up to a somewhat thick head this morning. Circled by the never-ending sound of quacks and clucks.

This is our penultimate day. It's only 8 a.m. and we drive to Stourport and park up by the fairground. Tony's struggling this week with sleeping rough and wants to go home today. We discuss his dilemma and he decides to go for a walk. This has done him the world of good. He says he's got his mind together and he's cleared the build up of this week's wobbly ways and agrees on one more night out. We nip into the local café for a bite to eat, before driving to the furthest point on today's run the *Masons Arms* (Wadborough). With the opening ale of the day very slowly consumed, we travel back through Worcester to a rather unusually situated pub the *Mug House* (Claines). This is off the main road down a quiet little lane that actually leads to a churchyard and stands on consecrated ground. We park on the road and walk to this pub, which is literally a coffin's throw from the graveyard. It's an old brick and beamed building with superb little rooms and is well worth a passing pint.

The day's run continues, eventually finishing off in the *Lenchford Hotel* (Shrawley) just outside Stourport. Although not a Banks's pub it's got a bostin (great) beer garden, next to the river and is ideal for tonight's kip. Downing the final pint of the day, I ask the barman if he's got some bread to spare. To our surprise he gives us half a loaf. I thank him. For the first time this week, on leaving the hotel, we get out the camping stove and warm some soup up. We desperately need some fittle (food), to soak up today's belly building booze. There's lots of nasty little flies buzzing around our soup and some try out its flavour, it's no longer vegetable soup, as dozens of these tiny little blighters add a meat content to our diet. After our à la carte meal we settle down and before we know it we're woken up at 8 a.m. by an employee of the hotel who asks us politely to move on, before the paying residents see us and think it's a garden for refugees.

Into Bewdley now and a tour around the museum is followed by a sit on the riverbank with an ice cream, waiting for Saturday opening time on our final day. It's a smashing sunny day as we stroll leisurely from pub to pub until our task is complete. Now for the town of Kinver, stopping as long as the permitted dinnertime hours allow. To fill the gap until the evening session we drive to see the old Kinver cave dwellings. These are actually cut out of the sandstone hills and were once lived in and not all that long ago neither. While looking in these caves Tony says he's had enough now and wants to head home. This time we let him have his way and shoot off for our very last pub. Well it has been a fabulous experience as our beer run comes to an end at this week's eighty-ninth establishment the *George and Dragon*, known locally as the *Crown Yards*, (at Bradley) and not far from our home. This is run by a right character named Marvin, who has appeared on telly for playing his optics with his drumsticks. He also puts on his own glove puppet show, on top of the bar counter to the amazement of welcome strangers. I must say too that the Banks's Mild in here is the best I've ever tasted, with its superb aroma and a thick creamy head clinging tightly to the glass, until the very last drop slips inevitably past my lips.

Arriving back home yesterday from our 1,040 mile mammoth mouth-watering mission, I have quite a long sleep in this morning, I must get up and work out tonight's run to Kingswinford. We visit and we complete ten pubs. As I've another week off work the following day, Monday, we pop into Kidderminster to visit one of the lads from Dudley who put us up in their caravan on our tour last week. He works here in a local bank. He's shocked to see us. His dinner hour is in five minutes, so I said, "In ya dinner hour, we'll take yoe over the road for a couple of beers."

"I'd like that," he replied.

Tony says, "It will be our treat for yoe putting us up for the night."

In the bar we trot. We have an hour of reminiscing and we buy him three pints, a pie and a bag of scratchings. He seems slightly merry now, as he leaves and nips back to the bank."Tony, what do ya think?" I ask, as I have a little laugh to myself, "Shall we nip in later and ask him for a big cash withdrawal?"

"It could be worth a try the state he looked in," he joked back.

What a thirst quenching hour.

We can't believe the last of the Pint and Platter pubs is complete after visiting the remaining few on the 6th and 7th of August. Today Thursday 8th is our first appearance in a newspaper, under the heading: *'Pub pals hit booze trail for charity.'*

It's also the day we carry on to complete our mission of visiting every Banks's pub. Shooting off to Manchester, then all the way down to Barmouth, where Lionel's family is staying in a caravan. We arrive early evening and spend the night in the clubroom on site and have an entertaining few hours. We then sleep on the floor of their caravan. On wakening, Lionel's parents line our stomachs with a large fry-up. Tony decides he's going for a swim in the sea, but the only problem is he does it fully clothed. What a prize mawken [idiot] – he's got no change of clothes and has to drive home dripping wet!

Enough money has now been raised for our first donation of £600 to be presented to Russell's Hall Hospital, Dudley. To hand over the cheque, Rob Jones alias Leo and myself, have the pleasure of meeting deputy nursing officer Marian Joshi and Sister Maureen Smith. Some of this money is being used to buy a nebulizer, which enables throat suffers to inhale air and breathe more easily.

The next few weeks Cradley Heath, Quarry Bank, Gornal and many more Black Country locations are paid a visit. While walking to one of these pubs Lionel, who I've already said weighs a colossal 7 stone, said to two tough-looking chaps, "Hey lads, wheer's the next pub from here?"

They come over to him, loud-mouthed and a little aggressive, then all the rest of us turn the corner.

The turn around in their attitude was funny to watch, as they shakily said, "It's jjjust dddown ttthere mate."

Amazing what a few numbers can do isn't it?

During early September, Oggy suggests a rather intrepid adventure. It seems that last year when he and his fellow members of the Moonshiner's Motorcycle Club toured Europe, they met a gaffer of a pub while in West Germany called Gunther. Oggy said he had a great time in this bloke's pub and would love to see him again and tells us about an incident that happened while on his visit there. Oggy had said to Gunther, "Gunther, I bet I've got a better physique than you."

Then he tells us, both of them took their shirts off. "I told ya so, my belly's bigger than yours. Us English like our beer. That's one-nil to us," said Oggy,

He goes on to explain that he grabbed his own belly with both hands and gave it a shake.

"Ja! You win, but beat this then." Gunther replied, before slapping his knob on the table.

"Let's call it one each." Oggy sheepishly said.

Oggy says he was flabbergasted at the size of it. It was like a piece of cod.

This is a fine recollection of his first acquaintance with Gunther.

I think we'll have to keep an eye on him, but his idea of a Europe trip sounds interesting and could be a memorable one.

Why not! A totally out-of-the-ordinary trip, the only trouble is we don't have his address. All Oggy can remember is it's near the town of Neustadt. No matter, we'll give it a go. I book the ferry, buy the maps and everything else is organised for the planned departure date for a Wednesday 25th September 1985. In the meantime we visit the *Foxcote* (Wollescote) where the gaffer asks us to come back when he's got some entertainment on, for a good-night get together. This is now stored in our memory banks.

CHAPTER 2

GUNTHER, GUNTHER GIVE US A WAVE

The day Wednesday 25th September 1985 has arrived for our first expedition to foreign parts, a dozen of us fill three cars and meet at my gran's house at 9 a.m. Everyone is kitted out in a Union Jack T-shirt and our usual beer towel coats and to be honest we make a colourful sight.

I said, "Now I know yoe lot. Make sure yoe've all got ya passports and money, especially yoe Lionel and yoe Tony."

This is a very important point, as both are known for being forgetful after a few bevvies.

We drive now towards Dover stopping off at the occasional alehouse for refreshment, before arriving early evening. After a filling meal in one of the boozers and a few pints, we leave for our late night ferry crossing. While hanging around the docks for loading and boarding ship we're stopped by the custom officials.

"You lot, line up there and hand over your passports," they said.

When we asked why, we were told that they wanted to know the motives and the purpose of our journey.

With our passports confiscated (all bar Oggy who refuses) we're beginning to wonder if we'll ever set foot on foreign soil. Our names and addresses are taken down and we're told to behave ourselves. It turns out we're being harassed for wearing our T-shirts and are suspected of a rendezvous with Neo-Nazi's while over in Europe.

What a start to our first trip overseas, it's a good job we're only going for a drink!

With this unfortunate misunderstanding out of the way we board ship. Our eagerly awaited crossing to Ostend is filled in by tonight's entertainment in the bar. We happen to be the only ones in here but we all have a good loff [laugh] singing and dancing to a chap on the organ and a female singer. With the four-hour drinking session having taken place our ship arrives at the docks. Now the adventure begins, as we alter our watches forward by one hour. Dense fog is a hazard on our journey through Belgium so, unable to see any further, we pull over at 4 a.m. and park up in what we think is a quiet and safe place somewhere down a country lane. It's very damp and visibility is virtually nil, so the majority of us sleep in the car with a couple braving the elements and dossing down outside.

We have an uncomfortable three hours' kip from which we're woken not only by the heavy traffic and the noise of the passing trains but by the police too. It turns out, unfortunately, that we're obstructing the highway. In the early hours in the fog we've parked by a roundabout, with our cars on the road by it, effectively cutting the two lanes into one. After a caution about the predicament we've got ourselves in we're told to move on, but not before asking them which road to take. Our first serious stop today is in Luxembourg and by now I'm clammed [starved] and could do with a good meal. The rest of the lads agree, so we park up and head to the nearest pub. To our disappointment due to the recent behaviour of English football fans we're banned from entering. All the pubs we stop at give us the same charming welcome. One bar owner allows us in for one drink but even he refuses to serve us food. While miserably supping our much sought after beer, we get yapping to two chaps from New Zealand.

"Do you know why Aussies call you Pommies?" they ask.

Neither one of our bunch of banana brains know the answer, so we listen to their theory.

They proceed to say, "Well, the then government of Great Britain, on deporting convicts to Australia, had their documents stamped with the words Prisoner of Mother England on them, hence the initials P.O.M.E."

"Thanks for that. I thought it was from the sound that our big guns made! Shows what I know then," I replied.

Mind you, their theory does sound more feasible than mine. Finishing off our beers, we continue on our journey as far away from this place as possible. On returning to the cars, Lionel's has got a puncture, so there is a short delay replacing his wheel before hitting the road again.

We head now towards *Neustadt an der Weinstrasse*, where Oggy thinks Gunther's pub is. On arriving, surprise, surprise, as expected Oggy can't remember a single thing of the whereabouts of Gunther's establishment. Then he said, "I think I remember an oss [horse] trough."

Great! All the way to West Germany and we've got to look for an oss trough. We cruise around this town for an hour, looking for this contraption, before we decide to call it a day. Then we come to a halt to discuss our next move. With the debate over, the decision is to find a pub and stop the night anyway.

It's back on the road and Lionel somehow manages to dodge an oncoming car and lives to see another day. We eventually find an excellent car-park with a few pubs at walking distance. I walk over to Doc and said, "Yoe was all lucky when Lionel forgot which side of the road he was on."

"I've had my eyes shut since we arrived in Europe, I don't want to see what hits us," Doc replied.

In the first pub we go in we think it's time we satisfied our appetites, so we all order a large steak with all the trimmings apiece (except Graham, who's a vegetarian), plus not forgetting our liquid refreshments. On completion of our delicious meal some of us order another one. Graham, at smelling our mouth-watering succulent steaks succumbs to the way of the meat-eater and orders two for himself. Meanwhile, while we eat, the others wander out of the pub for a ramble around the area, till we catch them up later. But, before we finish they're back. Rob Hill, nicknamed Cuzz, because he has the same surname as me, said, "Hilly we're ideally placed for sex shows, brothels and conker picking."

"Let's goo exploring then," and so say all of us.

We tell the owner of the pub that it's time to evacuate his premises, but we'll be back.

Well, with visions of wobbly flesh and dangley bits seen to, it's back to the pub. The gaffer said, "Ever heard of a drink called, 'Red Eye?"

"No mate, we'll try some though," I said.

The only thing I know that's in this drink is Tabasco sauce, so I take a bottle as a souvenir. After all these Red Eyes, a couple of us have now got 'Shut Eyes'.

We end up calling these drinks 'Zoonie's,' after the creature in the 1960s puppet show *Fireball XL5*. The reason for this is we now resemble him, even down to his speech. Especially Doc, who's gone slightly further than most and has flaked out down the steps of the pub and is now lying on the pavement outside, in a right state.

Yes, unbeknown to us, this bar is below a brothel and we hadn't realised it. Doc's antics upset the local leg-openers and they shout down from their bedroom windows above this pub, "Get him out of here, he's ruining our trade!"

I see their point, as Doc is blocking the entrance and no passers-by will bother going up to them. Trying to lift Doc is a bit of a task, he's a bit of a fat lad. It makes it more difficult because we have to dodge the fags and rubbery things the prostitutes hurl at us. They're still gobbing off at us. Bollocks! we reply.

They keep on mouthing a few more obscenities. Double bollocks! we reply.

All rather intoxicated, Cuzz, Graham and me struggle to carry Doc to the car park which is not too far away. Laying him on the tarmac by our cars and covering him over with his sleeping bag, it's then our turn to sleep. Graham, while this has been going on, is having a bash at building the 8th wonder of the world, with pyramid-type mounds of meat particles scattered over the tarmac. We all drift off to sleep eventually, only to be woken up by two Polizei. They wake Leo up and without opening his eyes and not knowing who's disturbing his rest, said, "Come back tomorrow."

They proceed in waking us all up. Thinking we're all in for it, to our surprise all they want to do is move us away from the entrance of the car-park, as it's used early in the morning and they don't want us to get run over.

"Thank you officers, guten nacht." I'm a bit of a cunning linguist you know!

We wake to the sound of bells from the church over the road and to find lots of kids all going to school with pockets full of conkers from the trees over the wall. The one's that we should have had. Well bang goes our little conker competition we were arranging. Wandering over to the bogs, by the church, we're startled by the cleaner coming out of the door as we're going in. He resembles Quasimodo and with the bells still ringing it could be. Not far away is the town of Heidelberg and its time to move on. All of us walk down the traffic-free high street in the modern part of this town. It's packed with shoppers, who all stare at us as we walk by. You could hear a marble roll. This is an eerie and weird feeling, which I personally don't want to experience again. None of us feel comfortable in this place so we have a quick, quiet drink and off.

Our schedule now takes us towards Rhudesheim, about 50 miles away. On arriving on the wrong side of the river, we just manage to catch the last ferry across the River Rhine. As this is a popular old town we decide to take off our beer towel coats, trainers and boots and have a good wash and brush up in the bogs by the railway station where we've parked the cars for the night. Looking for a good time here, we change into our best shirts and shoes. All the pubs are close together and most have entertainment on. Now for the first drink of the evening but, to our dismay, the licensee of this pub refuses us entry. Cuzz can't be bothered to even answer him, so undeterred we try another and the same thing happens again. Bar after bar we're refused until three of us get into a plain unexciting dump, Lionel gets the beers in and we sit down. Totally despondent at the moment after such high hopes tonight, six Germans approach us say, "You English are in our seats!"

Swat a squarehead springs to mind, but before anything occurs, in walk the remaining nine of us and it's flyaway Fritz and auf wiedersehen Hans and company. Talk about a welcome, Bomber Harris would have been proud. One of our most unfortunate and unforeseen incidents yet.

We all go back to the cars and it's back on with our general attire, then back into town. We're all rather agitated at the moment and on our approach to our first pub we are anticipating refusal once again. To our joy the licensee allows us to enter. No wonder; there's not a soul in here. We all relax at long last on one long table and the ale starts to flow. Happy hours and alcohol-filled jubilant jugs of juice are drunk without further interference. In the end, although we've been in the bar all on our own, we do enjoy ourselves. Leaving now we walk to the railway station, where we form a barrier with the three of our cars in a U-shape for protection against the arrival during the night of any further heavy vehicles that could turn us into hedgehogs. This works on our port side, but on the starboard side we're unable to stop the thunderous sound of the trains going by.

It's a lovely sunny morning and not a very pleasant sleep is had by anyone. Stoves at the ready we cook beans on toast and tins of soup. Off now for a stroll round town, to buy some souvenirs. From here we can see chairlifts rising to some German monument. The chairlifts are good fun and on reaching the summit, we find the monument dedicated to a war they won back in the 1800s. It's a smashing view up here, as you can take in the Rhine and the vineyards. With our curiosity complete, back down we come, all separated in small groups, to rummage in the gift shops. Again it's Lionel who gets hassled by a few locals. What is up with these people? There's no messing around this morning and we run them into a vineyard and cover them with bunches of squashed grapes and that's that.

Rudesheim is getting us really irritable, so let's get out of here. Joe has bought two twelve-foot balloons, about twelve inches in diameter and decides to blow them up while travelling along in the car. There's not enough room for these, so I open the window to relieve the strain. On doing so, the only map we have, which I'm reading is sucked out the gap and gets ripped and torn to pieces by the other cars behind before blowing into the Rhine. Lionel who's driving has a wooty on him (a word we use between us for being sulky or throwing a wobbly) because it's his map and moans we'll never find our way home now. Oh dear, my little mate's flipped so we stop at the next service station to get a new one. The lads in the two cars behind us are all still laughing and find it hilarious. Lionel though has still to be convinced. Our itinerary now takes us on about a 120-mile trip into Aachen. On the way here, Joe said, "This is a big town ay [isn't] it lads?"

"Which town's that then Joe?" I enquired.

"This one here look, we're just passing it again," he indicated.

"Joe my old pal, that sign says Ausfahrt! It ay a town name, it's German for exit!"

What a plonker!

Destination reached, it's all in the first pub we come to, where we stop for liquor, nutrition and a bladder movement. Ten of us request a steak meal and numerous drinks and then all put our leftover deutschmarks in a dish. When this is gone we'll be gone. We've all spent a fair bit of money in this place, only for the despicable gaffer to go over to Wayne – who's bought our last round out of the kitty – and say angrily.

"You haven't given me enough money, you're two deutschmarks (about 60p) short."

"I gave you the correct money, it's all we had left in our kitty," replied Wayne.

An argument breaks out between them and he threatens to call the police.

I go over and say to him. "I can't believe your attitude, after all we've spent in your pub. Arguing over such a trivial amount."

He insists on his payment and between us all we just manage to find the miserly amount he requires. We hand it over to this hateful bastard. With everyone out of German money, we head towards the Dutch border. Anything to get away from this pon [pan] hole. On the whole, an awful and unpleasant first tour into West Germany. It's certainly all been totally kraut of order. Nothing else can go wrong, can it? Yes! The police stop Graham, the driver of our third car, because one of his lights is out. We ask the police if we can put him in the middle of our cars, would it be okay to carry on to the border as we've got no money until we get there. This they dubiously let us do. At the border we all change our English money into whatever amount of guilders each of us require, while Graham buys a bulb for the light on his motor.

We then journey on to the nearest Dutch village, finding one of two pubs it has to offer, we get yapping to the locals and receive a warm welcome. The Dutch chaps and wenches (girls) are a good bunch and we agree on stopping and supping the night away in here. Fun and laughter is had by all. One couple we're talking to say in perfect porn-star English, "Ver are you schleeping tonight?"

"Outside where we normally sleep," said Fast Eddy. "No you mush schleep at our flat," they insisted.

"Very nice of you to ask but there's too many of us. We're better off outside," replied Leo.

They spake [speak] good English in this pub. One word I have to pick the locals up for saying is 'ond, meaning hand which is also the Black Country word for it. This word might have its roots going back centuries when the invasion by the Angles, Saxons and Jutes occurred, yoe [you] never know. With all my theories on parts of the English language over with, it's now 3 a.m. Our quaffing has come to an end and the offer of a warm flat has been refused. So it's outside the pub, a handier place. With not many hours left before morning there's no messing about. It's straight to sleep.

I'm woken up by a trickle of piddle running down the small bank above my head. My pillow has become a sponge. I shout out, "Who's been piddling on top of the bonk [bank], it's like a waterfall?" To my surprise Lionel's still up there and he hasn't finished.

"I day [didn't] see ya down theer Hilly."

One day I swear I'll lynch this little twat. Could it be payback time over his lost map? Our destination today is to be a smashing, popular and interesting small village called Sluis, on the Dutch and Belgium border.

Our daily jaunt begins and after about fifty miles on the road, we're lost in Antwerp, until a helpful Belgium bloke directs us out of a maze of streets and puts us on the right road to Sluis. Eventually we reach our destination and park by the quaint flowing river, with its charming working windmill, restaurants, coffee houses and sex shops. After a peek or two, (well, two hours more like) around these eye-popping porn parlours, it's all into a bustling bar. Here we all ravenously dispose of a fabulous steak meal. Mind you, any more scoffing chunks of cow and I'll be eating grass. A gargle of glowing golden beers will now quench our thirst during the remainder of the afternoon. A couple of us try the strong bottled beer called Duvel, this is potent.

What a glorious few hours spent sitting on the patio watching all the girls go by. Then, nipping in the gift shop to get rid of our remaining guilders, we buy gifts and borrow some carved walking sticks. Sadly it's time to move on as we've got a ferry to catch at Dunkirk. Again we get lost on approaching this town. Our usual signalling system that has worked well during our entire trip is beginning to fail us and exhaustion seems to be setting in. The 'system' we have is that the third car that is always at the rear should flash the second car and the second flashes the lead car, which then pulls over until we're all in one line again. Something hasn't worked out right as we've all lost each other. It's not until approaching the boarding of the ferry we meet up again. Our crossing allows us to recuperate for the long journey over to Dover. It's during this crossing that we come close to colliding with a ship. Luckily, we survive any major incident.

From Dover we drive non-stop arriving home at 6 a.m. because Tim, who has left the army now, works as an ambulance driver and his shift starts soon. I take my hat off to this lad, because I'm off to bed. This has been an expedition I wouldn't have missed for the world, albeit not the most welcoming. Possibly due to the number of lads, the locals didn't look at it as a visit more of an invasion. Who knows? I lie awake, reflecting on the past few days and wondering in the future who will carry on visiting pubs and who will disappear, leaving me with just the memories.

But at the moment let's carry on with the Banks's pubs, which have almost been completed. We're returning to one though, the *Foxcote* (Wollescote) as arranged by the gaffer a few weeks ago. On arrival at 7 p.m. with the entertainment being set up in the corner of the pub, we ask to speak to the gaffer. We're told he's not in just yet, he'll be in later. Never mind we'll stop anyway and wait for him to turn up. The clock strikes nine and we're all having a great night, singing and dancing but, alas, no sign of the landlord. Towards the end of the night our table is now full of numerous empties. All of the locals have their photos taken with us. They have enjoyed our company immensely and it's a shame the gaffer never showed his face. He missed a marvellous evening session.

Two days later and I now find my souvenir bottle of Tabasco sauce, obtained in Neustadt, on last week's adventure. On reading the label on the bottle it says *made in Worcestershire* – so much for my rare find. October 12th is upon us and none of us can believe it's our last Banks's and Hanson's pub all 748 of them. First, we must visit our penultimate pub the *Red Cow* (Gornal). Then a fitting finale is organised at the *Glynne Arms,* known locally as the *Crooked House*, (Himley). Free sandwiches have been kindly provided for us at this unique and fitting pub, which on entering you feel like your legs are in your pockets. The walls are lop-sided, so are the doors and windows etc, all due to mining subsidence. You can even roll a marble on the windowsill and it appears to roll uphill, a must for any visitor in this area. Gornal folk have always called the pub the 'Siden House' (sunken house). A Gornal rhyme written many years ago perfectly describes this landmark building.

Cum in an av sum um brewd erl,
Stop as lung as yoem erbal
At a public called the Siden House
Weer the bottel runs up the terbul.

The intention is to stop here all night but there's no television and there's a big fight on the telly soon. So it's back to the *Red Cow*, just up the road from this one.

We're all excited about this live championship fight as it's a local lad from Warley, to be precise, Barry Cowdell versus Azumah Nelson. Wayne, ah kid (My brother) said, "Hurry up lads, the fight starts in two minutes," as they're standing in front of the telly.

"Hang on a minute, we're still being served," replied Doc, Fast Eddy and Tim, who are getting everyone's order.

It's a small lounge in this pub, there's not enough seats for everybody, most of us settle down cross-legged on the floor. The lads pass the ale over and we all sit in anticipation as two excellent boxers are ready to knock the cack out of each other. Ding, ding, 'Round One'. We all relax and have a sip of our beer, all shouting Cowdell on, then out of the blue, it's Ding, dong, our man cops a punch from nowhere and Cowdell hits the floor, it's a first round knockout. Bloody hell, what a pisser, he never even had time to warm up and neither did we. The vote is unanimous and we drink up and it's off back to base at the *Yew Tree* (West Bromwich). An anticlimax tonight to the completion of all our designated Banks's and Hansons' pubs. We all reflect on the trips and adventures we've had since November last year, when we decided to tour pubs for charity. Agreeing between us that it's been an exceptional experience.

The following week at the *Yew Tree*, a disco and raffle is organised on our behalf to add more funds to the £500 we've raised for Heath Lane Hospital. We hand over our cheque to Mrs Ethel Hale, senior nurse manager. The money we're told will be going towards research equipment. Ethel and her three associates are enjoying their night so much they decide to stay. Our second entry in the local paper reads, *A Year's Cheers For Charity*. The general conversation tonight revolves around the prospect of further travels around Great Britain. "Shall we carry on raising money for charity and round our adventures off at 1,000 pubs?"

Jazza and Dennis explained that they've achieved their target and that's it for them.

CHAPTER 3

A THOUSAND MEMORIES

With a magical target of one thousand pubs to aim for, we take on board visiting all the Batham's, Holt's and Holden's pubs all situated in the Black Country. This moves us into January 1986. Touring local, we stumble on a most unusual pub. Even though it's only four miles away in Upper Gornal, the *Britannia* is a Gem. It's the most untouched place I've ever seen and we couldn't even tell it was a pub from the outside. There's a narrow passage on entry, with the first door to your left, a locked up defunct butcher's shop. The second door to your left however is a unique small taproom. Nobody is in at the moment so being first in we all sit down. To our amazement a little old lady walks in.

"What would you like to drink?" she asks.

"Anything you have on offer, please," says Leo. We can't see any bar counter.

"I only have Whitbread keg Mild," she explained and we said that would be fine. "Please remain seated and I will bring your drinks over for you."

I've never seen this before, as she pours our beer out of the old tap by where the disused hand pulls are in the old wall unit. She brings them over individually and we happily pay the lady. We ask her, her name. "Sally Williams," she replies.

Around the walls are photographs going back to the turn of the century. There's one of Sally as a young girl on the wall, she has lived here all her life. A roaring coal fire makes this room really cosy and on top of the solid marble mantelpiece, piled high are boxes of sweets and snacks. Sally says, "Those sweets never melt on top of the marble as the solid marble never gets hot."

After taking a few internal shots of the taproom, I ask Sally if my mate can take a photograph of the two of us. I can't believe it – my film has run out in my camera. This is really annoying as I think this would have been a unique photo for my records. What a remarkable old lady, we wish her all the best and leave. I've now got lots of affection for this pub and when the time comes when Sally is no longer capable of running this pub, like so many fascinating buildings in England this will undoubtedly be altered in some way. Fingers crossed it won't. The worst scenario is it could be demolished – we shall have to wait and see.

Anyway, off to the *Wharf* (Old Hill) by the cut [canal]. A quick pint is had, as it's packed and a little uncomfortable standing up. Lionel's car is first off the unlit car-park and he misses the narrow steep short dirt track exit and bumps over the edge, leaving his front two wheels hanging over a four-foot drop. We all steadily jump out and nip round to the front of his car, where we all give it a good old heave-ho eventually freeing him. We finish off at the *Manor House* (West Bromwich) a Banks's boozer recently purchased off Ansells. This is a superb thirteenth century old beamed pub with a moat surrounding it and is definitely worth a look.

It's February 16th 1986 and a visit to the *Vine* (Brierley Hill), known locally as the *Bull and Bladder* and headquarters of the Batham's Brewery, is first on our list and what an excellent classic alehouse. Next stop is nicknamed *Ma Pardoe's* (Netherton) after the long-standing landlady Doris Pardoe. Its proper name is the *Old Swan*. This is an old Victorian pub with enamelled ceiling and has a small cosy snug room, one of only four home-brew pubs left in the whole of England in the 1970s. The others are the *Three Tuns* (Bishops Castle), Shropshire, the *All Nations Inn* (Coalport Road) near Blists Hill Museum, Shropshire, and finally the *Blue Anchor* (Helston) in Cornwall.

Not too far away from the *Old Swan* and rather difficult to find is the *Little Dry Dock* (Netherton). This is owned by a chap called Colm O'Rourke whose idea about pubs is very different to any other and he is hoping to expand his pub ownership in the near future. He's definitely got weird ideas about the themes of his pubs, they are quite fascinating. Inside the *Little Dry Dock* is a complete narrowboat, which is now actually the bar! Desperate Dan pies are the pub's speciality meals. This is a massive pie with pastry horns on top. A young couple couldn't quite manage eating their pies and leave, so Oggy and myself sit down and intend to finish them off. The only problem is that the one I try eating has mustard on it, which totally takes me by surprise, as I don't like the stuff and I have to leave it. Oggy gets a shock too, as I tell him the young couple who left are on the way back in. They aren't really but Oggy's face was a picture to see. A short walk away is the Netherton Tunnel. A stroll along the towpath through this tunnel with the cut (canal) only feet away is quite scary, especially without a torch. You should try it some day.

Our final supping house of the night is the *Royal Exchange* (Bilston); a well-known jazz pub nicknamed the *Trumpet*. On coming out of this place, Tony discovers his car's been naffed (stolen). All of the lads who were in his car very quickly pile into the other motors so it's all a bit crammed. Poor old Tony is shown no sympathy about the whereabouts of his beloved car. No matter, he has to cadge a lift with the rest of us, all the way home. A strange night to say the least.

March arrives and our next home-brew pub the *All Nations Inn* (Coalport Road) is visited. Everybody for some strange reason comes out of the woodwork tonight as twenty of us in five cars fill the small bar room of this pub. The gaffer thinks a coach has pulled up. This isn't a visit; it's more of an invasion. We stop for a few excellent thirst-quenching pints, then it's on to one more pub nearby, then home.

Lionel has come up with the idea of making an appearance at the highest pub in Great Britain none of us have a clue where it is. "I've found it out lads; it's the *Cat and Fiddle*, on the road to Buxton, past the village of Flash, in Derbyshire," said an excited Lionel.

With a thin covering of snow and it being a cold wintry day, it's off on another mission. It's March 30th. After almost two hours of driving we arrive at our chosen pub. Yes, it's 1,690 feet above sea level; the only problem is it's the second highest. At this everyone feels like rolling Lionel up in a little ball and making a snowman out of him. All the same we stop for a lovely pint of Robinson's Old Tom. While up in the peak district or on a day like today the bleak district, we visit ten more pubs.

April arrives and it's our longest Sunday night journey to date, to the *Bickerton Poacher*, (Bickerton) Cheshire, which has a skeleton holding a pint at the bottom of a well inside the bar. Then it's off to the *Wilymoor Lock* (Wilymoor), to get to this one you have to balance across a lock over the cut (canal), a tricky manoeuvre at this time of night. A devastating week follows, as my grandmother, who means so much to me passes away, at the age of ninety, after a fall at home. At her funeral all the lads and many more besides turn up to pay their respects. Her home is where we have been meeting for the past two years. Gran's favourite song is April Showers by Al Jolson and as the burial takes place the sun shines down on the lads carrying the coffin and for a brief two minutes we actually have an April shower. This is a very fitting tribute to my wonderful and much loved grandmother. The wake at our local is a real emotional but joyful occasion with sing-songs, stories and jokes, courtesy of Foxy, one of Oggy's old motorbike pals. With plenty of flowing beers, Oggy, my dad, makes a speech.

"All drink to my mother and her memory, let's give her a night her'd (she'd) have loved to be part of!"

I think we've taken it as far as we can tonight. It's now 1.30 a.m. and what a wake it's been.

With the worst possible week over and with normal service resumed we pay a visit to Gloucestershire. We drop in a delightful isolated stoon (stone) built pub in the Cotswolds, a Donnington brewery owned inn, called the *Plough* (Ford). This was originally an old Court House and the cellar was the gaol. The interior has a flagstone floor, hops hanging off the ceiling, solid wood tables, a large open log fire and a gaffer who's chuffed we're visiting his boozer. Les

Carter is his name and what a character he is. Sitting our side of the bar on his stool constantly swigging away on his whisky and having a good old chit-chat with us. He says before we leave, "I'd love to see you lads again, come back and see me I'll put you up for the night."

It's darker than a chewed up blackjack around these windy narrow roads. All of sudden there's a very sharp bend at the bottom of the hill. I said to Graham the driver, "Slow down a bit mate, it's tricky round here."

"It's alright Hilly, I'm following the cats' eyes."

Somehow the cats went walkabout (Percy Shaw will turn in his grave) as Graham fails miserably to navigate a bend and ends up going nesting, leaving our car up to its belly in bibbles (pebbles). We're stuck in an escape lane. With nine of us pushing and a car pulling we finally manage to get it out of the gravel and on the way home our car sounds like a babby's (baby's) rattle.

After our merriment at the *Plough* last night, we plan a tour of all sixteen of the remaining Donnington hostelries. We waste no time and before we know it, we're off. It's a glorious sunny May day where a dozen alehouses have our stamp of approval, finishing off at Les's pub. Only a couple more pints are tasted in here, due to us all being slightly intoxicated. Les keeps his word and puts us up for the night above a converted old barn in the courtyard. There's lots of old junk up here, but it won't bother us as we bed down in-between it. Morning arrives to the sound of belches, farty flatulence and Ann – Les's missus, who shouts up the steps, "Lads your breakfast is ready, don't hang about or it will go cold."

This is something we hadn't counted on, so it's up and into the pub for our fittle (food).

What hospitality from a smashing couple!

Our intrepid team mobilises for today's remaining four pubs. On the way to these, the left-hand side of the road Lionel's driving on is cordoned off by cones. Lionel pulls round them, driving on the right now, when Doc said, "Lionel there's a bloody great big lorry coming towards us."

"I was here first," snarls Lionel.

We're all crapping a bibble now and remind him that it's bigger than we are.

In the nick of time Lionel swerves into the cones and the lorry thunders by.

What a stubborn prick Lionel can be! Anyway the four pubs are visited, and then it's off on a drive to take a nose around Donnington brewery itself. Situated in a splendid and attractive setting, with a nearby trout farm, its lake, black swans and impressive old brewery, this will take some beating, as it's beautiful here. This is what pub-crawling is about. Saying that, their pubs are superb too, some being by rivers, others in quaint villages and most with a magnificent country view. The beer isn't bad either. Magic is the word most appropriate for this unforgettable, tipsy tour.

June is here and we travel to the *Fleece* (Bretforton). It's a true, classic English unspoilt pub that you must see and only a visit will confirm the reason why. The landlady of thirty years Lola Taplin died in 1977 at the age of eighty-three and left the *Fleece* to the National Trust. Inside is a pewter collection believed to have been left by Oliver Cromwell in exchange for the family silver. When in season, asparagus is auctioned off at this pub and we stand and watch as this gets under way. Our next pub is a rare one indeed the *Shoulder of Mutton* (Broad Marston). This must be someone's house as we walk through the gate and up the path. A little old lady escorts us into a small back room in this superb thatched cottage, with a scrubbed table, old wood plank benches and a dartboard. The ceiling is so low that the darts have worn a groove in the ceiling on the way into the board, she then fetches our scrumpy cider the only drink available in a jug, and pours them in our glasses. Her husband signs my book and saying our farewells we leave, this unusual place is totally fascinating.

July comes and goes with two dozen pubs visited. It is now August, my brother Wayne and his family, along with John Bungle and his girlfriend Jayne, have gone on their holidays. So what better excuse do we need for a beer run? We'll turn up and take them by surprise. It's getting late starting our tour down towards Mawnen Smith in Cornwall. Being too far for us to make it before closing time, we find an isolated spot off a country lane to bed down for the night. Talk about being dark – this is darker than dark. Some sleep in the car. Tony Bungle and myself doss down on the ground by secluded woodland. It's a bit scary lying near long grass and we can both hear something rustling in it.

I'm crapping it a little and I ask Tony to go and have a look if there's something there.

Tony declined.

Both of us look at each other and neither one of us are prepared to investigate. Then it pounces. We let out loud screams and fight the beast off, only to discover it's Drewy, a new recruit, egged on by Gav, playing about. What a daft prat, he almost gave us a runny leg apiece.

I'm glad to get the night over with but it's a gloomy, dismal morning, so let's venture on. Arriving at our destination, our presence is not totally appreciated by the women of the holiday party, as they've travelled here to get away from us. Since we're not welcome, I think we'll nip into the town of Falmouth, out of their way. A few hours pass abusing the local ale here. We now drive to Maenporth as the lads fancy a swim in the sea. Freezing is the apt term for the water today, as they strip off to their skiddies and jump in. Meanwhile, I stop on dry sand and it's a nice hot cup of tea and a Kit Kat from the beach hut for me, overlooking a deserted Maenporth beach as the heavens open up. On coming out of the sea they're a sorry sight to see, as they've all got a bad case of winkie shrink as they change into dry underwear. I've seen better physiques on sea slugs.

Back into Falmouth for fish and chips then back to Maenporth in the *Seahorse Inn*, where the intention is to stop for the remainder of the drinking day. This is a really good pub as we have parked the car on the beach and walked to this one. This means all of us can have a good few pints. Plus, the beach is where we intend to sleep, for a peaceful night. What a change this will be. It's late as we wake up on another dreary morning so we agree to drive to Bristol; Tony's got some unfinished business with a girl he knows there. We eventually find the pub Tony's after, the *Old Inn*, (Congresbury). While he sorts things out with this wench (girl) called Helen, we end up stopping all day, finally settling for the evening over the road on a Rugby pitch. Talk about damp; it is damp and there are snails, slugs and woodlice everywhere, what nice things to wake up to in the morning. Things haven't gone quite to plan for Tony, so home is now the order of the day.

Twelve months have nearly passed since our first European trip and a suggestion for another shows signs of encouragement. The eight lads who fancy another bash are Leo, Lionel, Graham, Doc, Wayne, Joe, Gav and myself. Graham said, "I don't fancy the arrangement we had last year, with so many cars it was a pain trying to keep everybody together."

Wayne pipes up saying, "Why not hire a minibus?"

A good idea, so it's agreed by all to arrange a departure date and organise a travel route to wherever we fancy. Surely if we descend on West Germany again it can't be as bad as last year, can it?

September 23rd 1986 and so begins our second invasion of Europe. To save money we're leaving on Tuesday and our return will be Sunday 28th on the 21.45 ferry. Cost of the minibus is £255, the crossing £182 and £200 in the petrol kitty. I've had £90 off each explorer. It's taken a few weeks of planning places to visit, interesting sites, mileage, foreign currency, canned foods, a couple of pounds of bacon, milk, the camping stove and hopefully everything else to get us through the forthcoming six days. Gav and myself go to pick up our transport at 9 a.m. It doesn't arrive until 9.30 a.m. then the door jams and it takes the mechanic another half-hour to free it. Then I break the key in the petrol lock; another delay. Finally, one hour thirty minutes late, we're free to collect the other lads. We set the milometer to nought and away we go. The first stop is the *Rose and Crown* (Hartwell) Northamptonshire. There we play darts and pool, some relax on the kids' swings and climbing frames. On the road again, as a game of cards starts up in the back of the van and a fitting sing-along,

From a Jack to a King. A café near Canterbury, a traditional ale at the *Mermaid* (Bishopbourne) and a final stop at the *Chance Inn* (Guston) before we board the ferry. In this pub, out come the darts and we play games called 'Killer', 'Half It' and 'Leave It', most of the darts are ending up in the tyre by now, as a few ales have been sunk. We continue our journey and I top the minibus up with petrol and then we board the 10 p.m. ferry, arriving in Ostend 2.10 a.m. The lads who have watches put them forward by one hour and we drive on. Missing the ring road in Brussels and getting lost, ending up on a service station in Leuven where we sleep until 7.30 a.m. on the grass verge.

Up and off, pulling in at a nice picnic area lay-by, where we're all looking forward to our breakfast. As we sing together, "It's all egggg, bbbacon, beeeans and a frieddd slice," a record sung by Madness.

My mouth is wairtering (watering) at the thought of bunging down my breakfast. Alas, some clown has forgot to bring the frying pon (pan), so we all end up with tinned soup. I take a long swig of milk now and I'm almost sick as it's gone off. Our epic expedition starts again, until coming to a halt at a bar in Hambach, by Diez near Frankfurt. The beer in here is lovely. I said to the woman in charge, "Do… you… have… a… frying… pan?"

This isn't going down that well as she can't understand me. So with a piece of paper and pen I draw a pan with eggs in it and then show it to her. Bingo! We've got one as a souvenir. Meanwhile Graham, who's brought with him one hundred pre-decimal shilling pieces in a bag, is emptying the pub's fag machine. Unbeknown to us, four of these old-shilling coins (worth 5p each) can get you a pack of twenty fags in return. The West German exchange rate is working out at 2.90 marks to the £1. The beer is two marks for about half a pint. We leave here after a pleasant afternoon's drinking arriving at 5 p.m. in Wurzburg, stopping to savour our very late breakfast.

Next stop is a pub in the village of Hilpolstein. While in the boozer, the gaffer comes over and asks which of us smokes. "None of us actually mate, so why the question?" I reply.

"Because all of the cigarettes in my machine have gone, that's why," he says sharply.

We're soon to find out, as bloody Graham has sneaked off and used up his remaining old shilling coins and he's totally emptied the gaffer's fag machine. Next thing we know the landlord bans us and wants us out of his pub, so we're forced to leave. It wouldn't be that bad if we all smoked and he shared them out, but he's taking them home for his missus. Walking around this village, we notice terrorist pictures on the wall of the police station. Gav said, "I bet that last gaffer in the pub thought we were terrorists."

We loff (laugh) at this, but not for long as the windows open in the cop shop and the police come running out." You are not welcome in our village," they say. So sleeping in this place as gone up the suff. (down the drain). We carry on walking. It seems the word's out in the village that some English are here. Next a Hell's Angel stops us on his motorbike. As we thought, his gang have heard we're here and he said to us, "How would you like to come to an all night party?"

Thank the lord for that, I thought he'd come to lamp us up. Anyway I replied, "No thanks, the police have told us we have to move on."

"Let's move," said the lads.

I think this is a safer option.

We travel only a short distance from that slightly unpleasant village Hilpolstein to another remote village, called Eichstatt. Why waste valuable drinking time? Let's get in the nearest distillery den. In this place we get on well with the licensees and a bloke about fifty years old, named Rudolph Hess, I don't believe this chap but he produces his passport to confirm his identity. Rudy, as we call him, buys us all a bowl of soup and bread, what a friendly gesture. He speaks quite good English and we get on admirably. By now a group of fifteen German youths have arrived and are all supping away noisily about three yards away from us. While eating our soup one of them who's had a few beers goes up to Wayne, yapping on about something in his kraut lingo and smashes a glass on the floor at my brother's feet. His mate fetches him back and our stiff upper lip wins this round. The next thing to come over is a cushion, which knocks our beers over. I pick up a large ashtray intending to give him a 'Brucie bonus'. Rudy said, as he grabs my wrist, "Leave it to me, I'll sort it out." So we do and for the moment he does.

Wayne and Gav now go to the bogs to ask a couple of the locals who have gone in there why they don't like the English. While they are in there, another cushion comes flying over like a V2 rocket, again spilling our beer. This time it kicks off and the kraut that chucked it cops a direct hit to his eye, just like a Spitfire by my well-aimed fist. At this moment I'm thinking we're in for a right thumping as we're outnumbered two to one. By the time Wayne and Gav return this chap's eye is a black blob and they're wondering what all the commotion is. Amazingly none of his pals start a thing and the gaffer throws all of them out. Well, what a stroke of luck that was. Now we can relax again and enjoy a good humoured conversation with Rudy and the licensees.

An elderly local bloke enters the pub and said. "Little... man... drowning... in... river!"

We thought this might be a trap to get us outside, but we rush out to help regardless. Where we find Lionel, he's spewing up in the river lying on his belly. So we carry him to the minibus and put him to bed. Back in the pub until 3 a.m. by now my head feels like Florence spinning round on her magic roundabout and the doors and walls are no longer in a fixed position. We thank everyone involved in making it a welcoming, if somewhat eventful night and fall asleep outside this pub. It's brass-monkey weather tonight and at daybreak it's still too early to rise. The plastic bag I'm sleeping in looks more like a used Johnny, while Joe's been lying on a tatty old sofa and resembles Worzel Gummidge. What a potent evening we had.

Having set off, we now stop for a rare wash in the toilets on the A8 Munich to Saltzburg road. The town of Berchtesgaden at 12.30 p.m. is a welcome rest for us. This is the place Adolf Hitler resided at, called the 'Eagle's Nest'. It's too misty up in the hills to bother with this, so we walk around this most desirable part of Bavaria. All quite parched, we hear jubilant rejoicing coming from the local town hall.

As we approach, dozens of German's totter and fall out of this building, where there's a beer festival going on. We fancy going in here but after last night's escapade we probably won't be welcome, so we give it a miss, preferring a quieter stimulant elsewhere. Now it's over the border into Austria and the idyllic village of Strobl. The first Hughie (throw up of the day) belongs to Lionel, as he feeds the fish in the lake. Watch out for low flying cheese, as Graham and I have a slight disagreement over me taking a nibble out of Wayne's cheese. We similarly conquer St Wolfgang, as we indulge in a drop of the hard stuff in the *White Horse Inn*. Around this scenic town are loads of glass cases containing facial woodcarvings. Mind you we've got a couple of woodentops in our group. Leaving and rolling on over the 'Gschutt' pass we arrive in Zell am Zee. It's a dead hole. There's not a soul about, so after a quick drink and with it getting late our stomachs need satisfying. For supper we warm some grub up on our stoves and then we bed down opposite a railway line on a car-park and slowly nod off.

We wake up to a somewhat comical situation, all of us are bone dry, except Joe and myself. "Hilly, was it raining last night?"

"I doe (don't) think so Joe."

"Why are we so wet then?" moans Joe.

The other lads have a good giggle at this. They had found the culprit, it was a rag stuck in the guttering above our heads and all night it's been dripping water on us. "Yoe pair look like a pair of living wet socks," says Leo.

After cleaning us up, we all go to the café for a cup of tea and a piece of cake, for forty shilling. I said to the lads, "This Austrian money is very simple to work out providing yoe can remember the old pre-decimal English money, because the exchange rate is exactly twenty shilling to the £1."

(This is precisely the amount of shillings that was in our sadly missed pre-decimal £1).

Less of the nostalgia, it's now 8.30 a.m. and the moist air, mist and cold now descends on the town. So we decide to move on. Advancing into Kaprun, we've come here to view the dams, which are high up in the mountains. I'm driving this morning and to get to the dams we must drive up a steep narrow mountain road. The gradient is unreal. I'm in first gear with my foot right down on the pedal and we're only just doing 5 m.p.h. This is a terrifying ascent with everyone wondering if we're going to stall and roll back over the edge. Talk about shitting a brick, this is the closest I've ever understood to the real meaning of panic! What a relief to get to our destination, which is still nowhere near the top. This is where we have to park the minibus and have to pay the equivalent of £7 each to carry on and view the dams. From now on it's all uphill. Travelling on a coach now at 45 m.p.h. swerving through a single road tunnel certainly puts the wind up us, again we're all glad to get off. Thinking this was the end of our hazardous climb, how mistaken we are, now having to board a large cable platform continuing our perilous journey to the summit through thick fog.

Surely it can't be much further. We'll be having lunch with God's dog at this rate.

On our exit from another tunnel an amazing sight greets us. It's certainly been worth all the nerve-racking moments to get to the pinnacle of this trip. We're now above the clouds and it's like being on an Apollo space mission. The view is breathtaking with majestic snow-covered mountains and the colossal dams. While the other tourists have a lecture off the courier, we do our own thing and walk around taking photos, admiring the spectacular sights, breathing in the clean fresh air, the… bloody hell where's everybody gone? The clouds engulf us completely and we can see no further than two feet in front of us. At this altitude we begin to think we'll never be found alive and it takes a good half-hour of fairy steps before we find the coach, where the rest of the other poor tourists have missed everything due to their long lecture. Back now for our descent, on what I can only say has been the most exhilarating experience of my life to date.

All that clean air has made our mouths quite dry and it's time for a tipple. So onward to the beautiful village of Krimml, with its grass so green and the cows with their jingle bells round their necks. This is an ideal location for a thoughtful and peaceful pint. Not far from here is Europe's highest waterfall, not to be missed. On approaching this, we stumble into two old ladies from the Black Country town of Walsall. One of them said, with a grin on her face, "Wheer yoe from?"

"Not fer from wheer yoe live," said Gav.

Yoe'd never believe it would ya? It's amazing who yoe can bump into.

I love it round here and what a splendid scene the cascading waterfall makes. We drink from the stream, while getting soaked by the spray. Joe turns round and says, "Hilly, there's no hops in this."

A good point, so I think it's time we found some water with them in and, with the viewing complete, our merry band of munchkins now set off for Maynhofen, paying a toll of £3.50 to cross the Gerlos pass. A sign tells you it's 1,628 metres above sea level. There's lots of bogey bends to navigate through this pass, taking one and a half hours to travel roughly twenty miles, arriving at this popular tourist town at 4.30 p.m.

An excellent English bar is found called the *Scotland Yard*, where we consume large quantities of the good stuff, play darts and all bought a T-shirt with the pub name on. For a break of scenery we pop out down the road to a Bavarian bar, but at £2 for half a pint we're soon back to the original watering hole. The night gets more blurred and as our bunch of bleary-eyed boozers depart and make their way back to the minibus, Leo said, "I ay been scrumping in years."

Then each apple tree we find is stripped of its fruit. This is scrumping at its very best. The minibus all this time has been parked on a large hotel car-park and this is where our memorable day comes to a close, on the grass outside the hotel kitchens.

We are woken abruptly early in the morning to the clattering sound of tin lids from the kitchens and the hotel staff all gawping at us. They must find it amusing as they're all up the windows laughing at such a peculiar pile of polythene moving about the grass with little heads popping out. "Morning ladies!" we all shout.

To our dismay we have to ditch our plastic bags due to them being covered in the dog muck we've been lying on all night. They're in a right mess. Good job we've got spare ones. The bin-men arrive to the puzzling sight of all the litter-bins being full. I can't think why. Having had a short walk around this appealing town, stopping for tea and cheesecake, we now have to buy three litres of oil as the minibus is feeling the strain of chugging us around these big hills. We leave for a drive through a road with numerous bends and superb views on what can only be described as a Scalextric track. *The Fern Pass* at 1,209 metres (what's that in yards?) above sea level. Off this road we stop for refreshment at Fussen, then pay a visit to *Neuschwanstein* Castle, which was used in the film *'Chitty, Chitty, Bang, Bang.'* After a pleasant drive through what's known as the 'Romantic Route' – basically it's a drive down a country road. We called for a pint in Peiting, before stopping to cook beans, eggs and tinned stew on top of some bins in a lay-by on the way to Ausburg. To wash it all down on arrival in Ausburg we enter a bar for a pint or two. While in here I get yapping to Hans, an old German officer. He said to me, "I served in the Africa Korps in World War II and I was a P.O.W for three years."

He then asks our names. I said, "Peter, Karl–" and before I could finish, he replied, "Those are good old German names."

"They're also good old English names as well Hans."

We leave now for a four and a half hour drive and I take the wheel, to a town we all remember from last year, *Neustadt an der Weinstrasse*. We park on the same car-park as last year and enter the same establishment as last year, only to be told it's the licensee's night off. Never mind we'll stop for a bite to eat and we pay the equivalent of £5 for a rubbish steak and cold chips. To be honest it stinks in here and so does the barmaid come to think of it. We can't stomach the slop they've dished up, which is very unusual for us. A total contrast from our last visit.

I said to Wayne, "I know I'm driving but if you take the wheel, I'll read the map for ten minutes so we can find the right road we need to get out of here."

Wayne agrees and we walk back to the car park. There, we find Graham relieving himself up the side of the bus. Nobody notices the police watching us from over the road. Wayne jumps in the driver's seat and we all pile in but before he's got the key in the ignition, over comes the Gestapo. I can't believe this, after all the driving I've done today, I think we're really in for it now. The reason being, Wayne has no driving licence and no insurance. I tell Wayne to give them my name and address.

The policeman said, "What's your name and address?"

Wayne gives them my name. Well, so far so good. "Can I see your driving licence."

Almost made it as Wayne shows them my driving licence. "Now can I see your passport."

Well, our little game's up. Now what? Thinking the worst, Graham shouts from the back, "We came here last year, officers!"

One officer said, "It isn't you lot who slept on the car park is it?"

"Yes, officer," came the reply.

It turns out these are the same two policemen that had us last year and they remember us well.

They both say together, with disbelief, written across their faces. "Go on, continue your journey."

After this minor miracle, I take over the driving and we say our thanks and it's off as quick as the legal speed limit allows us. What a stroke of luck that was and a hundred miles later we arrive at Inglis near the Luxembourg border. With us now stationary, four of us dash into the nearest pub, as it's now 1 a.m. The other four mess around in the back of the bus. We just manage to get served but unfortunately the other four slow bones are locked outside and can't get a drink. Instead of us quenching our thirst in this pub we buy a dozen bottles of beer and go back to the bus to share what we've bought with the others. Half-hour later we're crossing the border and settle down on a car-park, swig the remaining beers and get ready for what is now becoming a very chilly night. I've got on, my T-shirt, three jumpers, my beer towel coat as well as being inside my sleeping bag and plastic bag and I'm still freezing. Roll on the morning!

Early birds this morning, as we rise to the noise of rowdy turkeys and mooing cows, three feet away in a field. Dew is everywhere at this time of day and most of us are wet. Joe resembles a giant silkworm. Graham though is counting the phenomenal amount of fags he's collected with his old shilling pieces. All because the lady loves cancer. We are off now on a non-stop drive through the mist into a favourite location of ours, Sluis. Arriving at 12.30 p.m. on Sunday 28th September we are pleased to note that the clocks go back one hour. So we've extra drinking time, but first food, food, food. Our first destination is last year's favourite booze and binge bar-cum-restaurant the Friestag. Between us we indulge in half an abattoir of meat and consume numerous bottles of Duvel beers. It's all been fabulous, delicious and certainly required. The gaffer in here drops some coffee granules on the bar counter and we think it's Wayne's money turning to dust as it's his round and the beer hasn't arrived yet. A short tour around the working windmill is next, where you get an excellent view of the surrounding farmland and all the smells that go with it. It must be muck spreading time today. Leo bored by windmill sails said, "Any chance of a nip in the naughty shops for a peek of the female form?"

Grinding corn isn't what Leo's really bothered about, unless he's hungry and fancies a couple of slices of bread. He's got a point though and we pop in a few for a very nice hour or so. W-w-well, back to the bars and drink I think. Yet again we spend a splendid afternoon in Sluis but, alas, must move on now towards Ostend.

On arrival with an hour to kill before boarding, we go into a bar run by an English chap, for a game of table football and pool. At the docks the custom officials stop and search our minibus with sniffer dogs – nothing is found and we are allowed to drive on. All aboard, as we catch the 9.45 p.m. ferry. Slumped in our seats with a few cans of beers and bottles of Blue Nun, we start up a game called Buzz. This is an easy game where all can play. The first person shouts out the number ONE, the second number TWO, and so on, until you reach number SEVEN, nobody is allowed to say this number so they must say 'Buzz'. Then it continues eight-nine-ten-etc. any denomination that seven goes into is forbidden. If someone does say seven, fourteen, twenty-one etc, they are out of the game. That's the general idea of the game anyway. Graham and myself eventually fall asleep and get our shoelaces tied together. This is a little awkward, when I wake up to use the bog. It's foggy, it's Dover, and it's 3 a.m. Along the A2 near Canterbury we park up in a dead end country lane and sleep until 8 a.m. Wakening up sore and itching, due to lying in bunches of stinging nettles, we pack up and have breakfast at a Little Chef. Joe decides to phone his mom and said to her, "Hello mom, we've arrived safely back in England."

"What time was your arrival?" said his mom. "Hang on mom, I'll ask the lads." We've all had a few and Joe's had more than most.

"It's 8.30 a.m. Joe!" we all shout.

"Is it day-time or night-time?" replied Joe with a bewildered look on his face.

Yes, it seems Joe has certainly overdone the ales. We've all overdone it this holiday and I think most of our brains are pickled. Last stop on our tour – just to make sure, is the *George* (Roade) Northamptonshire. Then it's back home after our epic marathon and the journey ends late afternoon, after covering a total of 2,200 miles. We've successfully completed a memorable drive across Europe. We must do it again.

Not much happens during October with only five alehouses visited. It's November and two new Banks's pubs have been built in the Manchester area so a visit to these is arranged. I've also found out the location of the highest pub in Great Britain on the North Yorkshire/Durham border, so a minibus is hired again. A few new lads come on this trip. Foxy, Little Derv', Mick (Billy boy), Jase and two other chaps I've never met before, but they're welcome – if only for this trip. Our journey begins and our first three pubs to have our seal of approval are the *Railway* (Cheadle), the *Station* (Cheadle), and the *Milestone* (Burbage). Old brick in newly built 1980s public house design is certainly in fashion at the moment. Again we drive to another three pubs then it's on our way towards our ultimate aim, the highest pub. Each yard we travel to get here is like being on a different planet. It's a secluded landscape of bleakness and isolation. There's nothing for miles as the minibus twists in and out down this dark narrow windy road. Eventually we spot this totally out of the way oasis and what a pleasing sight it is.

A triumphant accomplishment now needs christening, so in we go, into the *Tan Hill* high on the moors at 1,732ft above sea level, on the Pennine way. Margaret and Alec Baines are the licensees and Margaret signs my book. They have been at the pub since early 1985. Every year since 1951 there has been an annual *Tan Hill* open Swaledale sheep show. The *Tan Hill* is also well known for the double glazing television advert featuring Ted Moult, where he drops a feather by the windows in this pub and it floats down to the floor. It's a good job he didn't drop it by the door today because the draught through this would have blown it to Carlisle. Maybe his next advertisement will be for double glazed doors? The room itself has stone walls and a flagstone floor: scrubbed wood tables with chairs: a grandfather clock and a roaring log fire. A great place to unwind. The Theakston's 'Old Peculier' is sinking faster than a bibble in a millpond in here and the amount that's now passed my little old wazzin has finally reached the balancing agents needed to walk properly and the visual effects are quite extraordinary. I could have sworn on going to pick my glass up that I only ordered one pint. When at last the time comes to leave, on exit the fresh air clonks me on my noggen and the next thing I know I'm kissing the ground. Somehow I find myself all wrapped up and lying curled up in my plastic bag, huddled together with some of the other lads. A howling wind and driving rain is making sleeping outside at this time of year and at this altitude very uncomfortable, especially when you're well past the alcohol level and need to have a gypsy's kiss.

How relieved I am when daylight comes, having struggled through the horrendous night's downpour. To my horror, there's only me left outside here in the cold and the others are sitting in the warmth of the pub in front of the log fire, eating breakfast. I'm feeling really rough this morning and on entering the pub and smelling the smoke and fumes of the burning fire, I rush to the bogs, to the call of the porcelain. On entering the cubicle surprisingly Lowey is in here. He's already on his hands and knees praying his stomach will stay in one piece. I quickly said to him, "Lowey, shift quick!" I just make it, as all the money I spent on beer last night disappears down the pan. "Hilly! It's my turn now," Lowey cries as he carries on emptying his belly too.

So there's the two of us, me with one hand on the pan and one hand on Lowey's collar and visa versa, pulling each other up by our collars when our turn was necessary. After both of us have taken it in turns to throw up, it's back in the bar. I now hear the full story of my involvement and intimate association with a nice loveable alcoholic beverage called 'Old Peculier' as told to me by the ones who put me to bed. I assume, to the best of my knowledge, that in future I shall have to lay off the slightly higher gravity beers in such quantities. "Had a rough night Hilly?" says John. "Me and some of the lads found a dry place to kip last night. A small cave. It smelt of piddle and dog shit but at least it was dry."

Mick, a guest on our run, quite smugly said, "I found an even better place. Some caravan, out back."

How I wished I'd have stayed sober.

Walking back to the minibus the wind has now picked up again and it's gale force, Leo finds out how strong the wind is as he opens the minibus door and it's ripped from his hand and dents all the side of our hired transport. It's bitter cold and the heavens open up as we journey on through the sheep and barren terrain surrounding this isolated inn. I still feel like meeting my maker, so I wind down the window and let yesterday's fermented ingredients loose. This I do without the knowledge of what direction the wind is blowing. The result of this is I now have the largest cobweb I've ever been entangled in, all in my hair over my face and down my neck. Lowey on seeing me be sick shouts, "Shift Hilly quick, out my way!"

The direction of his spew fails miserably and he puts the map of the world all down my back and over my pillow, which I'm still resting my head on. At this my pillow decides on a better life roaming the Pennine way with the sheep population. We drive now into Blackpool for the remainder of the afternoon. I did try drinking in the first pub but the lads couldn't stand the smell wafting off me, so I went and sat back in the bus and kept Lowey company. He doesn't smell too good either. Achieving our happy aim of visiting Britain's highest pub, the lads jump in the minibus and it's home. This trip has definitely been thirst quenching.

The West Midlands, Nottinghamshire, Leicestershire and Staffordshire all get whirlwind visits, taking us into a New Year, 1987. An old pub we visit is well worth seeking out is the *Manor Arms* (Rushall) near Walsall. This has no bar counter and delightful small rooms. It is accessible by car and narrowboat and is next to a nature reserve, making it that more interesting too. A mention for the *Whittington Arms* (Whittington) near Kinver shouldn't go amiss neither. A charming fourteenth century timber-framed pub, with beams, wood panelling and great open fires inside. It is a well-authenticated fact that Charles II, stayed here after the disastrous defeat of Worcester. April is quickly upon us and a massive milestone finally arrives – our 1,000th pub. A surprisingly subdued affair, there are no major celebrations, no special accomplishment, just a fairly short dinner-time drive sees us venture into a new Bank's owned pub the *Old Wharf* (Digbeth) in Birmingham. Then off back home for dinner and out again for the evening run into Derbyshire.

It's an entry in the 1983 *Guinness Book of Records* that brings us in this part of the World. The *Mount Pleasant* (Repton) reputedly has the longest bar in Great Britain, at seventy-one feet, eleven inches. There are bouncers on the door on arrival, who kindly let us in. For seven nights a week this is a disco pub and the bar isn't one long bar, it's a square one with twenty-nine dispensers on it. This is somewhat disappointing to us because we expected a continuous long bar. No matter, we find a much more interesting hostelry the *John Thompson* (Ingleby). A converted fifteenth century farmhouse, we try their home-brewed ales, which is a lovely end to the night. We talk over whether we continue or disband, now the magical figure of one thousand pubs has been reached. It's decided that we'll carry on for a while longer. Graham, however said, to my surprise, "Sorry Hilly, sorry lads, I've had a great time, but enough is enough, I'm calling it a day."

And so Graham now becomes another casualty of pub tours and will now remain a memory.

CHAPTER 4

BATS GO BANKS'S

It's been a while since we've stopped out overnight, so what better morale boosting exercise can you get. Jazza, Dennis and Foxy, although not regular members any more, organise a trip and we tag along; how refreshing to have someone else plan things for a change. Our route takes us into Shropshire, visiting three different pubs before finishing off at a revisit pub, the *Button Oak* (Kinlet), due to it having a nearby camping site. There's no sleeping in plastic bags tonight; we're going posh, because Jazza and Dennis have brought their eight-man tent. We stop in the pub for a steady session until closing time. On one of his regular visits to the toilet to relieve himself, Oggy bends over the pan and the lens falls out of his glasses into the mess someone forgot to flush away and he has the unpleasant task of retrieving it. The tent is pitched on a field in a place known as Hungry Hill. We've our own hungry hill, Oggy, who is now nominated as chief cook and beer swiller. Morning follows a noisy night of snoring. The smell of bum belches fills the air and is hanging stagnant in every corner of the tent. Chuff, phufftt and Foxy lets rip and creates another hole in the ozone – mustard gas has nothing on the whiff inside here. Most of us have breath like an old bog brush, but this soon disappears with the taste of bacon, eggs and a can of beer apiece. Outside the tent Jazza shouts, "Look at that squirrel jumping from tree to tree."

Dennis replied. "That's no squirrel, it's Foxy's underpants!"

We couldn't stop laughing at this quip. We pack up the tent and drive into Bewdley for a couple of pints before heading home. For me it's been a lovely little break and the weathers been sunny too.

All the talk had been about seriously disbanding our drinking gang. However at the last minute a 1984 good beer guide is given us and Tim said, "Let's visit a few of these."

"Sounds good to me," I replied.

With the continuation of our travels now confirmed, I start to realise our charity pub-crawl is developing into more than this. I decide that as well has having my book signed, I shall start and record the décor, beers, and location of all the pubs we visit in an A4 lever arch folder and take photographs where possible. April sees Jase join as a permanent member of our merry mob together with his mate Mark. Both have only just turned eighteen and fancy exploring this great country of ours. Marston's brewery, at the moment, have a promotion on, if you visit any twenty five of the pubs listed on their leaflet and get the leaflet stamped by the publican in each pub, you receive a free Marston's pub trail T-shirt. In no time we've completed them and our prize is sent to us through the post. The cost of a pint of beer now is around 65p, with lager at 90p, so it's off on our first 1984 guide visit into Herefordshire. The first one being the *Forge and Ferry* (Fownhope), it's an evening trip today and we have to wait fifteen minutes for opening time at 6 p.m. Each minute is eagerly counted down, but to fill in time we stroll down to the nearby open air baths – the River Wye – until opening time. Yippee, time for a drink. Twenty minutes pass in this boozer, when two local yokels, both one over the eight and a little wuss (worse) for wear come in covered in daffodils. One stands on top of a stool and starts shouting, "Beep, beep, I'm a Jeep, sorry, sorry, I'm a lorry!"

Then the other one starts and both start howling, "I can't read and I can't write, but I can drive a tractor!"

What a pair of prats. The gaffer tells them to shut up and asks them where the daffodils have come from. It turns out they've pinched them out of his flowerpots. I think it would be quite sensible to move on now. The *Butchers Arms* is next at (Woolhope), where we sit in the beer garden with its ornamental disused large grinding wheel, overlooking lovely countryside. Next is the *Cottage of Content* (Carey) which opened its doors to the thirsty in 1485 and is now paid a visit by the thirsty in 1987. Now as our travels continue we end up getting lost on the way to the *Loughpool* (Sellack). Having taken the wrong road we end up in Mr John Edward's stables the famous local National Hunt trainer, who has had many a winner around various racecourses. Hooray, at last we find our final stop for the evening, a remote black and white half-timbered country inn situated in pleasant and scenic surroundings. We're as dry as old dusters, so we hurriedly order our beers and mine empties rapidly. I get chatting to an elderly chap called Fred, who said, "I've been using this boozer for fifty years."

That's what you call a loyal customer, so we buy him a drink.

We tell him how we got lost on the way here and where we ended up.

Fred points over to the door and said, "There's the man, just walking in."

It's only the man himself, Mr John Edwards.

I'd love to have a chat with him for a tip or two, but a few nice looking girls surround him, so I think I'll leave him to it.

The landlord, on hearing about our quest to raise money for charity, buys us a pint of Guinness each and signs my book. A pleasurable session is had by all, with us being the last left in the pub. The gaffer said, "You are quite welcome to sleep outside my pub by that old grinding wheel."

"Fair play gaffer, that will be great," I said.

Rising to the sound of horses' hooves clobbering past very early in the morning, I suddenly realise that I'm not such a big fan of horse racing after all. I doze on and off for a while then later I go for a walk in the woods. Anything to make the morning move a bit quicker. It's a fine sunny start to the day as I wake up the other hibernating beer buffs, for an outdoor feast of a full English breakfast cooked on our stove. With my Vauxhall Victor now part of some by-gone era, we get in my newly purchased Ford Cortina Mk 5 for our long drive to one of the oldest pubs in Great Britain mentioned in *The Guinness Book of Records* the *Royalist Hotel* (Stow on the Wold). Nice town, modern hotel where the oldest part of this building is probably a stump of wood built into it. Even older maybe is the gutter stones in the kerb outside, which were made in West Bromwich. Stow on the Wold is the Cotswold's highest town at 750 feet above sea level. We then leave for a quick hello, pint and goodbye at Les's the *Plough* (Ford). Then onto Ann Hathaway's cottage for a nose around, the home of William Shakespeare's old trout, arriving home at 5 p.m.

A couple of weeks pass sampling brews in Worcestershire pubs, with the most interesting one being the *Live and Let Live* (Bringsty Common). Blink and you'll miss the turning to this small unusual country pub as it's down a dirt track situated in delightful countryside. Again we're off to visit two new Banks's pubs in the Manchester area, the *Tollgate* (Old Trafford) and the *Sparking Clog* (Radcliffe). There are twelve of us on today's tour all with our beer towel coats on. The first stop is the *Clog*. Yes, it's that new brick design again. While sitting out of view of the landlord, three of us go up to get the beer. On approaching the bar the licensee after signing my book said, "I'll get you all a beer lads."

So I order twelve pints. He thinks we're joking but to his amazement the others on hearing of his generosity all appear from around the corner to collect their freebies.

The licensee gloomily said, "I didn't realise there were so many of you."

"We'll pay for them gaffer, seeing as there's been a misunderstanding."

But, the gaffer does keep his word and honours his statement. A very nice chap indeed. On entering the second one the *Tollgate,* all we can hear is someone saying, "Out, out!"

Taking no notice of this we carry on walking to the bar. It turns out it's directed at us. The landlord said. "I don't want your sort or anyone of your description using this pub."

Explaining to him is difficult, eventually getting through to him he calms down and serves us. It's funny how you can get two totally different welcomes, off individual gaffers, working for the same company. The longest named pub as mentioned in the 1983 *Guinness Book of Records* is the *Thirteen Volunteer Cheshire Mounted Rifleman Inn* (Stalybridge) and this is our next destination.

Map reading is not the strong point of Jase's navigational skills at the moment. Mind you, he is only a novice and all the practice he'll get can only make him better, as we get lost again and end up in the *Grapes* (Heyrod). The gaffer here is a friendly bloke, who after our drink invites us to an overtime session later on and a breakfast in the morning. The point is it's only 8.30 p.m. and we haven't reached our goal for today, so we have to decline his generous offer. Back on the road to the longest named pub, we finally find it. Gav and me play table skittles whilst Jase and John are having a secret drinking challenge against one another. Jase brags and says to John, "I can run three miles uphill in twelve minutes."

John agrees and replies, "You probably can, tied to the back of a motorbike."

Meanwhile, Wayne's eyes are now beginning to roll around.

We've decided to make our last port of call, the *Snake Pass Inn* (Snake Pass). To get here you must negotiate numerous bogey (sharp) bends in the road, so watch how you drive. On entering this pub we find it busy and expensive, bed and breakfast is £33 for a single room and £47 for a double. We were hoping for a quiet out-in-the-wilds cosy place. Never mind though, we order three pints apiece as it's getting late and settle down.

Then the manager comes over and said, "What are you doing in here?"

"Just having a quiet drink," replied Leo.

I tell him of our previous excursions and what it's all in aid of and I ask him if it's okay for us to sleep on the grass over the other side of the car park.

"Most certainly not, sleep anywhere near here and I'll call the police," he nastily replied.

What a friendly bloke this prat is.

We gulp our pints down and head back to the *Grapes*. I don't think we'll make it though because it's too far away. Jase has now done a terrific job of reading the map and we're in a yard at the back of a police station. Wayne breaks the longest throwing-up record in history as he keeps the car door ajar covering the road with sick all the way to the *Grapes*. On arrival it's closed. With nowhere else open we cross the road and park further down the street. Then jumping a wall onto the railway embankment, which overlooks the sinister shape of the cooling tower. No torches available at the moment due to them being used to get all our clobber out of the cars, it's difficult to see a blade of grass to bed down on. Suddenly in the darkness we hear a yell and a scream as one of us falls down the twenty-foot embankment onto the railway lines. Rushing to get the torch we discover it's Jase who fell. He's pissed after his private little drinking session with John and his legs have turned to jelly.

John shouts down, "Yoe all right mate!"

"I think so."

"Well get off the rails then."

To make sure he was okay a couple of the lads go down and struggle getting him back up the bonk (bank). Tony and myself share a sandwich and a little chewed-up piece is rubbed on John's lips. He immediately starts chucking up and blames me for this, not the numerous pints consumed challenging Jase. Millions of stars are out on this quiet tranquil night and we fall asleep, until the sound of thunderous trains passing disturbs some of us. Especially Gav and Jase who wake up at 4.30 a.m. on a very early sunny morning. They can't get back to sleep so they go for a walk and are now throwing small bricks at everyone, what a pair of arseholes. I annoyingly shout, "You won't wake me up throwing them!"

Achieving their aim of getting us all up they then both decide it's too early to get up themselves and too long a wait for the pubs to open, so they bed down too. They nod off, leaving the ones they woke wide-awake. More shuteye is needed.

Blimey it's hot as I rise at 8.30 a.m. I wake the remaining – should I say, 'railway sleepers'? On doing so John honks up and feeds the worms again. Looking across at the huge cooling tower, none of us notice an old lady sneak upon us from the opposite direction. Thinking we're all in for a rollocking about the noise we're making, she surprised us by saying, "How would you all like a cup of tea and biscuits?"

"We'd love it!" was the reply.

That's a smashing offer, too good to refuse. We all assume she owns a café but to our astonishment she invites all of us into her cottage. What generosity, as pots of tea and tins of biscuits are joyfully swallowed. Jabbering on for over an hour about our past exploits, she now tells us where to get a good breakfast in a place called Holmfirth.

We discuss on our departure how amazing it is in this day and age for a charming little old lady to invite so many strangers into her home and actually let us use her toilet, too.

On the way to our selected appointment we notice a pub. It's 10 a.m. but it seems open so we pile in. The licensee says, "What would you like first, a breakfast or a round of drinks?"

This is a great start to the day. "We'll all have a pint please."

"Where's the rest of your coach party?" He enquired.

"We're not with one. We're in our cars."

It's a slight mistake telling him this, as he now throws us out, as he's expecting a pre-booked group. On coming out of here Jase, still recovering from last night's booze, lets rip and gets a terrapin's neck in his pants. This delays us for ten minutes, as he sees to his slight mishap in the pub's toilet. We journey on to Holmfirth, which is incidentally the home of television's longest running sitcom in the world *Last of the Summer Wine,* which started back in 1972. Had a filling breakfast in the town's famous café before having a few photos took outside Nora Batty's house. The boozers are still not open, so we travel on until opening time, settling in the *Little John* and then the *Plough* both in Hathersage, Derbyshire. Finishing off with a game of pool in the *Miners Arms* (Winster). Wayne's struggling this afternoon and sips his lemonade. There are some beautiful landscapes around this area. We drive past Sudbury prison where an old pal of mine is currently working for the Queen for six months. Another enjoyable eventful trip ends, covering 300 miles.

It's the 25th May 1987 and after yesterday's return off our weekend run, an early start is made to another pub claiming to be the oldest (it's our second of four mentioned in the record books). It's *Ye Olde Fighting Cocks* (St Albans). On arrival in this town we stride towards this pub passing under an ancient stone archway and a quick look in the magnificent cathedral of St Albans before finally finding the pub. The pub's original foundations date back to circa 793 and was formerly called the *Olde Round House* but rebuilt after the flood of 1599. This reputedly is where Oliver Cromwell nipped in for a tankard of ale or two during the English Civil War and we've actually brought one of his troops along with us today, Oggy. In Stuart times up one of the corners of the building was a cock fighting pit and it is still there. When the sport was banned in 1849 it was renamed *The Fisherman* for a while before reverting to its original title. This is a nice old place but too busy to stop for too long.

Out and off for an alehouse which has a rather unusually shaped chimney and unsurprisingly is called the *Crooked Chimney* (Lemsford). In we go for a beer, walking up to the bar the gaffer shouts. "Out, I'm not serving you lot with those beer towel coats on!"

"Why not?" we reply to his outburst.

"I don't want to."

So we proceed to take off our coats. The pompous bag of piss then says to us, "I'm still not serving you."

Undeterred I ask him if he'll sign my book then. "What for?" he said.

"It's our hobby and we raise money for charity and it's proof of our visit."

I can't believe his reply, "Yes, but what for?"

At this Oggy walks out.

I just answer now in a state of frustration and annoyance. "To prove we have a meal in every pub," I say sarcastically.

Amazingly he only goes and tells me that the pub doesn't serve meals. "Can we have a drink then?" I said.

So he pours us a drink and signs my book. We can't work this bloke out, not for the life of us. What a weirdo this bloke is. It's 2.30 p.m. and thankfully this place is now closing after the dinner-time session, so it's off to Bury St Edmunds.

Arriving here with all the boozers shut until six, we have time to kill. A casual hour is spent in the impressive cathedral, where Leo and me sign the visitor's book. At last, the bong of the church bells ring out, 6 p.m. Beer hour! We've come to this town to clock in at Great Britain's smallest pub the *Nutshell*, only to find it is still shut. Mark asks a passing policeman when it opens and he tells us 7 p.m. Never mind we'll be back later. Meanwhile we find *Ye Olde One Bull* not too far away to wallop down a couple of wazzin warmers. We share a good-humoured hour telling the landlord about our dinner-time experience where we were told to take of our beer towel coats. "Dress restrictions don't apply in here," said the gaffer.

Just as he said this, a chap walks in with a suit and tie on. "Oi, you can't come in here dressed like that," the gaffer shouts over. We couldn't stop loffin' (laughing) at the alarmed look on the chap's face as he about turned and went to walk out the door, before the landlord said to him, "It's only a joke mate."

Fair play to the suity-boy, because he took it all in good fun. Back now to the *Nutshell*, only to be told this time, by a local, that due to it being Bank Holiday Monday and the church owning the ground the pub stands on, it doesn't open at all today. Dejected and with head bowed, we venture back to the cars.

We are all down in the doldrums at the minute, but we soon snap out of it when I tell the lads our next stop is to be the third of the four oldest pubs in the record books. It's dark now as we pull up outside *Ye Olde Ferry Boat Inn* (Holywell), Cambridgeshire. Although being by the River Ouse and with a part thatched roof, this is very disappointing to us, because it's more of a restaurant than a pub. But it does have a slab in the floor that marks the grave of a seventeen-year-old girl who was buried there in AD 1050 called Juliet Tewsley, a lovesick girl who hung herself over a broken romance. To relax here and sleep outside is now cancelled. Down in the dumps again we drink up and head off on the A14. Pulling off at junction fourteen, it's late and we're all hungry. The sign says Titchmarsh, this will do as we look around for a fish and chip shop, without success. So it's into the nearest pub, the *Wheatsheaf* at 10.05 p.m. I ask the landlady if it's possible to fix us up with some cheese sandwiches. She said, "Sorry food finished at 10 o'clock."

Oggy looks around at the plates of leftovers on the tables and eats the batters off the fish someone's failed to eat. A little more hospitality would have kept us in here, but as there's another pub down the road in the same village we leave here and head for that one. It's called the *Dog and Partridge*, and an excellent pint of Charles Wells bitter is the first to disappear down our gullets. The landlord, whose name we forgot to ask, makes us plates of sandwiches and tells us we're okay to drink over until 1 a.m. We take full advantage of this and continue whopping the pints down. The gaffer then said, "Where are your sleeping quarters tonight?"

"Outside by the cars I suppose," we reply.

"No you're not, I've a buffs club room at the back of the building you can sleep in there and the heaters on too." Beyond any of our expectations, again we've dropped lucky. No need for the plastic bags tonight, just our sleeping bags. Mark, who has a habit of howling in his sleep, only occasionally interrupts a good night's kip.

The gaffer wakes us at 9 a.m. He's brought us cups of tea, more sandwiches and leaves us to help ourselves. We agree on a whip-round for him for the generosity that he has shown us. Mark whispers over and announces, "If that's the case, I'll put his wall clock back then." Which happens to be stuck up his jumper. We say our farewells and thanks to one of the best licensees we've ever met. He refuses the collection we have raised for him and so off on the road we go.

After a long drive we enter the *Navigation* (Wooton Wawen), where the lads play pool and I check a 10p accumulator I had on eight ossis (horses) yesterday. I'm almost running round the room like I've won the pools as I have the first seven winners only to find the last nag comes a lousy second. What a celebration this would have been. In a somewhat subdued mood I soon cheer up as we arrive at *Ye Olde Bulls Head* (Wootton Wawen). As we pull up, we notice a coach load of women walking over to the pub, so getting a quick spurt on we manage to get our drinks at the bar before they do. We journey on to the *Masons Arms* (Wilmcote) then take a short tour around the nearby Mary Arden's House, mother of William Shakespeare. Steadily we drive home after a trip certainly worth travelling 400 miles for.

At the moment our ambition is to visit every entry mentioned in the 1983 *Guinness book of Records* that refers to pubs. Our tour tonight the 31st May, takes us to one of those described in the book as being the licensed premises with the longest name and most words, the *Green Man and Black's Head Royal Hotel* (Ashbourne), Derbyshire. The inn sign of this establishment sits proudly at twenty odd feet high and spanning across one side of the road to the other. Ashbourne is the place to be, if you are fit and strong, fancy a black eye, broken legs or arms, because for two days every year they have a 'Shrovetide Rough and Tumble' football match and another on Ash Wednesday. This is played between the Upards or Downards, (depending on if you were born north or south of the river) by hundreds of lads in a game of football that lasts from 2 p.m. and 10 p.m. The goals are three miles apart and the game is played with very few rules.

Wandering further into enchanting countryside it's a cloudy night when we reach the *George* (Alstonefield). This has facilities for camping around the back. On leaving through the villages of Wetton and Butterton we come to a steep incline in the road. The majority of our motors easily manage this incline. But on getting to the top after travelling for a further five minutes we notice John's car is nowhere to be seen. We turn around to see what's up, only to see one of the most hysterical scenes we've ever come across. A bloke on a pushbike passes John's motor, which is overladen with our fellow beer drinkers. John's car, being a 950cc Datsun Cherry, is incapable and failing miserably in negotiating the steep slope with the weight of its passengers. As the lads now all jump out of his car and start pushing it uphill. Triumphantly it reaches the brow of the hill.

"Hip, hip hooray!" we all chant.

"Surely ya car should be able to get up that hill John?"

"Yoe'd have thought so Hilly."

It turns out John's car mat has rolled up underneath his accelerator pedal so it wouldn't fully compress to the floor.

Accelerating, car mat-free to the *Jervis Arms* (Onecote) we find a lovely beer garden here by the river but, alas, it's starting to rain. The Bungle brothers like the look of the garden umbrella and try to fit it in the car boot. The gaffer clocks them doing this and shouts, "Naughty, naughty!"

"We were only seeing if yoe was game for a laugh, gaffer," replied a startled Tony. John now puts it back in its rightful position. So, drinking up quickly we move on, finishing in our last pub of the night the *Yew Tree* (Cauldon). What a gem of a pub, packed with old antiques, grandfather clocks, polyphons, pianolas, symphonions the landlady gives me a couple of old pennies to put in and all these old music machines actually work. One of these machines plays Swanee River. This is a pub interior full of character, run by two old dears and a pleasant chap named Alan East, who's wearing a dicky bow and he signs my book. How enjoyable it is to finish off in a place like this. It's an absolutely fascinating place. Supping away happily, Jase turns and says, "It's about time we had a name for our beer group."

"Well, somebody suggest some then," replied the Bungle brothers.

Various names are thrown about, and we agree that it has to start with the word Black Country. "What about the Black Country beer boys." Gav said. "Black Country beer tasters is better," replies Leo.

Then I said, "We need a Black Country word in it, so what about Black Country Ale Tairsters?"

"This sounds great to me," replied Jase.

Our name is born, as we order another round of M&B mild. "We can call us the 'BATS' for short," Leo cheerfully said, "I can get some cards printed at the place I work at."

"Good idea." I said. "I'll get designing it when I get home. Quicker we get them printed the quicker we can hand them over to the licensees of every pub we go in," I replied excitedly.

We head home now ending tonight's momentous occasion.

Through June we knock off various local pubs, passing into July where on the 11th we're off on our first Ludlow trip. Our brand new cards have been printed and are ready to hand out. During our visit here in the *Wheatsheaf*, Gav said to the gaffer, "Where's the nearest police station? I want to report an old bloke who's been following us all day."

Oggy comes over to me and says, "Hilly, the gaffer keeps giving me funny looks."

"He would Dad, Gav's told him yoe'm a pervert."

"Never, let's get out of here quick!" replies a panic stricken Oggy.

After six more pubs, John, who's brought his girlfriend Jayne out said to her, "Am yoe sure yoe'll be able to take all this beer tonight?"

Jayne quick as a flash replies, "Yes, will you?"

At our ninth pub of the evening John has a belly bunging binge in the waste bin outside the pub. Jayne for some reason has a big smirk across her face, and I can't think why. With the evening drawing in, a departure to a more convenient part of Shropshire for the night's shuteye is due. However a last supping stop is spotted on the way called the *Cottagers Comfort* (Leintwardine). We have three pints apiece until a rather late closing at 12.30 a.m. A ten-minute drive from here takes us to an isolated field. It's an enchanting evening with clear skies, lovely and warm and lots of stars. Gav will be seeing more of them if he don't shut up as he keeps rambling on. Gav thinks he's the new Patrick Moore and points to the names of the star clusters, "Those are known as the saucepan, that shape is called the frying pan."

Ar and if he keeps on I'll hit him with one, he's got a gob as big as a bucket tonight. Finally the astrologer nods off into orbit; at last peace and quiet.

I'm woken early by a cockerel, cock-a-doodle-doing somewhere in the woods, sheep bleating, John honking again – real sounds of the countryside – I love 'em. The rest of the living dead begin to rise. We load up the cars and our destination is a café back in Ludlow. With our bellies full of bacon we stroll over to the *Feathers Hotel* dating back to 1603. A beautiful carved timber-framed façade. It has an interesting interior that is made even better by a walk up the stairs to view two magnificent wood-panelled rooms with moulded ceilings. These are for residents only. Gav gets yapping to an elderly married couple, who ask him if he's travelled far. "Oh yes," says Gav, "it took us 1 hour and 10 minutes to get here, are you local yourselves?"

"No, actually we're from Melbourne, Australia," was the reply.

Oggy laughs his socks off at this and with Gav being blown away we exit the pub. The two tourists are filming the frontage of this building and Gav reaps revenge on Oggy for laughing at his cock-up, by grabbing hold of him and giving him a big kiss in front of the filming tourists. He's now immortally captured on celluloid! A few choice words are expressed by Oggy before we venture down to more watering holes, finishing off at the *Bridge*. An Ex-guardsman runs this pub and the whole of the interior is full of military objects, artefacts and memorabilia. It's the most brilliant collection of military stuff I've ever come across and certainly makes this more of a museum than a pub. Now for the drive back home, but not before stopping for a few punnets from a 'pick your own strawberries' farm. During July, a tour to Kenilworth is on. Oggy decides to read the map and what a big mistake this is. We pass the same castle ruins three times, which is getting really annoying. On this run we talk about an epic journey north to visit a short list of boozers all named after racehorses that I've cut out of the newspaper. A departure date is arranged for Saturday 25th July 1987. Before embarking on this, I write a letter to Banks's brewery explaining our achievement of visiting all their licensed establishments and they have organised a brewery visit for us on Thursday 23rd July. A bit late, but better late than never.

The day arrives and the BATS go Banks's. Fifteen make it this evening arriving at 7.30 p.m. A friendly chap called Adrian Willis greets us, he's the marketing manager and we are shown to the hospitality room. Adrian said, "Before the short film and the brewery trip starts, I would like to present to you all a specially engraved tankard each commemorating your achievement."

One by one we collect our tankard. We're all over the moon with this. "Help yourselves to the free Banks's mild, lads."

We then sit down to a short film that tells us that the water for their beers comes from the river in nearby Tettenhall. It should be served to the general public at about 55°F and ideally last for three days. By our own drinking experience some must have had it on for two weeks. Wolverhampton & Dudley Breweries Ltd was formed on May 14th 1890. Our brewery expert Dave has now arrived to show us around the brewery. It's our first tour of a large brewery and on approaching the 'copper' where the hops are added we noticed they we're made in Oldbury at Hunt Brothers. Amazingly Oggy worked there in the early 1970s. We've never heard of finings before. Dave explained, "These are our bags of fish bladders, the finings. They are pure proteins and when in contact with the beer can turn it from being cloudy to a crystal clear drink. It costs £15 a pound to buy in."

Each room of the brewery is visited. The hop room is next where we're told only the seed of the hop is used in brewing, the waste goes either for pig feed or manure. At the moment Worcestershire hops are being used. The fermenting room follows, this is what I want to see. What a wonderful smell, and a wonderful sight as we view the large open-top fermenting vats all bubbling away. It makes you feel like jumping in. The yeast is working well tonight and a couple of us ask Dave if we can taste some. He gets a long rod with a small cup on the end and Tony and me have a taste first. It's very sweet, thick and sickly at the moment, but I'm glad I sampled it. Now the barrelling department and storage room, then it's back into the hospitality room after our one-hour trip around the brewery. Everybody gets down to the serious stuff of drinking all this free beer. Dave uncovers a large table of food and again it's all help yourself to whatever you fancy. We all sing our BATS anthem which is Dean Martin's *Little old wine drinker me*. Followed by our Banks's song that goes like this;

> *"If you come to the Midlands you will see,*
> *Banks's and Hansons' Brewery,*
> *We don't drink whisky we don't drink rum,*
> *Because we cor afford 'em."*

I tell Adrian that I've recently had an old price list given to me from 1961. "What was the price of a pint of mild in those days?" he asks. "One and threppence." (Just over 6p in today's money).

A tremendous evening is had by all and we leave at 12.30 a.m. Between eight and fourteen pints are quaffed each. Thank you Banks's, their motto is *'Unspoilt by Progress,'* but tonight, we're just spoilt.

During the week, after a slight disagreement with Fast Eddy, Tim and Cuzz they no longer want to carry on and decide to finish with the pub-crawling. Good lads these, I hope we can still keep in touch, I've had some fabulous times with them and I shall miss them all.

CHAPTER 5

THE PINT NORTH

The ale trail that is going to take us to the remote northern places has now arrived: The 'Pint North Trip.' Our excursion begins with eight of us in two cars, there's my car and John has borrowed Tony's 1300 Escort. Moving off and it's away we go, listening to tapes of Mel and Kim and Madness. Leo decides he's going to be the diarist on this trip. I ask him if he knows shorthand. He hands me a sheet of paper with the words; *How's this for shorthand, B******s*. Our first pub is the *White Horse* (Littleborough) a landmark situated high on the Pennines, 1,300 feet above sea level, with superb views of the surrounding moorland and Hollingworth Lake far below. A Roman road is close by too. Taylor's Mild is consumed in our next alehouse the *Old Bridge* (Ripponden) before a drive into Haworth arriving at 1.25 p.m. We have a four-hour break here eating our sandwiches and completing five pubs. While in one of the boozers here, in the *Black Bull* the gaffer said, "If you are members of 'Camra,' I won't sign your book."

"We don't really know who 'Camra' are, gaffer," I replied, "and we're not members anyway."

Haworth is a cracking, steep, cobbled stone village, where the famous Brontë family lived in the parsonage. Here, three of the Brontë girls became famous authors with books called *Wuthering Heights* by Emily, *Jane Eyre* by Charlotte and *Tenant of Wildfell Hall* by Anne. You've got to pay to get into the parsonage, so we give it a miss. We bought some souvenirs instead from one of the many little gift shops.

It's situated close to the Worth Valley Steam Railway too. Engaging our engines we leave for the village of Esholt and to the *Commercial Inn* used in the popular television soap *Emmerdale Farm* (first episode transmitted on 16th October 1972) and better known as the *Woolpack*. To our disappointment it's only the exterior they use and the interior is completely different. Mark cleans his teeth in the lounge here and swills his mouth out with his beer. A local tells us Seth Armstrong, a character off *Emmerdale*, drinks in a pub not that far away.

So we go to meet him at the *Old Star* (East Keswick) and sadly there's no guest appearance by the man himself on our visit. Our fourth of the four oldest pubs mentioned in the record books is now successfully found *The Bingley Arms* (*Bardsey)*, is my personal favourite of the four. Although it is a popular meals pub it retains more character than the others we've been to, and it dates back to 953 AD, it was called the *Priest's Inn* until 1780, when Baron Bingley changed it to its present day name. A Dutch oven dating from 1738 is in the adjoining bar and it is one of only a few remaining in its original position in England. There's also a well-lit priest's hideout up the chimney. Jayne has her photo taken outside the ladies' bogs. The sign on the door reads 'Wenches' which is a Black Country word for girls. The local Yorkshire stone used in the inn is the same as that used in the church where the Saxon tower is in a perfect state of preservation and is one of the finest examples in Europe. We intend to sleep outside here but can't find a suitable place. Our journey now finishes off at the *Alice Hawthorne* (Wheldrake), the first of the pubs named after a racehorse. This horse won fifty-one races between 1841-1845. There's no chance of a late drink in here as the landlady is very strict on drinking up time. This means leaving earlier than planned making it a long night ahead of us. Mind you, outside here is a disused car-park so no need to look any further; out come the plastic bags and down with our heads. Ferocious flocking bats spend their happy hunting hours whizzing menacingly above us for most of the dark hours. Oggy wakes up screaming and shouts, "Bugger me something's attacking me, it's a giant three-foot black and white rabbit!"

Personally I think it's the consumption of too much ale because we get up and can't find a rowdy rabid rabbit anywhere.

On waking up on a warm sunny Sunday morning, Oggy still strangely insists the bunny beast attacked him. We go for a breakfast at the Little Chef before passing Beverley racecourse and spending an hour throwing stones in the sea at Hornsea. Waiting for opening time we're bored, so we drove to a second pub on our list named after a racehorse the *Altisidora* (Bishop Burton). This is a pub-cum-restaurant in a nice little village with a pond. One corner of the village green is where the Methodist John Wesley preached and every year a service is held to commemorate his visit. The oss (horse) itself was locally trained and won the 1813 St Leger. Third one on our list is the 1839 St Leger winner the *Charles XII* (Heslington). We have a quick drink in here and the gaffer tells us where we can get a value for money dinner. We're hungry and want a dinner before the Sunday deadline of 2 p.m. as this pub doesn't do food. We dash into York, just catching the *Cross Keys* open. The licensees very kindly say we'll be okay for a dinner. I have a pork and beef meal for £2.95. Excellent!

With plenty of time before opening tonight at 7 p.m. Lionel suggests a walk round the York Minster.

Leo agrees and says, "Good idea, this will give our food a chance ter goo down."

It's free to enter the Minster and it is a must for any visitor to York. It's the largest Gothic church in England. We're really enjoying it in here when over comes an arrogant security guard who reminds us this is a Minster not Wembley. With our beer towel coats on, this thicko thinks we're football supporters. He then said, "There's no smoking in here so don't light up any of your fags, okay."

We don't even smoke and all this prat achieves is spoiling our visit to an immense and magnificent piece of architecture. We leave to visit the Jorvik Viking Centre, after waving goodbye to Mr Big the security man. There's a long queue and it's £2.50 in. So we have a stroll down a delightful little street called the Shambles, then jump in our cars.

We travel on to Castle Howard about five miles from Malton.

This is where they filmed the television programme *Brideshead Revisited*. A stately home built for the third Earl of Carlisle in 1700, with pleasant gardens, fountains and peacocks. We think Mark's fallen in love with one of these peacocks as he's chasing it and making mating calls. We all then pay a pound to view the 'Fashion through the Ages' rooms, where I get a telling off by the woman attendant because I'm about to take a photograph in here and it's forbidden.

Pursuing our journey now to the *Star* (Harome), there's fifteen minutes to wait here until the 7 p.m. opening, so we listen to the Top Forty on the radio. This is a thatched pub and it serves a decent drop of ale. We then drive to the *Malt Shovel* (Oswaldkirk). This was built as a manor house in 1610 and converted to a coaching inn in the eighteenth century. This place is full of young toffs. We sample the excellent house beer. Mark, for some reason, decides to put a colander on his head off the food trolley. He thinks he's a German! It's now tipping down with rain as we move on to the southern edge of the North Yorkshire moors. Where we nip in the *White Swan* (Ampleforth) before settling in the *Fauconberg Arms* (Coxwold) a seventeenth-century inn. A disappointing place, with nothing of interest apart from the gaffer who has a check coat on and dicky bow and he's strict on closing time. He tells us that this pub featured on the television programme *Treasure Hunt*. It's still raining really heavy and we've got to find somewhere to doss down for the night.

Driving a few miles we spot an old barn. I stop my car and said to Lionel, "What a great place this will be. Park ya car across the entrance to the barn and we'll bed down in there."

All settled down, Jase's appetite and mine needs satisfying, so when John passes out we naff (pinch) some chicken legs out of his bag. The sheep in the back of the barn behave themselves and are not too noisy. During our warm and welcome overnight stay in this dry shelter, the only interruption to the sheep and our sleep is the sound of John throwing up.

An early rise for me on this Monday morning as I wake at 7 a.m. I leave the others asleep and go for a short walkabout, exploring the area. To my horror I find we're actually sleeping in a farmer's barn on his land, next to the Golden Square Caravan Park. I dash back to tell the others, to get them up before the farmer comes. At 7.30 a.m. a woman in her Land Rover stops and asks, "What you are doing on this land?"

"We're doing nothing, we're going now," I hastily reply.

She drove off and I said, "Quick hurry up and get the stuff in the cars, I bet her's gone to tell the farmer."

We've almost finished packing our clobber, when, you've guessed it, the farmer arrives.

He said, "That will be £9 for sleeping in my barn."

"We haven't been sleeping in it mate, we just stopped to tidy out the boot of our cars," I protested.

So who comes walking out of the barn with his sleeping bag over his shoulder but Oggy, who shouts to the farmer, "Thanks for the use of the barn mate, it was a sound night's kip!"

After five minutes trying to talk him out of charging us for the Yorkshire hospitality, he said, "For £9 then, I'll let you use the toilet facilities on the caravan site."

It's agreed we could all do with a wash. It turns out value for money as it's the fust (first) drop of wairta (water) that's touched our skin since our journey began.

We drove back to Coxwold now to visit the Newburgh Priory founded by Roger de Mowbray in 1145, where Oliver Cromwell's remains are hidden. Except for his embalmed head which since 25th March 1960 has been kept at Sidney Sussex College in Cambridge. This is where he was a student in 1616-7. The only problem is it's closed and only opens to the public on Wednesdays. The gates are open however so we go in anyway, driving round the grounds. All of a sudden we notice men walking over to us from all directions. The scene, early this morning with a slight mist, made them look like zombies. Not waiting to find out if they were, we're off out of this place. Travelling a mile or so, we discover Leo is missing. He's not in my car. Turning round, we go back to see where he is. As it happens, he got out of my car before our short and sharp trip around the Priory and popped into the local shop to buy a film for his camera!

It's still early in the morning so we stop at the large Kilburn White Horse figure embedded in the limestone up on the hillside since 1857. It's more of a grey colour. Lionel volunteers to cook breakfast. Jase comes up with a bit of a yampy idea and says, "Let's have a small wager. The first one to stand on top of the White Horse wins the bet."

So Jase, John, Leo, Mark and myself throw a quid in the hat and we're off. The problem is, the steps are so steep to get there, neither one of us make it without a rest. We're about as fast as a slug and I'm not really bothered who wins. It's the most knackering thing I've tried since I last bought a round of drinks. With my legs like jelly babies and after taking sharp intakes of breath I eventually reach what I'll never reach again – the top! Who won? I couldn't care less, all I know it's not me. The view though is amazing, but watch out for low flying hang-gliders because a couple of nutters are jumping off the top here. Back down for our beans on toast, where I now feel a bit light headed after my exercise regime.

Beer waits for no man (or woman) so, because the pubs are now open, we manage to get a couple of early ones in before arriving at Knaresborough. Where we spend quite awhile in the *Mother Shipton's Inn*, named after a fourteenth-century prophetess. This has a table, reputedly owned by Guy Fawkes in the bar room. After chucking-out time at 2.30 p.m. we head to Mother Shipton's Cave and Petrifying Well. It's £2 in, but I've got some leaflets from out of the nearby petrol garage when filling up earlier and we all get 25p knocked off our entry. The first thing we come to is an unbelievable sight to see. Anything porous can be hung under the flowing water coming down from the rocks called the 'Dropping Well' and, in a few months, the objects petrify and they look like stone. It's all to do with different minerals being in the water. For a small fee you can personally leave a sock, teddy bear, hat or numerous other things then come back later in the year to collect your much heavier item.

"How much is it if we leave Lionel?" I ask.

We have plenty of time to fill in, so some of us hire rowing boats out and have a pleasurable hour floating up and down the River Nidd. Time now to carry on boozing and we leave Knaresborough at a sedate pace, dropping on the *Guy Fawkes Arms* (Scotton). The gaffer tells us this is the village where the bonfire boy himself was alleged to have lived, before trying to blow up the Houses of Parliament. The fourth racehorse pub on our list is next, the *Little Wonder* (Harrogate). Named after the 1840 Derby winner, it doesn't open until 7 p.m. While waiting, Mark does his Tarzan act and falls out of the tree that he's been climbing. At last the pub opens and what a disappointment it is. On getting served Jayne asks for a Britvic orange and is told they are out of date. This place needs a good clane (clean) so a quick drink and off is our best bet here. Out into the country now to our fifth racehorse pub, named after an 1850s champion the *Flying Dutchman* (Summerbridge). Which has cottage accommodation, beer garden, lunch and evening meals. I get yapping to an ex-Navy bloke who visits here ever year and he buys me a beer. His daughter is twenty-one today and is very pretty too. I didn't want to leave this place because I haven't found out her name yet. Alas our schedule must be kept, so begrudgingly we set off again.

Still out in open countryside we enter a smashing little village and alehouse the *Foresters Arms* (Grassington). We leave this popular pub and just down the road is another idyllic boozer called the *Fountaine Inn* (Linton-in-Craven). To get to this pub you have to cross a small stone bridge spanning a stream. Oggy tries out a game in the bar room of this pub called 'Ring the Bull' which involves a small ring on a long length of string to be swung over a hook attached to the wall, from a few feet away. This he successfully accomplishes. This village has been voted one of the loveliest in North England. Defiantly, our troop march on to a coaching inn on the B6160 the *Buck Inn* (Buckden). Buckden Pike at 2,305 ft above sea level lies behind this inn and is an ideal setting for the hotel and our plastic bags. B&B is £17 for a single room. With a drink overtime and a game of darts against two local women, we find a comfortable piece of grass to lie on by the car-park and a twenty-four hour toilet facility.

It's a warm, close evening, so we all lie on top of our bags. This place is over-run with rabbits and at least they are the small ones and not like the three-foot one's Oggy saw way back at the *Alice Hawthorne* back in Wheldrake. Drifting off, nobody wakes up until we hear John and Jayne shouting about a loud buzzing noise. None of us have a clue what it is, until Leo spots a mass mob of moaning midges, which hover above our heads and fancy a drink of blood for breakfast. Sleep is now impossible with these about, as we're all getting bitten and have to go in the cars to finish the remainder of our nap.

We rise at 8 a.m. on Tuesday July 28th, with everybody covered in red bite marks. Jase fancies a rabbit for breakfast and chases a few, while I scrape a large squashed slug off my arm. Moving on we all have a satisfying sausage and egg sandwich in a café in Leyburn. Then we begin the drinking day in the *White Bear* (Masham). It has an interesting interior with a stuffed polar bear's head at the back of the bar and a stuffed fox dressed up as a barman in hunting regalia smoking a fag, holding a glass and wearing a top hat. There's various other collectables around the room. Four more boozers are visited then a trip to view the River Ure and the Aysgarth Falls by the old former cotton mill, which is now the Yorkshire Dales Carriage Museum. Here, the cascading flow of this brown-coloured water resembles mild ale and it's making my mouth water. In a café near to the falls we have cold tea and a stale bun each. We complain about these and are basically ignored, so a booklet on Yorkshire places to visit walks out the door with us.

Hawes is our next jaunt where we go to see a rope maker at work. Yippee, put the flags out, at last it's opening time. We sit on the benches with fish and chips and our pints outside the *Board Hotel*. Whilst sitting here I spot a girl carrying a box of groceries trying to open the pub door.

"Excuse me, would you like some help?" I asked.

"Yes please," was the relieved reply.

My good deed for the day comes unstuck rather abruptly, as I carry it and the bottom falls out of the box sending the contents rolling down the steps. Oggy meanwhile is strutting round the street with one of our hand-made nylon bushy tails on the back of his trousers. This reminds us of 'Operation Molten Knot', back at the Hilly House, Dudley in July 1985. Advancing ever onwards, we negotiate lots of ups and downs along the roads of remotest Yorkshire, and a welcome break is had at the *Moorcock Inn* (Coverdale). Another one of our racehorse pubs named after the three times winner of the Richmond Gold Cup winner, but the pub sign's got a cockerel on it.

John is struggling with the driving today and Jayne says to us, "We need a good night's rest, somewhere that does bed and breakfast, does the *Tan Hill*?"

"I think so Jayne, give 'em a ring," I replied.

They get a double room there for £16. The *Kings Arms* (Askrigg) is our next port of call and like so many others up this way this also has featured on television in the well known series *'All Creatures Great and Small.'* Oggy now shows Mark his trick where it appears a chalk dot travels through the table onto his hand, Mark's bamboozled at this. Three more pubs, the *Crown* (Askrigg), the *Victoria Arms* (Worton) with an eccentric gaffer and the *Farmers Arms* (Muker) are paid a visit before we arrive at the *Tan Hill* our final one for today.

One thing I'm grateful for when I order my beer is that Theakston's Old Peculier isn't on. Back in November, on my last visit here it knocked me clean out. The midnight hour strikes and the loving couple climb the wooden hills to recuperate and charge their batteries for more adventurous pub miles tomorrow. The remaining few now watch a local pot-holer demonstrate the art of how to crawl through small spaces by wriggling in and out of two wooden stools put together. Rubberman is the only name I can think of to call this chap. We have a game of pool in the back room and after a more sober night in here compared to my last visit and being the only ones left in this pub, it's time to sort out the sleeping arrangements.

Leo, Jase, Mark and Lionel come over and Jase said, "We've all found that cave yoe told us about Hilly and we're dossing down theer." Oggy and myself sleep outside the kitchen window of the pub. With some old planks of wood and a few bricks I make a small shelter to cover our heads. The weather in the middle of the night now turns into torrential rain and severe gusts of wind. A combination of the two fills up our plastic bags with air, water and mud, which is running off the wood planks, and we're getting saturated. Oggy can't take this any longer and succumbs to a drier environment in the car. A monstrous few hours are spent in this hellhole, then hearing the sound of clinking cutlery I wake up.

My sleeping bag is now sodden and my 'Benny' hat is soaked. The plastic bag I'm in is filled with half-an-inch of rainwater, so to say I'm slightly damp is an understatement as I wring out my pillow. I've no watch on and wonder what the time is. I'm sure I can hear the rest of the group enjoying their breakfast through the window on a wet Wednesday morning. I walk over and wake Oggy up and we both enter the pub. It's 9.30 a.m. and I'm right as they are all sitting down eating breakfast and I'm annoyed a little at this. "How come none of yoe lot woke me or Oggy up?" I angrily said.

"We never saw ya and didn't know where yoe dossed down," Jase replied. "Anyway there's nothing left we've eaten it all and it was only £2.50," said John.

Pissed off at this I go for a scenic stroll outside. I can now appreciate the surroundings of this isolated inn now the heavens have zipped up. Mind you, I do have a headache this morning, as a result of either too much beer last night or the lack of a good sleep, I'll blame the latter. Mobile again we're off to one of the highest market towns in England, at an altitude of almost 1000 feet. We arrive at Alston for opening time.

Three taverns and three beers are tasted before leaving Alston. Moving on to the *Shepherds Inn* (Melmerby). It is a nice village with a local bakery using grain from a local mill and a local duck who resides in a little house in the middle of a stream opposite the pub. At last sunshine and I'm almost dry now. We get on the motorway to Scotland and we stop at Hamilton service station early evening. Everyone has something to eat but I'm in desperate need of forty winks so I nod off in the car for thirty minutes, then have a quick swill to refresh myself. Feeling much better now I round up the 'BATS.' as we need to move on.

Our continuous drive takes us all the way to the beautifully situated *Inverberg Hotel* opposite Loch Lomond. Then a drive and into the *Bridge of Orchy* and finally the *Clachaig Inn* (Glencoe). This has a large square bar room where Mark tries to have an intelligent conversation with some foreigners and ends up selling them two of his cigarettes. Oggy bellows over to him and said, "Yoe better make a quicker conversation with the barman and order the beer!"

Mark comes back to the table with a tray full of pints and said to Oggy, "Here, stop moaning, that's your pint on the left."

Oggy goes to pick his glass up and none of us knew what was going to happen next. As he grabs hold of it, all of the glass wobbles and bends all over the place, losing most of his beer in the process. This is very funny, but Oggy isn't too amused. Without us suspecting a thing Mark's been and bought a rubber pint glass. The gaffer finds this hilarious and said, "If you're stuck for a place to sleep I have a small bunkhouse at the rear of the pub and you can use that."

There's no need to ask us twice as we drink up and it's first to get in there gets the best bed. Lionel at the moment misses this as he's got his head stuck down the bog being sick. It's a smaller bunkhouse than imagined and squashing up tightly we all just fit in. All undercover for a change so nothing eventful can possibly occur. But as the night goes on Jase decides he's too hot so takes his jumper off, then he goes cold and puts it back on, he's hot and off it comes again; he's getting a real pain in the arse now. Because it's like the black hole of Calcutta in here and we are so crammed and it's a major job every time he does this. Mark then opens the window he's also too hot but I shut it again because there's lots of nibbling gnats eyeing me up. Leo gasps for air, he needs the window open. Oggy meanwhile sounds like a road drill and Mark's now fallen asleep and he's moaning like a werewolf. So all in all, an action-packed night.

We didn't realise until getting up this morning on Thursday July 30th that the location of this pub is out of this world, a majestic mountain valley surrounds us. Jase and myself notice a big chunk of tat [scrap metal] by the side of the pub. I bet it's worth a bit of money, it happens to be a large metal anvil but it's too heavy to pick up and put in the boot of our car, so we have to leave it. We have breakfast and walk a little way up Ben Nevis. The walk is too long to the summit, so it's on to the Commando Memorial at Spean Bridge. American tourists are taking photos of this and I shout, for a laugh, "Hand grenade!" and chuck a large stone across the ground.

Most of them dive on the floor. I've never seen so many people move so fast, I think I've frightened half of them to death. It was only a joke but it didn't go down too well. The ultimate reason for coming on the 'Pint North' trip is to spend a couple of days on the Isle of Skye and visit the highest pub there.

So quickly supping down a pint in the *Cluanie Inn* by the loch of the same name our journey continues to the Kyle of Lochalsh. The short ferry ride costs £4.14 one way and it takes about five minutes to get to the other side. The image of a quaint old village with lots of stone built pubs is, to our dismay, quite wide of the mark and it is a built-up area by some scruffy railway. The weather is deteriorating and the clouds are above us like a massive hangover, but we must soldier on. First stop is the *Sconcer Lodge Hotel*, built in 1881 as a hunting lodge and set on the water's edge with breathtaking views. It is ideally situated for walks or cycling in the Cuillin Hills and guests can enjoy the adjoining golf course or try their hand at clay pigeon shooting. From here we visit the tourist attraction called the Crofters Cottage; it's 2.05 p.m. and they stop serving snacks at 2 p.m. even a little begging fails to work as they refuse to serve us any food. Three miles down a narrow lane to our next pint at the *Misty Isle Hotel* (Kilmuir). In the bar is a penny-farthing cycle and a large old weighing scale made at Salter's in West Bromwich. The highest pub on the Isle of Skye is the *Stein Bridge Inn* this is our next stop. The gaffer intervenes and said. "Lads it's been shut for a while due to the landlord being put behind a different sort of bar for smuggling."

It's hard to take in after travelling 954 miles to visit this pub.

On hearing this disappointing news we unanimously decide to get off this isle and hopefully catch the last ferry back to the mainland. Trucking down yet again on narrow roads we pass a coach that's gone in a ditch. The nearby *Edinbane Hotel* is handy, so a drink is consumed in here with all the American passengers off the stranded coach all having the same idea. Jase and Lionel play pool whilst I have a walk round in the large adjoining sports hall, where a young girl is playing records on her disco units to an empty room. The last drink on the isle is in the *Pier Hotel* near the ferry crossing at Portree, which comes from the Gaelic word for King's Port. John heads for the small seafood stall and buys some herrings in sherry sauce, which end up where they originally came from, in the sea. All a little miffed with our findings on the Isle of Skye we pay our return fare of £4.14 and are relieved to make it back on the mainland.

The first stop back on the mainland is the *Balmacara Hotel* (Balmacara), followed by the *Clachan* (Dornie) where I beat Oggy 3-0 at darts. This overlooks a spectacular spooky view of Eilean Donan Castle, made even more mysterious with the light now fading and the clouds surrounding the loch. The castle was established in the thirteenth century as a royal stronghold. Then our tour takes us into the *Glenmoriston Hotel* (Invermoriston) the lads play 'Chase the Ace,' while I sit outside, admiring the night sky by the small stream and get peffled (covered) in nibbling, munching midges yet again. Thinking the pubs close at 11 p.m. we dash off to the *Lewiston Hotel* (Lewiston), only to find our efforts are unnecessary due to the fact this place doesn't close until 1 a.m. The bar room is packed with folk but the lounge is more to our taste and there are plenty of seats available. Lionel is recorded in our notes for buying a round of drinks. Leo says, "God bless him."

Lazily lounging about having an enjoyable night, the gaffer said, "Come back in the morning and I'll cook you all a breakfast."

Now for an opportunity which cannot be missed. The chance to sleep in the grounds of Urghart castle, on the banks of Loch Ness; a dream had by many of us, with all its myths and legends that surround this place. Conveniently parking on the empty coach and bus spaces. Oggy isn't fit enough for the next obstacle course and says, "I'll sleep in the car, I'll be safer in this."

Fearlessly carrying our kipping clobber, jumping two gates, I boldly lead the way. I have my torch in my mouth, sleeping bag under one arm and a large stick in the other (just in case Nessie pops his head up). Striding down the steps, crossing over a wall and finally with this commando mission over, we settle down in the castle ruins, right on the edge of Loch Ness. It begins to drizzle with rain and I drift into my dreams before getting up at dawn to relieve my bladder. I wake to a sight more sinister than can ever be imagined; a setting to be seen at least once in everyone's life. The mist hangs over the top of the still and silent water, the haunting silhouette of the Castle and the only sound to be heard are the howls of Mark in his sleep. Too early to rise and too scared I quickly bed back down.

It's 7.30 a.m. it's raining, it's Friday 31st July and it's time to get up. John disappointingly said, "The monster never turned up then?"

"He probably couldn't stand the smell," replied Leo.

I grab a stone out of the loch for a souvenir.

It's time to go. If any tourists start arriving, there's the possibility of getting caught in the grounds and being forced to pay the entrance fee. Back at the cars, John's has been moved; it turns out the bus inspector arrived and made Oggy move it, so a tourist coach can park in it's proper place. It's now raining heavily and we drive back to our promised breakfast, only to be told on arrival that the gaffer's changed his mind and we cannot have one. What a twat! We find a roadside café and petrol station instead, to satisfy our appetite and fill our cars up.

Instinctively, it's pedals to the metal and a quick drink in the *Spean Bridge Hotel*. Next on today's agenda is the oldest pub in Scotland the *King's House Hotel* (near Glencoe) just off the A82. What a terrible track leading down to this place. Bumpy and full of pot holes for about 300 yards. In this hostelry it's got a bar, lounge, restaurant and hiking facilities, but I'm a little disappointed with the interior in this place. Commencing on our journey we arrive at an old stone-built pub the *Inverarnan House Hotel* (Inverarnan), north of

Loch Lomond, known as the *Drovers Inn*. A unique interior, it can only be described as a typical old Scottish pub and my favourite on our trip so far. The gaffer and the bar staff are all dressed in traditional dress with their kilts on. The walls are adorned with stuffed animals and fish. There is a welcoming log fire and plenty of various Scotch Whiskies are available. Tomorrow we're told the yearly Highland Games are to be held on the adjacent large field. In the hallway of this pub is a large stone said to weigh over a hundredweight (112 pounds). The gaffer said to me, "Why don't you try and lift it?"

"No thanks mate, I don't fancy my bag of suck hanging on the floor," I reply.

Meanwhile, a few locals were having a bash at lifting this and all fail, so curiosity gets the better of me, and now, with no one about, I decide to have a go. On my first try I lift it to my waist, my second attempt it slips out of my hands and makes a tremendous bang as it lands on the old wooden floorboards. At this, everybody comes running out of the bar to see what all the racket is, tourists and locals alike.

One old Jock said, "Nobody can lift that in here and even if they did, it would have gone through the floor if it was dropped."

"I did lift it mate," I confirmed.

With something to prove I psyche myself up and in one steady movement, I get it to my chest and make the lift above my head. After a round of applause the gaffer panics a little now and said, "Don't get dropping it this time, from that height it will definitely go through the floorboards."

"There's nothing to worry about gaffer," I said, as I slowly lower the stone and place it in its original position. A smile and a nod to the old Jock says it all. I'm now asked if I want to compete in tomorrow's games. I had to decline because our mission is to travel to pubs. I did fancy having a go, though.

Stopping off at a service station, Jase fancies a change of scene and goes to purchase a top shelf soft porn book. On approaching the counter he notices a young girl assistant at the till. He bottles out and Mark, 'the man' buys it for him. Gretna Green is now our destination. This I imagine as being a tiny charming village, with a thatched blacksmith's shop, where young couples elope to get married, so why not have a peek around? The blacksmith's shop is as expected, but to my disappointment there's a large café and a council estate by it. The *Hazeldean* is the local alehouse and is our first stop. The locals tell me they have lots of trouble in the village, because after the pubs shut in England at 10.30 p.m. the English nip over the border for extended drinking hours and a punch up. We leave for Brampton, where in the *Nags Head* and then the *Scotch Arms*, we merrily drink away. In the middle of this place is a village green and what better place to get our heads down than under the memorial shelter, Trying to fall asleep is difficult tonight because we're near the main road and it's noisier than we first thought. No matter, we'll have to stick it out.

It's been a fairly uncomfortable night as we all wake up on our penultimate day of our tour to the downpour of heavy rain. I'm as wet as the inside of a beer drinker's belly, so it's all off to the village café for food and a dry out where we eat our excellent breakfast for £2.30 each, all except Lionel who's sneaked out of the door without paying. Steam is now rising off our clothes and the effects of the drying process are well under way. We agree on a site-seeing tour to Hadrian's Wall, as none of us has ever seen this spectacle before. The image is of a ten-foot high wall running the breadth of England roughly seventy-five miles from Wallsend on the River Tyne to Bowness at the head of the Solway Firth. With the rain now easing off, it's been fifteen miles of travelling up, down, round and across, looking for this bloody wall. We eventually stop to ask a local where it is. He turns out to be German and doesn't understand us. Out in the wilds, continuing our journey, a signpost is spotted, on it the words 'Ancient Roman Ruin.' At last, it can't be far away now. Our eagle eyes are peering over the landscape looking for this high wall but it's still not in vision. Coming to a halt in a cutting at the side of the road, a little walk across the fields is undertaken to see if a wall can be found. Quite excited and looking forward to discovering this bit of history, we suddenly bump into a three-foot high, four-foot wide stone wall. Surely this can't be it? What a massive disappointment; to our dismay it is. While it does stretch in parts for a few miles it's nothing compared to the wall we thought existed. So, a call of nature is had by all.

Disheartened at our findings, the tour continues and our band of explorers head to the Lake District. Our first two pubs are the *Sun* (Bassenthwaite) followed by the *Pheasant Inn* (Bassenthwaite Lake) this is really the only lake in the Lake District as all the others are called waters or meres. The word 'thwaite' means 'clearing' and is an old Scandinavian word. Whilst supping away in the *Pheasant*, I overhear a couple in their fifties, who have clocked us sitting at the bar, say to the gaffer, "Is there another room we could eat our dinner in, as we do not fancy eating in here now?"

The snotty-toffee-nosed twits. Mind you, bed and breakfast is expensive at £28 for a single room. Anyway it's off to the *Sticklebarn Tavern* (Great Langdale) with its cheap hiking bunkhouses at the rear and then the *Britannia* (Elterwater), with a pretty barmaid. We sit in the small lounge for our last drink of the afternoon.

Oggy said, "What's on the agenda now? There's nothing to do around here."

I get the map out and find a visit to the 'Nuclear Reactor Plant at Sellafield' could be interesting, but mainly it's to pass a few hours until the pubs reopen. I notice a short cut can be taken through a road called the 'Hardknot Pass'.

Passing through wonderful countryside, this single-track road with its severe gradients of one in three is in sight, the 'Hardknot Pass'! This road can only be described as a 'helter skelter,' a clutch burning nightmare, as one minute you are looking up at the bonnet of your car and the next down at the tarmac. There's an old Roman fort called the 'Mediobogdum' along here and it's easily missed, so if you are up this neck of the woods keep an eye out for it. This is a unique road; designed specifically for their chariots, at a guess? Stupendous! Is how to describe this view with its gigantic bits of rock covered in lumpy grass, shrouded by fluffy clouds. Leo said, "Open the sunroof

Hilly, I want to tek some photos of this scenery."

"Okay mate." So he pops his head out.

"Hilly, my best hat's blew off, stop the car!"

Too late, and his hat is never to be seen again as it floats away over this windy pass. Near the end, stuck on this road is a young couple in a sports car, which has failed miserably attempting to negotiate this pass, with its clutch burnt out. Jumping out and pushing their car to a safe passing point is the only way out for us. What a superb experience, the Hardknott Pass is. It takes us 1¼ hours to navigate over these really sharp bends which require extreme caution. A challenge that driver's should attempt at least once in their 'car's' life.

Arriving at Sellafied, there's a coach that takes you around the site. We miss the last one, so our happy bunch of travellers pose for a picture taken outside the visitors' and exhibition centre. Entering here and viewing the exhibits, Mark finds a more interesting display: they're packets of balloons. He takes a dozen of these and disappears. We spend an hour in this place, keeping warm until it's time for the pubs to open. Mark turns up and says, "Come and have a look what I've done."

What's he been up to now? I thought. On approaching our cars it's easy to find out what. He's blown the balloons up and he's tied them all onto the cars. A site to behold as we zoom off with all these brightly coloured balloons waving in the air. Thankfully we arrive for a drink in the *Bower House Inn* (Eskdale Green) where we bost (burst) all the balloons. The *George* (Eskdale) is our next one, then the *Sun* (Coniston) and the *Red Lion* (Hawkeshead). The last pub planned for tonight is the *Queens Head* (Troutbeck), but our navigational skills go amiss and we find ourselves with five minutes to go before closing time on a caravan site. Rushing in the clubroom I said, "Are we okay for a drink, or are we too late?"

"No problem, what would you like?" says the barman.

Ordering two pints each, it's time to rest our bones and wind down, talking about the day's events.

Unreal, five minutes pass and the gaffer comes over and says, "Drink up it's time to go, we're closing now."

"Not until our drinks are finished," says Jase.

At this, the gaffer fetches a few of his henchmen. I explain to him our aim, purpose and adventure and he then allows us to drink up at our own pace. We are later given a personal escort off the grounds. Bang goes the idea of bedding down here then.

Moving on, stuck out in remote wilderness, climbing higher up this mountain road. It's bleak. We notice a light twinkling in the distance so we head for this. To our surprise it turns out to be an inn, called the *Kirkstone Pass*. Sadly it's closed, because it's now approaching the midnight hour. It's like a blackboard up here and you can't see a thing. I nip over to the car and fetch my torch, as this is an ideal spot to stretch out and nod away the night. Oggy's roamed off and is shouting, "Where is everybody, I can't see a thing?"

On finding him, there he is talking to a large piece of cardboard sticking out of a bin, thinking it's one of us. Oggy Magoo is his new nickname from now on (after the short-sighted cartoon character). An ideal place is found by a 'No Camping' sign, so on a lovely grass slope, on a peaceful evening, counting the stars, I'm in heaven.

We wake up on Sunday 2nd August, our final day, to a magnificent and idyllic mountain view and another sign 'Private Car Park.' We best move the cars then.

Leo then says to everyone's astonishment, "What an uncomfortable night's kip that was, it was like sleeping on ball bearing."

"How come Leo?" I said.

"I've been lying on hard round globular objects, called sheep shit!"

Well! Anyway, packing our stuff away we embark on a steady pleasurable drive taking in the scenery, when I notice a pub serving breakfast at 10 a.m. called the *Brotherswater Inn* (Patterdale). We stop to investigate this chance occurrence. This is a stroke of luck and a sizzling breakfast is gobbled down, followed by three pints apiece of early morning beers. The chap who's dished up our nosh, said, "The pub you slept by last night is the third highest pub in England, at 1500 feet above sea level."

We then head back up to the *Kirkstone Pass* formerly known years back as the *Traveller's Rest*. The road up to here is known locally as 'The Struggle'. Inside the inn today, candlelight and a log fire illuminate the room due to the generator being broke. There's also a three-foot diameter tree trunk in the middle of the room. This famous inn was built in 1496 and has a genuine stone half-spiral staircase, unique to the Lakeland area. We sup away our beers for a casual half-an-hour, whilst I read the following verse;

> If I were a lover and loved a lass,
> Who lived at the top of Kirkstone Pass,
> I'd swear by all that's true and tried,
> While I abode at Ambleside,
> To love and to cherish her ever and ever,
> But go up and visit? Never! No, Never.

Our travels continue, heading for the *Queen's Head* (Troutbeck) the pub we couldn't find last night. A superb pub built in 1617, the 'Mayor's Parlour' is a room full of interest, with a massive old carved oak bar, carved old chairs and a wealth of original oak beams. Some of us play pool in the small back room. We travel on to the *Crown* (High Newton) just making it for last orders and this is our last pub before heading home. What a mammoth and fascinating adventure it's been! Most of us are now quite worn out as the gruelling week of travel is taking its toll. On our long journey homeward we stop off at Morecambe for fish and chips. With £2 left in my pocket I'm determined to go home skint, so I have my last pint in the *Coachmakers Arms* (Wednesbury) and this brings the 'Pint North Trip' to an end: seventy six pubs and 1,754 miles later.

CHAPTER 6

HIGHER, LOWER! LOWER!!

Foxy, an old pal of mine, has sent a letter to the Old Codgers page in the *Daily Mirror* asking them if they know the whereabouts of the lowest pub in England. This has started a somewhat large dispute and disagreement amongst various publicans. The *Mirror* concludes that three are in line for this accolade, the *Admiral Wells* (Holme), the *Bridge Hotel* (Clayhithe) both in Cambridgeshire and the *Ship* (Dunwich) Suffolk. To make sure we visit the right one, a visit to each is planned. A bright summer's morning has arrived. Foxy makes a guest appearance for this trip, so it's off to the *Admiral Wells*. This is a country pub with a beautiful beer garden, where, in the fields nearby is a sign on a pole telling you that you are now eight feet below sea level. The *Nutshell* (Bury St Edmunds) the smallest pub is now our aim. Please let it be open!

Blow me down, would you believe it – it's market day in Bury St Edmunds and one of the few pubs allowed to open all day in the whole of England is the *Nutshell*. What a smashing little interior; the room measures 15ft 10ins x 7ft 6ins and most people are standing outside drinking their beers as obviously there's not much space indoors. Oggy pays a visit to the bogs that are upstairs in this three-storey building and, while widdling away, most of the folk outside can see him due to the windowsill being quite low. There are lots of curiosities around the walls and ceiling. Jacquai Knott the landlady points out to us a mummified cat and woolly nipple warmers. It was definitely worth the effort to come and see this unique alehouse – and it was open too! Foxy, who is today's guide said, "Right lads, the next pub is claiming to be the lowest due to the fact that in the 1800s the original village and all the building were claimed by the sea."

"I suppose we'll all need a snorkel for this one then Foxy?" I replied.

"Don't be saft Hilly, there's one left in the village that the sea hasn't reached yet."

The *Ship* is found and it's not open, so we stroll along the shingle beach and we sit in the empty boats watching the waves wash away a bit more of England. This passes a thoughtful few minutes. Craving for a pint, the pub opens at last. We quench our thirst and enjoy a game of darts.

On leaving here, the rear brakes in my car start making the occasional grinding noise, but we carry on regardless. The *White Horse* (Badingham), *Victoria* (Earl Soham) a home-brew pub and then one of the other pubs claiming to be one of the lowest in England the *Bridge Hotel* (Clayhithe) are visited in that order. The final two pubs of the day are the *Anchor* (Sutton Gault) and the *Mermaid* (Ellington) and with no chance of a drink over in here, we drive for a couple of miles and settle down on a grass verge. We all agree that the *Admiral Wells* was the lowest pub. Wrapped up and warm, we're rudely disturbed by a bloke with a torch who arrogantly said, "I live in that house over the road, what are you all doing here?"

We tell him we're trying to get some sleep, then off he goes.

Ten minutes later the police arrive. The prick has only gone and shopped us. It turns out that because we are being quiet and causing no one any harm, they'll let us stay put. With a beautiful clear night and lots of shooting stars, I fall asleep.

Morning arrives and the same bloke who woke us up last night sets his Irish wolfhound on us. Foxy, who's zipped up to his neck in his red sleeping bag looking like a red hot chilli pepper, somehow manages to frighten this scruffy mutt off. This plonker then calls his dog and runs in the house before we retaliate. After escaping the jaws of death, it's into the café at Banbury bus station. By now the grinding noise in my car off my rear brakes sounds pretty bad. It's the brake shoes, they've worn out and they're failing to stop the car when I want them to. As a member of the *AA*, I must think of somewhere to park up while waiting for them that still allows us to visit a few pubs. Looking through my map Hook Norton is not too far away.

My judgement for once proves correct as we arrive here with enough boozers to keep us satisfied. To our surprise there's a unique old brewery called Hook Norton. This was rebuilt and completed in 1900 as a tower brewery rising to six floors with one of their prized possessions being its twenty-five horsepower stationary steam engine. Next to the brewery is the *Pear Tree*. There's five minutes before opening and seeing a small window open and a little old lady sitting beneath it doing her knitting, I thought I'd lean through and tap her on the shoulder and ask her if she's opening soon. "Excuse me, can y–" before I could finish my sentence she's jumped six inches out of her chair, drops her knitting on the floor and yells, "You silly sod! Are you trying to give me a heart attack?"

Mind you, it did get the pub open. An excellent tipple of Old Hooky bitter is tasted, and Mary the charming lady I almost frightened to death is relief manageress for Iris and Harry Blackwell the licensees, whilst they are away on holiday. She said to us all, "If you wait long enough you'll see the Hook Norton dray and shire horses locally delivering their beers."

This I must see, so another round is bought.

Mary's husband Jeff arrives. He buys us two pints apiece and tells us he was born in Bretforton, the same village as Les Carter our favourite gaffer from the *Plough* at Ford. A great old tradition now greets us as the Hook Norton dray pulled by three shire horses goes by. At this, we said our goodbyes to a very hospitable couple. Just down the road are two pubs together, the *Red Lion* and the *Sun*. This is an ideal place to park the car and phone up the repair service. While waiting, in we go for a drink. The beer garden at the rear of the *Sun* is a pet sanctuary for pheasants, rabbits and peacocks. Should this place be renamed the Animal Magic? Nipping next door to the *Red Lion,* is when the very nice man from the *AA* arrives and while he works on my brakes, we visit the other pub down the street, the *Bell*. This has the first circular, swivelled pool table any one of us has seen, so we play a game. The landlord comes over and gives me a leaflet advertising the first ever Hook Norton beer festival. All funds raised at this festival will be going to the restoration of the church and the local fire brigade. This is a village certainly worth travelling to. Back now to my fully functional automobile, I thank the AA chap and give him a well-earned tip. After such a blissful afternoon, it's off to Cirencester for fish and chips.

By chance, travelling the country lanes we find the enchanting village of Bibury. Here there is a long row of old cotton weavers' cottages called Arlington Row, a trout stream and more importantly two pubs called the *Catherine Wheel* and the *Swan Hotel*. Another detour takes us into the *Earl Grey* (Quenington), a small bar resembling someone's living room, then onto two more pubs before heading to our final happy-hop-house, owned by 'Ye Olde boozer' the man himself Les Carter at the *Plough*. He's over the moon to see us again and of course the offer of accommodation is too good an offer to refuse. It's so nice to see his missus, Ann, who reminds us not to get up too late in the morning and miss breakfast. That happens to be a long way off at the moment, so for a change scrumpy cider is called for. I tell Les of our meeting with Mary in the *Pear Tree*, He says he knew her really, really well in his younger days. Les who's always smiling says to Jase, "Here's my cider, the proper cloudy stuff – you taste that."

Jase asks about the thing in the bottom of his glass. He said it looked like a soggy old slug." Don't worry about that, it's pure protein and it will put hairs on your chest," said Les. Confirming it is indeed a slug.

A cheerful glass-gargling session is enjoyed by all. Lionel was legless, Jase was spaced, Foxy was fermented, Oggy is groggy and myself – well, the less said the better. Up to the old barn now, where halfway up the steps Jase gives Les's mobile lawnmower something to work on in the morning as he chucks up over the railings. Good night lads, sleep tight and don't let the bedbugs bite.

Ann calls us for our breakfast at £3 per head. After finishing our fittle (food) we thank our hosts and it's off to a pub I must revisit, the *Shoulder of Mutton* (Broad Marston). This time I'm going to take some photos of the interior and the old landlady. On our arrival Friday August 7th 1987 there's a sign on the gate saying, *'We regret that due to illness the pub has now closed. We thank you for your custom in the past.'* This is heartbreaking news, as I would love to have met the landlady again. Sadly, yet again a classic pub bites the dust – another one gone. I shall personally never forget the experience of actually drinking in this rare establishment. Devoted to our cause we despondently embark on route to the *Manor Hotel* (Pershore), where the gaffer of 'Wilson's Fun Fair' is happily supping away and tells us of the Wilson's history and all the fun of the fair. With 600 miles of pure adventure and nineteen pubs visited. Another memorable tour is completed.

A mediocre few weeks pass. During this time we discuss a third European trip. This is due to us watching a programme on the telly called *The Secret Hunters*, about a parish priest in the small village of Moussey in France who offered his life in exchange for his parishioners in World War II. The Germans had captured all the men of the village for supporting the British and sent them off to concentration camps. The British SAS soldiers who were also captured were taken into the forest and shot. On the last Sunday in September every year he tends the graves of these SAS men who were found years later and reburied in the graveyard. Wreaths are laid on their graves. "Let's go and see if we can find him, if he's still alive that is," I suggested.

"It would be great if he was, he's a bit of British history," replies Wayne.

Leo's not so sure and said. "It will be a miracle if he is alive and at the church too, he must be in his 90s now!"

"No matter my old pal, if he's not I've found out where the world's strongest lager is made. It's called Samichlaus Dark 1987, it's 14.93 per cent alcohol by volume and brewed in Switzerland. We can go there if we can't find him," I said.

Seven of us put our names down for this trip. I must start organising it. First it's the deposits off all the lads for the minibus, petrol and road tolls. Then there's the booking of the ferry, RAC cover, and forms for health care and accidents, first aid box and extra driver insurance. I shall have to get a move on, I've worked out £115 per person should cover everything. I also need a picture of the parish priest if possible so I go up to the library in West Bromwich and look through *The Secret Hunters* book. To my relief there is one of him in it so I get a copy.

Jase has now passed his driving test. He's got a car and it's taken on its maiden voyage to the *Vernon Arms* (Hanbury) where there's an 'Elvis' tribute night on commemorating the tenth anniversary of his death. While in here Mark tries out the rubber glass trick on Lowey, who, horrified at the wobbly feel of the glass drops it all over the lounge floor of the pub. Time to leave I think. The *Live and Let Live* (Cutnall Green) is next, where three of the BATS have the pub in stitches. Lionel is sitting stiffly on Gav's lap and Gav's hand is up the back of his jumper. Gav then throws him about like a ventriloquist's dummy while Lionel keeps saying. "Gottle of geer, gottle of geer."

Mark takes his turn now sitting on Gav's lap and does his Orville the duck impression singing, "I wish I could fly way up to the sky but I can't."

It's truly hilarious and bellyaching entertainment.

As it's T-shirt weather tonight, we sit outside the next pub and try to educate Jase on the Highway Code. He's finding it difficult work navigating his motor and it's been up numerous gutters and round an island the wrong way. Lionel on the other hand has bought some brand new spotlights for his motor and tries them out for the first time. He flicks a switch and the whole of the night sky is illuminated. Well, at least it was for a very brief moment as all the lights on his car short circuit. He has to stop in the middle of the remaining two motors to get home safely. To our relief tonight's survival run comes to an end.

It's Sunday 30th August and Kinver is our destination and we stop at what, in our opinion, is the best pub in town, the *Old Plough*. It's a smart old place full of brasses. The gaffer on hearing of our tour said, "My dad, Mr Creed, was from Carters Green in West Bromwich. Back in 1932 he started hiking around the world."

He then shows me a thick book he had left him when his dad passed away two years ago. It's full of newspaper cutting from every place he visited. "Did he ever complete his mission?" I said,

"No, he got as far as Australia then the war broke out," he replied.

"Bloody Hell gaffer, that was bad luck, I hope we don't have the same trouble."

This was a magnificent document. If only I had time to read it.

It's Bank Holiday Monday, so for a change of scenery we go to Oxfordshire. Woodstock to be precise. We drop on a couple of interesting pubs worth a mention. The *Bear Hotel* is an original coaching inn of Old England. Which has been dispensing hospitality for over 500 years. The other pub is the *King's Head* known locally as the spud-pub. Here you can scoff various fillings of baked potatoes. On the wall is a seven-verse poem called *Ode to Potatoes,* this is about one potato called Harvey and the last verse goes as follows.

But Harvey was baked, with Sid and his mate,
Then covered with chicken and curry,
Put on a plate,
And suddenly ate,
He was gone in a terrible hurry.
Poor old Harvey.

They also sell various cocktails and coffee specials named after Henry VIII and his wives: Katherine of Aragon, Anne Boleyn, Jane Seymour, Anne of Cleves, Katherine Howard and Katherine Parr all at £1.10 a glass. Beer back home is 65p a pint but we're paying roughly 90p in this town. Now afternoon closing arrives and to pass the time we decide to walk to Blenheim Palace. This was designed by a chap named Sir John Vanburgh for John Churchill 1st Duke of Marlborough as a token by Queen Anne on behalf of the country after his victory over the French at the battle of Blenheim in 1704.

Capability Brown landscaped the beautiful park with its boating lake. Sir Winston Churchill was born here in 1874 and is buried in the quiet churchyard nearby at Bladon. Approaching the entrance we're abruptly stopped in our tracks by the £4 fee to view inside the palace. "Bugger that," said Leo. "There must be a cheaper way in?"

We pay 50p and enter the park grounds and then take a longish walk down to the lake. Oggy refuses to walk that far and lies down on the grass for forty winks, with the sun beating down on his walnut whip hairstyle he soon nods off. Leo notices a possible way into the palace, so we jump a fence, down a ditch, scramble along a wall and enter the palace from the exit. Inside are wonderful statues and lots of history about the Churchill family. Two hours are spent absorbing English history.

"Let's find Oggy," said Leo.

Leo and I can't believe our luck because we're locked in the grounds. The gates are locked and there's no sign of Oggy. The only way out is to scale an eight foot wall so over we go. There's a handy little café close by that will be a good vantage point to spot the 'Woodstock Walnut Whip Wanderer'. Satisfying our appetite and thirst with a bun and a cup of tea, half-hour passes and the man himself comes hobbling past looking totally lost and bemused. Shouting him over a rather annoyed Oggy bellows back, "Wheer yoe lot bin? I've bin walking round for ages."

It turns out that upon waking up and finding the gates locked he couldn't climb over the wall and had to walk the long way round to get out of the place. Leo now discovers he's lost his front door key when he conquered the high wall earlier. We go back for a look but it's a lost cause. Before my belly thinks my wazzin's (throat's) been cut a pint of the pure brown ale is urgently required. A new Banks's pub is not too far away situated in the Jericho area of Oxford. It's called the *Victoria Arms*. Standing at the bar, the licensee comes up to me and said, "I remember you well mate, I signed your book when I was licensee in the *Bella Pais* [Aldridge]."

"Yes, I had £5 off you for our charity collection, but you never bought us a drink did you?" as I jokingly nudge him. This seems to have done the trick, as he buys us all a round of drinks. Then a drinking group approaches me in here and one of them says, "What's all this then, are you some sort of beer tasters?"

"Pub visitors really chaps, we're called the BATS," I explained.

"We're called the JARS, the Jericho Association of the Rarely Sober."

We make our acquaintance and exchange our different tales and exploits, stopping here for four hours consuming numerous pints of ale. The licensee offers us the chance to sleep in his pub. As it's back to work tomorrow we have to decline his kind offer. Still it has been a grand day out and we listen to Elvis tapes on the way back home, stopping a few times for Leo to be sick.

The Hook Norton's first ever 'Beer Festival' arrives at last and we're going. It's Saturday 19th September 1987. There's six of us squashed in my car and trying to find the village proves a problem. Mark the map-reader today has got us lost in some remote road. By chance there's a pub here called the *Norman Knight* (Whichford) so why mess around any longer? Let's get a drink! The landlord in here puts us in the right direction. Eagerly keen on sampling our first beer at the festival we arrive in torrential rain in the field just up the hill from the *Pear Tree* pub. The Sealed Knot Society are well into their re-enactment of an English Civil War battle and approaching the beer marquee we're now up to our ankles in mud.

There's twenty-one different beers, selling at £1 a pint. It doesn't take us long to figure out with our plastic pint glasses that if we leave half-inch at the bottom of the glass and ask for half-pint the barmaids were filling them up to the top. So happily we start working our way through all the beers available. The toilets are a long way off across the muddy field outside so everyone's piddling up the side of the marquee instead.

I notice that there are boxes of old and new beer towels on sale for 50p each.

The organiser approaches me and said, "Lads I would like to thank you all for coming today, because before you came in not one beer towel was sold. People only saw you lot walk in with those beer towel coats on and we've sold out,"

"No problem, glad to help out," I reply.

The festival closes at 5 p.m. and with thirty minutes left the beer is now sold for 50p a pint. This doesn't really bother us as we've been getting friendly with the barmaids and have been getting ours for nothing. An enjoyable afternoon comes to an end. Walking back across a sea of mud to the cars, Oggy thinks he's a toboggan and slides down the small grass bank on his arse then rolls over a bit and now resembles a chocolate soldier.

Travelling to the nearest pub so he can clean himself up we arrive at the *Gate Hangs High* near Hook Norton. Oggy gets through a whole roller towel in the bogs at this pub trying to get all the mud off his clothes. The *Railway* also near Hook Norton is where we watch two old blokes in their seventies have a short fight with each other. We then revisit three pubs in the village the first being the *Red Lion*, where we have a game of darts and eat half a chicken each. I phone up two of the other members of our gang who will meet us later tonight to tell them we'll meet them in the *Bell* down the road. By now, 2 x 2 = 5 and I've never seen so many pool balls on one table. Nature calls and, whilst sitting comfortably and going about my business, I get quite annoyed at the number of people knocking on the closet door. On opening it I find to my horror there's a queue of women waiting to use the toilet. I'm actually sitting in the ladies' bogs and it's the only one available to them in the pub. Embarrassed I apologise to all concerned and on coming out I forget the step down into the lounge and go flying across the floor knocking the lads' beers and Oggy's double whisky off the table. The Bungle brothers arrive with their girls plus Doug, a new member. We now move on to the *Pear Tree*.

Six of them decide to walk down, but Tony decides to drive the remaining five of us. Off he speeds, trying to get in the pub first. However, not realising how close it was he misses the turning, bumps up the gutter, crosses the grass and comes to a halt just before ramming a lamp post. "What a twat, Tony," I said. We should have walked.

It's a great night in the *Pear Tree* with us all having a sing-song till the early hours. Surprisingly, our late arrivals all have to head off home. The original crew of six decides to sleep in the graveyard opposite the *Red Lion* where my car had already been parked up for the night. The rain finally stops and we all bed down for our final resting-place of the day. In the early hours, bright shining lights coming towards us disturbs our rest. Still pissed and out of focus, we all think a car is travelling towards us.

Gav said, "It's the bloody police with their torches!"

"Oh shit, there's no way I can move tonight." I groaned.

"Have you lot been to the beer festival today?" said one of the officers.

"Yes we have but we've had too much to drink and drive, so we thought we'd kip here for the night," Lionel replies.

"As long as you don't cause any commotion and promise to keep quiet you can remain here for the rest of the night."

This is good news as I'm out of my noggen.

Indebted to the local bobbies, Leo is now jumping up and down like a kangaroo trying to get out of his sleeping bag for a slash. The zip is stuck and by the time he's free, there's a nasty smell in the air. He's been hopping in dog shit and the smell is vile.

Trying to get back to sleep is a nightmare. Gav has left his trainers on and they are screeching down the plastic bag he's in. Mark's moaning like he's risen from the dead and now a coach pulls up playing loud music for half-hour until the police arrive to move them on. Finally I manage to drift off, waking up to the sound of organ music. Where this is coming from is anyone's guess as it's only 4.30 a.m. so again I try to nod off. Managing to get three hours' sleep I'm now woken by loads of pigeons flying above me and nesting in the church roof. They are having a lovely time seeing which one of them can score a direct hit on my head with a fair deal of success. I give in and I just lie on my back trying to dodge the droppings. The early morning mist is now clearing and when the Sunday worshippers arrive they take one look at us and seem too frightened to come past us. The gaffer of the *Red Lion* sees the predicament they are in through the window of his pub and comes over and asks us all if we'd like an early morning cup of tea.

"Not arf gaffer, we're parched."

Thank the landlord for this.

"What a night gaffer," says Gav, who explains to him how so much can happen in such a short time in such an isolated spot. He finds it amazing too. We say our thanks and goodbyes and then it's off to the Little Chef for breakfast in Chipping Norton. Lionel's belly bales yesterday's ingredients out in here and he can't eat his brekkie. The lucky person who grabs his breakfast first gets to eat it. Leaving for Henley in Arden we arrive one hour before opening time so we've got to find something to amuse us until then. All buying an ice cream we sit outside the *Golden Cross Inn*, laughing about old *Candid Camera* clips. Oggy said, "I remember one where two people carried a piece of imaginary glass." He then told Gav and Mark how it was done.

"Let's play the trick on some passing motorists," says Mark.

So pretending to hold a large sheet of glass between them, about six feet apart, both holding handkerchiefs in their hands with their arms outstretched proceed to walk across the road. The drivers of the vehicles kindly stop and let them cross to the other side. This is really funny and it works every time. It's mine and Leo's turn now as Leo goes one side of the road and me the other, we bend down together and pretend to pick up an invisible length of string, then we stand up and pull it taut. The motorists soon come to a halt as they all believe that spanning the road is a real length of string. Hilarious and most drivers do see the humorous side of our little joke too. Lastly, with opening time almost upon us we all have a game of pool on a non-existent table on the pavement where many curious drivers slow down to see what's going on.

Anyway with all the clowning around concluded it's in the pub for a well-earned pint. Today there's a charity pram race through the main street and everybody's out watching this, leaving us to complete the remaining pubs in town without queuing at the bar. A brilliant boozing binge has been had by all, with the possible exception of Lionel who refuses to blame the beer for making him sick earlier in the day, blaming it on his cup of tea instead. Well, it's off home now to plan further intoxicating trips.

CHAPTER 7

BONSOIR MONSIEUR

It's Tuesday 29th September 1987 and our third European tour is to begin. Our mission is to find the parish priest in the village of Moussey, in France. He's the man who, in September 1943, offered his life in exchange for his parishioners. Every year he lays poppies and a wreath on the SAS graves in that village. To actually find this chap who is now part of British history, alive, would be unbelievable. If we are unsuccessful, then our other aim is to find the strongest beer in the world in Switzerland. The magnificent seven are ready to rumble: Wayne, John, Doc, Leo, Jase, Doug and myself. All dressed in combat trousers, boots and beer towel coats. This is to be a tour of military precision, I hope. Doug is the odd one out because he's wearing white Doc Marten boots. A minibus is hired from the same garage as last year. It's a long drive to the first pub on our adventure the *Jolly Farmer* (Cookham Dean). Tim Brooke-Taylor of *The Goodies* fame is part owner of this pub. The gaffer gives us a bucket to keep for emergency reasons. He pointed out that travelling long distances without a toilet on board could be painful. We leave at 3 p.m. for Canterbury, arriving at 5p.m. While waiting for the pubs to open we empty our bucket of piddle down the drain and go for a drink in a proper 'Tea Shop'. Various flavours are sampled in here, from strawberry to fruit and mango. Doc declines saying that none of these are his cup of tea!

The *Old Locomotive* is open so we go in for a drink. Lots of railway memorabilia adorn the walls. Our next pub is *Ye Olde Yew*

Tree Inn (Westbere), built as a medieval hall house around 1308 probably becoming an inn sometime in the sixteenth century. Sold by Whitbread brewery in 1980 it is now a free house. We then head straight into Dover as we continue our journey to our last pub before the ferry crossing, the *Elephant and Hind*. Before we sail we grab a Wimpy burger for £2.56 each and then board the ferry called *The Pride of Free Enterprise*. At the moment it's hard to stop John from saying, more tea vicar! I think he overdid the pots of tea in Canterbury. The beer on board is 80p a pint and we have a couple apiece before nodding off for an hour and arriving in Calais at 11.30 p.m. There's no need to turn the clocks forward by one hour due to France turning theirs back last week. We drive until 1.15 a.m. and park on a lay-by at a place called Arras. We sleep on the grass bank but it's a noisy night due to the heavy lorries pulling up. We wake up early on a freezing Wednesday morning and it's foggy. We don't mess around too long and grab a quick bite to eat then put the Beach Boys tape on, hoping the sound of their music can make us feel warmer. We fill up with petrol and pay our first toll fee of 240 francs (about £8.20) at Reims, our second fee at Metz for £5.70 and a final small toll at Faulquemont. Here is where we think it's time for a beer in the nearest pub we come to and it's called *Au Rallye*. There's a table football game in here. I'm a good player, but we make the mistake of playing doubles against the local French lads. They happen to be brilliant and we never win a game. Wayne, who's annoyed at losing, is wearing an Aussie cork hat and points to the badge he has clipped on the side of it and said with a whisper to the French lads, "SAS."

We all leave and whilst climbing in the minibus all the locals in the pub come rushing out and give us gifts, such as ash trays, calendars, glasses and maps. This got a little embarrassing. Wayne however found it all quite funny. On our map, the village of Moussey is about twenty miles away on the road to Mulhouse. On our arrival it turns out to be the wrong Moussey! Our visit here is not wasted and feeling rather parched, we go into the *Bowling Tabac* pub. The owner of this place tells us of another Moussey and points to roughly where the next one is. This 'other' Moussey is a distance of fifteen miles away in the Mouselle Valley. It's getting dark now and we get completely lost and drop in on the village of Senones where there's a pub. The gaffer in here looks like his head's on upside down. He's bald on top with a big black beard. I wonder if we'll ever find this village called Moussey and as I can't speak French and this bloke can't speak English, I show him my picture of the parish priest. He smiles and said, "Oui, Oui monsieur."

Waving his arms he guides us outside. He gets in his car and we follow him in our minibus. Up we go around narrow roads, high up in the hills, eventually coming to a halt in complete darkness at a spooky looking church."Yes this is it, this is the village we've been after all day!" I said.

Our guide from the Senones pub knocks the church door. A young chap opens the heavy wooden door and a conversation starts between them in French. Which leads to us being directed to the house next door. Thanking our guide for his help, he now leaves. The young chap knocks this door and an anxious few moments pass before it opens. Standing there straight in front of me is a small frail elderly man who must now be in his nineties. We can't get over our excitement – it's the parish priest, we're told his name is Abbé Molière. This is unbelievable. We're all chuffed to bits I said, "Bonsoir monsieur." The only phrase I knew. I now get the man himself to autograph the picture that I've brought with me and all of us have our photograph taken with him. To meet this man who during the War offered his life in exchange for his parishioners is an honour. For his bravery he was presented a SAS beret off that regiment and every year he pays his respects at their fallen colleagues' graves. Who would have thought we would actually meet this man? I for one didn't. It was just another excuse for a piss-up around Europe! I put my arm around the old priest and I now say my goodbye as a look of the SAS graves is next. These graves have their own special area set against a five foot high stone wall in the graveyard and we now place a poppy on each of the graves of these brave men. A sombre occasion.

After a while Leo clocked a pub nearby and said that it was time we paid it a visit. The pub is called *La Sympa*. On entering the pub only two other blokes are in here. The word quickly spreads in the village that some English are paying their local a visit. Before long all the locals are streaming in. Out of the two dozen folk who have now arrived only one can speak English. I told him what our mission was and he said, "You are very lucky to have caught Abbé Molière, as he lives in an old folks' home just outside Paris and he's only up here for two weeks so he can tend to the graves."

He goes on to tell me that this man also won the Medaille Militaire at Verdun in the Great War in 1916.

This chap is very handy indeed as our translator.

I'm asked where we are sleeping later tonight. When I tell him outside, I'm told to follow a chap who proceeds to take me in his van to the village community centre. Here I'm shown the floor that we can put our sleeping bags down on. The heaters are left on for us and I'm now given the door key to the place. He then takes me back to the pub. My translator tells me we're welcome to use the centre for the night. Not much ale has been consumed today and now all are on a high after our meeting with the priest, the beer starts to follow rather quickly. We carry on drinking into the early hours. Dancing, singing and beating all the locals at arm wrestling. As the night draws on most of us are paralytic and there's only us left in the pub. Wayne is the only one sober as he's driving in the morning.

All I remember upon coming out of this pub on the darkest night that I've ever known is shouting to Wayne, to tell him I've gone blind. I then flaked out on the pavement. I know nothing until the morning when I wake up by a metal pole. It's a bus stop. Situated outside the post office and people are looking down at me whilst waiting to catch the bus. I'm in a right state. Wayne comes over to me. He's been sleeping in the minibus and tells me what happened last night. "I've never known anything like it. John went to sleep early because he felt sick; Doug broke his glasses when he passed out and hit his head on the toilet bowl; Doc's still asleep in that hedge he fell through. Leo and Jase had a scuffle with each other and the outcome is Leo's cut his lip and nose. You had a mishap when you went for a crap before flaking out."

"What do ya mean ah kid?" I groggily replied.

He then points to an unfinished turd. It turns out that I had a dump forgetting that I had my bracers on and halfway through my job they twanged back up, so the other half is now in my trousers. So my motto is 'Don't wear bracers when you are drunk and need a dump.' The landlady of the pub opens up for us at 8 a.m. I give her the community centre key that we never used. The lads go in for a cup of coffee while I nip off to change into my clean jeans.

It's time to move on and at the Swiss border the police arrive and tell us to line up outside the minibus. One by one they ask the lads for their passports and to empty their pockets. Eventually they reach me. I'm last in line with my head now stuck in the bucket we brought along. The copper asks me for my passport. I tell him it's in the minibus, as I chuck up again in the bucket. He opens the door of the minibus and picks up my shitty trousers. The smell makes him heave but it does the trick, and they tell us we can move on. Another toll fee is paid and we have a long drive before a stop at Thun for a snack. Our tins of soup are keeping the lads well fed, but my soup refuses to stay down. Our mission now is to find the strongest lager in the world. I'm just wishing I had the strongest stomach!

We arrive in Lauterbrunnen in the Bernese Oberland with its fabulous scenery. Our mob of happy travellers view the Staubbach Falls, then we journey on a £6 mountain railway ride (there are some worried faces on this steep track). Finally we jump on a train to Mürren then back to a place called Grindelwald. We roam around a few bars here trying to find this strong Samichlaus Dark lager but to no avail. It's 11.30 p.m. and time for a sleep. We rest on a grass verge on the village car-park. All have drunk sensibly today, recharging our batteries for tomorrow's session. On waking up, it's a drive to the cable car ride at Grindelwald. This is fantastic but a bit scary. The view is amazing. There's a big mountain called the Jungfraü. Some clown now suggests a walk to an ice glacier cave, with our 'Brucie bonus sticks' which really are walking sticks that we had from Sluis in 1985. We march for a bloody hour. Along steep, narrow and rugged paths and arrive at some dirty looking glob of ice. We have a walk inside the ice cave and come back out. "Well, that was wuth [worth] the walk wasn't it?" I said with just enough breath to get my words out.

"Magic," was the reply.

The only good thing about this is that there is a mountain café bar nearby. What a great place to stop and rest, while supping down a couple of bottled beers apiece. Now for that long walk again. At midday we catch the cable car back down. We head to Brienz and being desperate for a wash, Jase and John jump in the Brienzsee Lake. I wash my hair in it and it's ffffreezing! Some bloke then passes by on a bike, verbally abuses us for polluting the water. Being wet on the outside it's now into the nearest bar to get wet on the inside. The beer is £1.60 a bottle. The Bernese Oberland is a must for anybody who visits Switzerland.

On leaving here and only a few miles away, we hit a notorious road high up in the mountains called the Susten Pass. The summit is 2,244 metres (What's that in yards?) high. It's a bit of a racket up here as numerous fighter planes are having a practice flight. Along this road you pass through tunnels, negotiate bogey bends, see waterfalls and our minibus is struggling at eight m.p.h in first gear. The minibus needs a rest so we stop at the summit. Jase and John find a metal bin lid to sit in and take it in turns sliding down the snow that's left in isolated pockets on this cold side of the mountain road. Suddenly, John's screaming that he can't stop. He has to take drastic action, diving off his sledge and gambolling over with the bin lid disappearing over the rocks. The trip down from the pass takes us two hours to complete fifty-one miles. A monotonous trip in the end and a drink is required. Our journey continues through Altdorf, famous for its William Tell connections. We then travel on to Vaduz with its castle on top of the hill and its small fair. Here we fill the minibus up with petrol and fill us up with beer. I have these joke teeth with me. They are a big set of black nashers, so I put them in my mouth to order the beer. The expression on the barmaid's face when I smiled at her was a picture. The dark strong lager we so desperately want to sample looks like it's never going to be found, as I ask again and fail.

The final stop of the night is in Brand, a dead-end village by a fast flowing river with a pub by it. We finish off with three pints each and a game of cards called 'Chase the Ace'. On leaving the pub at 12.30 a.m. we're now all slightly pissed, but as our minibus is parked up for the night it doesn't matter. We get our sleeping bags and out of the blue, a police car turns up. The gaffer of the pub has reported us – can you believe it? Two coppers get out and one said, "You can't sleep here, you must move on."

"We've all been drinking officer and none of us are fit to drive," said Wayne.

"Get in the van and you will be escorted out of the village to another place," he persisted.

This we are forced to do and they take us to a cutting in the forest next to some old derelict stone grinding factory. As it happens it's much quieter here as the roaring sound of the river can't be heard. All the lads get a good night's sleep, waking up at 7.30 a.m. We leave for Konstanz. On arrival we park by the lake and spend our last few coins on food in the supermarket and a last beer in a pub. We are hoping to find the world's strongest beer in here but alas it's not to be. We finally give up trying to find this potent ale and decide to move on. Back at the minibus we almost lose it in the lake, as the handbrake isn't on and it rolls towards the lake knocking a slab off the top of the wall before coming to a halt.

Only fifteen miles away is the famous Rhine Falls. This we really want to see. On our arrival it costs us 60p each to view this spectacular sight. We spend 1½ hours just gazing at the billions of gallons of water cascading over the falls. This is certainly worth the money. A bag of chips is had by our slightly undernourished adventurers and we share them with a few of the fat sparrows nearby. It's off to Schonwald now which is thirty miles away in the Black Forest. At a hotel here we have a beer, which surprisingly goes down very well with a large chunk of cake called Black Forest gateau. Germany's longest waterfall is nearby at Triberg and that is our next stop. Again this is only 60p and not as impressive as the last drop of water seen at the Rhine Falls. However it is in the forest and it is a pleasant walk. All feeling like wood beetles after our forest walk, by some remote chance we find a pub. It's warm enough to sit outside overlooking the trees cheerfully sampling our lagers. John now starts talking about wasps and more wasps and he's sending us to sleepppzzz! Another round of drinks is ordered and swallowed, then we journey on.

It's a long drive and while travelling north we notice that we're near the town of *Neustadt an der Weinstrasse*. We now take a detour for a quick look to see if we can find that elusive character Gunther, again. We fail and agree to never try and find this bloke ever again. Another five miles away heading north a pub is spotted so in we go. We meet a yank couple (man and wife) and started chatting to them while we order a meal and our beers. It turns out he's a commander over the European army bases and served in Vietnam. His missus is a typical yank – I've got this, I've got that, this is bigger and that is bigger. She then said to Doc, "All of our cars have got air conditioning."

"All of ours have got windows," replied Doc.

I thought this was quite witty coming from my old pal Doc. We stop in here for the rest of the evening and have a nice few hours drinking and talking about the day's events. Not too far away along the A62 is a place called Reichweiler. This is where our day comes to and end at 11.30 p.m. on the top of a bank at the side of the road in a cut out in the woods. It's good night from me and good night from him.

Up and back on the road early Sunday morning October 4th at 7.30 a.m. Filling up with fuel at Trier, we stop for a bite to eat at Namur. Then we're not stopping again until we reach our favourite destination, Sluis arriving here at 1.45 p.m. on a lovely sunny day. At least we can all relax after a tiring drive. Our normal shops and pubs are visited and John buys some sexy toys for his girlfriend back home. A pleasant five hours gently passes us by and now it's off to Ostend for the ferry. The crossing is rather boring listening to a chap playing an organ. It sounds like he's building a shed, because tonight the right musical notes desert him. He'd be better off using his feet. To pass the time I chill out and drink a bottle of Blue Nun, a well-known wine. It's

Dover and out! It's now we're pulled over by the custom officials and asked where we've been. After satisfying their curiosity we're on our way. The weather is horrendous. Thunder and lightning, heavy rain and gale force winds. It's hard to drive in these conditions along the A2, so we pull off at the village of Coldred. It's 2.45 a.m. and we certainly need to get our heads down. The village green with its big tree in the middle comes in handy and only five of us sleep outside in our plastic bags tonight. Doc and Wayne doss in the minibus. The rain continues to piss down and now it's gone really hot as an electrical storm sets in. We're in a silly place stuck under this big tree, but at least it's giving us shelter from tonight's bad weather.

Our final day, Monday 5th October and it's still hammering down. The five of us who slept outside are soaked, stuck in our plastic bags like soggy kippers way past our sell-by date. We feel as if we haven't had any sleep and all of us look dog rough this morning. Everything is now slung in the back of the minibus, but not our plastic bags, we leave these as presents to the village. Our journey takes us to the service station at Cobham and the Little Chef. It's here we dry off and have a bite to eat. A drink is what we need so it's in the minibus and off to find our first pub of the day. We're looking for the *Cuba* pub (New Bradwell) and we can't find it so it's into *Halley's bar* (New Bradwell) to ask for directions. An article in the *Daily Star* newspaper is the reason we're after the *Cuba*. This is because the gaffer of this pub has welded two stools together for one of his locals called Tone, who weighs twenty-six stone and as we're this way why not pop in and buy Tone a beer? The only problem is we still can't find it, so I approach a local and said, "Can you please tell me where the *Cubba* pub is?" and I show him the piece of paper with the name on.

"That doesn't say *Cubba* mate it says *Cuba*," he replied.

It's no wonder nobody knew where it is. All morning I've been pronouncing it wrong. I think I've got dry rot setting in. Anyway, Tone isn't in the pub so I take a photo of his stool. We make a convenience stop at a pub called the *Wheatsheaf* (Crick) situated not far from junction eighteen on the M1. We have a nice hour in here yapping to the barmaids before setting off and arriving home at 4.20

p.m. Doug's white boots are now a dull brown colour and our skin is almost the same colour too. A bit of maintenance on our bodies is needed. First stop, the soap! Although this trip has been tiring it's been fantastic and the memories will remain forever. At least I hope so, because it's taken 1,983 miles to remember them.

CHAPTER 8

WHEN THE CHIPS ARE DOWN

With a good many of our pub ambitions completed a new challenge is required. We are given a map featuring all the public houses in the whole of the two counties of Hereford and Worcester. A chap called Jimmy Young of the 'Better Pub Company' designed the map. He's in *The Guinness Book of Records* for claiming to have visited 23,338 public houses. I put the idea of drinking in all the pubs available on this map to the lads. It's at this moment that three more members decide to leave. It's goodbye to Doc, Lionel and Tony Bungle. We won't forget these three in a hurry. I decide to phone up Whitbread brewery and ask them if they would be interested in sponsoring us around all of their pubs in these two counties. Peter Grieve of Whitbread agrees to £1 for every one of their pubs we visit.

Determined not to hang around, our pub-crawl continues throughout October onto the towns of Bridgnorth, Upton upon Severn, Bewdley and Kidderminster. In Bewdley someone lets a firework off and it makes a loud bang! Gav said to me, "I didn't know John was using his car tonight!"

Then on to Kidderminster our last pub on the last Sunday of the month *Ye Olde Seven Stars*. John for some reason listens to a group called Smiley and the Hedge in the other room. John flips in here and has the biggest wooty (wobbly) he's ever had. It's all about the gaffer giving him a half-pint when he asked for a pint. He storms out the pub and the gaffer calls him back in, shakes his hand and apologises for any misunderstanding. Gav then takes John's fag out of his mouth and out the door goes John again. We follow him singing, *When you're smiling and Happy days, happy days.* This didn't go down too well as he starts shouting and flinging his arms about. I go over and calm him down and put him in the car where he falls asleep. We have a laugh about this on the way home.

November 1st, our usual Sunday night tour takes us to Stourport. While in the *Lord Nelson* Oggy tells us of an incident a few years ago involving Ted, his mate. He tells us that while they were in a pub the gaffer asked Ted if he knew anything about jukeboxes as the one in his pub had broken. Ted said, yes and asked for a screwdriver.

The gaffer passed him one and Ted unplugs the jukebox and takes the back off. After a minute or so Ted turned round to the gaffer and said, "I think I've found the trouble."

"What is it?" replied the grateful gaffer.

Ted then held up a big meat fly in-between his fingers and jokingly said, "The driver's dead!"

The gaffer hadn't seen the funny side of this little joke and chucked us out of his pub, Oggy explained.

Moving on now, we visit one more pub and drive towards home stopping at the Pensnett chip shop. There's a sign in here that said that if anyone finds a Yorkie could you please ring such and such. Gav said, "What's anybody want with a chocolate bar?" (Yorkie is not only a dog, it's also a chunky chocolate bar).

The chip shop owner not amused at this said, "Why don't you grow up?"

"I'm too old for that," replies Gav.

You could cut the atmosphere with a knife. We have our chips and head home.

The following Sunday it's back into Stourport for the last time. In the *Holly Bush* they have a coal fire with a large tortoise shell as a fireguard. Leo clocks this object and said, "It's a funny way for a tortoise to sleep."

Onto the eighth boozer of the night, the *Mitre Oak Hotel* (Crossway Green) and Mark buys lots of Remembrance Day poppies and pins them all over him. On the way home – somewhere around Stourport – one of our cars take the wrong road and we lose them. I carry on in my car to Pensnett chip shop where I stop for Lowey, Doug, Leo and Mark who all want a bag of chips. They seem a long while so I go in and stand at the back of the queue. I hear a drunken local bloke saying to his son of about eleven years of age, "Hold my coat son and I'll show you a bit of fun."

He walks up to Leo grabs him by the lapels and said, "Do you know your mate's a dick head."

"Well, he is a bit of a tilly nana," replies Leo.

I can't believe Leo said this. Then this bloke smacks Mark across the face. When the chips are down it's time for me to make a move. The gaffer of the chip shop now gives this bloke a bottle, what did he do that for? Then I remember what Gav said to him last week. So there I am squaring up to this bloke standing face to face. I tell the lads to go in the car and slowly I back out of the shop. On getting to my car, he comes running out like a loony. I just stand there and talk him out of doing anything silly and he goes back in the chip shop. What a prat!

Worcestershire is our destination on the second Sunday of November. We travel down the M5 south, getting off at junction seven. One of our pubs tonight is a gem, the *Monkey Cider House* (Woodmancote near Defford) on the A4104. This is hard enough to spot in the daytime let alone at night when it's pitch black. We just manage to see a single light bulb shining in a thatched building off the side of the road, so we pull up on a small dirt car-park to investigate. We walk down a muddy path and open a cow gate, then it's a walk down a path past a derelict shed and a large tree and then I spot a serving hatch. I tap the counter and a chap walks over and says the only drink available is rough cider straight out of the wooden barrels. We all have a pint each. The gaffer's name is Graham Collins and he signs my book, he's not the most welcoming of landlords but we've met worse. The only place you can shelter if it rains is a small square outbuilding, otherwise you stand outside. This is an unbelievable place to visit and so are the bogs. The gent's toilet is made up of a few breeze blocks about five foot high and when you have a widdle your head is popping over the top of them as there is no roof either hence its name the Observatory. We decide to stop for another drink in this rare cider house and we don't get home until 1 a.m. During the following week on 19th November, a brand new Banks's pub opens on the site of the previous old pub called the *King's Arms* (Tipton). For the last nine months a portacabin has been used by customers, so they could continue to fill their bellies with beer while it was being built. The next pub we go to is *Mad O'Rourke's Pie Factory* (Tipton), which was formerly the derelict *Doughty Arms* and built in 1923. This is the fourth pub owned by Colm O'Rourke. He owns the Bewdley-based Little Pub Company and signs my book. All his pubs have rather eccentric interiors and this one is no exception. It's decorated with abattoir equipment including plastic meat carcasses: pigs' heads, a giant meat slicer and sawdust on the floor. It's also upset local animal protection groups for being in bad taste. Sunday sees us travel to Worcestershire where the *Elms Hotel* (Abberley) is visited. An expensive place, where a single room costs £55 and it's £1.20 a pint. John tells us about how his nickname 'Crinkle Crisp' came about when he was younger. He said, "When I was a baby my ears stuck out and looked like crisps due to the way I slept, so I used a hard back book to rest my ears on to flatten them."

"It didn't work then," laughed Leo.

The *Bell* (Pensax) is also visited. This is a superb old pub out in the country with a good range of traditional draught beers. We are usually mild drinkers and most of these beers are bitters but we give them a go. The proprietors John and Christine Stroulger ask us how they taste. They are very good indeed – we might just get the taste for these! On the way home none of us are too sure if we should stop at Pensnett chip shop. So, the two drivers tonight, Jase and John can't make their minds up and then, both deciding on different manoeuvres, Jase hits the side of John's car. This must be our bogey fish and chip shop. On getting out to view the damage a car drives past and a chap inside it throws a bottle at us. From now on I think we'll drive home and stick to a piece of toast and a cup of tay (tea).

It's Drewy's and Leo's birthday and as it's the last weekend in November a night out is arranged. The Herefordshire town of Kington is our aim because there's an old lady who runs a pub there and it would be nice to meet her. Eight of us depart on this trip at 4.30 p.m. It's a steady drive that takes us 1¾ hours. In the third pub of the night in Kington, the *Oxford Arms Hotel,* we relax and watch the television comedy *'Allo 'Allo* and get talking to the licensees Charles and Stella O'Donnell. A smashing friendly couple and I ask them if they know anywhere we could get a breakfast in the morning. Charles said, "Give me 30-bob (£1.50) each and we'll cook you one."

We give him £2 each and tell him to put more food on our plates. Our next pub is the *Olde Tavern*. This is the one owned by the old lady who is ninety-six years old! To our immense disappointment we're told she is in hospital with a broken leg. It's a totally untouched pub with two rooms. There's a cupboard containing old beer bottles, a large wood settle and an old bloke with a white handlebar moustache. We're told the old varnish on all the woodwork in both rooms must be removed immediately for hygiene reasons. Well, we must move on. The *Stagg Inn* (Titley) is next, where Gav does his impression of Joan of Arc and an Irish minesweeper. Meanwhile, Mark is drowning his sorrows with quite a few Southern Comforts, as the reality of losing his job two days ago starts to sink in. Back now into Kington and the *Burton Hotel*. In here we get yapping to an old chap with his cap on, sitting all alone in the back room. His eyes light up when he sees us come in and he gets out his mouth organ and entertains us. We all join in singing along to all the tunes he played. Moving on to the *Wine Vaults,* Mark, Gav and Leo have all got this little game going where they shout, "Duck!" and all of them duck.

Then they shout, "It's coming back!" and they duck again. Most of the locals think they've all gone saft and I'm not going to argue with that. The *Lamb* is over the road and Drewy tries opening the door the wrong way with his shoulder and the pub door window smashes. At this Drewy legs it down the road and all the locals come out shouting. One comes over to me and said, "What bastard done this!"

I told them a drunk smashed it and ran off down the road. The gaffer comes out and I tell him the same. They then go running after him the wrong way. We find Drewy sprawled out in a shop doorway put him in the car and we all get out of town before the police arrive. Our last pub of the night is about five miles away, the *Swan Inn* (Huntington). It's an old country inn with a cosy bar and a stone fireplace with a real log fire. We all finish off with three pints and this finishes most of us off. Drewy's passed out by the fire and singes his trousers. John has given his last pint away. Mark throws up and flakes out in the car. Jase didn't feel too good. Oggy's got a bad case of what we call 'Hop Fever' and can't stop sneezing. Gav's showing off and says he can drink another and me and Leo can't manage any more. It's 11.45 p.m. The landlady says we can't sleep outside so we follow a local lad in his motor for two miles to a field in Powys.

Parked up for the night, Gav gets out the car first, falls in a ditch and throws up. Gav said it was only phlegm but he's never admitted being sick in his life. However, a photo of him will be a reminder of this so-called rare event. Our sleeping stuff is carried over the narrow road and over a gate into a sheep field. We might as well have a black hood over our heads because visibility is virtually nil. There's no light and no moon tonight. Mark's still passed out in the car and Jase says it's too cold to sleep outside. He's got a point as I put on three jumpers, two pair of socks and my 'Benny' hat before getting in my sleeping bag and covering that with a blanket I've brought with me. After half an hour of lying on the grass I think that next time I will bring my long johns, as my legs feel like two flakes in a 99 ice cream cornet. Mind you it's a real quiet evening. We're all woken up at 8 a.m. on a freezing foggy morning by the sound of Gav getting rid of some more phlegm. (Can Gav hold his beer?).

We all arrive for our breakfast at the *Oxford Arms Hotel*. Everybody's full up by the end. Except Gav, he disappeared to the bog and his bacon and eggs disappear in there too. Stella says we're okay for a beer and there's no hesitation as we order a round of drinks. We stop here until midday, say our goodbyes, then it's back down to the *Lamb,* the pub where Drewy put the window through last night. The gaffer hasn't messed around in repairing it and a new pane of glass is already installed. He doesn't mention anything about last night, much to our relief. We visit another four pubs and drive home. This has been a superb booze trip to remember.

A few weeks of mediocre pubs are visited, then on December 20th the *Old Bull Inn* (Inkberrow) is visited. The gaffer's a tight sod, he charges me 90p for two postcards. This pub is the 'Original home of the Archers' radio series. The next pub visited is the *Wheelbarrow Castle* (Radford). Oggy calls for the beer and the barmaid looks up at him. Oggy said, "I'm over here."

"I know, I'm looking at you," replied the barmaid.

Oggy hasn't realised the barmaid is cock-eyed and he goes as red as the birthmark on his face. The *Red Hart* (Kington) is a popular but quiet country pub until Leo tells the popular comedian Stan Boardman's joke about the Messerschmitt's and the Fokkers and we're asked to leave. It's been a fairly average run tonight.

The following week, with Christmas out of the way, a journey to the *March Hare* (Broughton Hackett) is our first stop of the night. There's a log fire, wood beamed ceiling and a deer's head on the wall. Oggy says."That deer must have been travelling at some speed when he hit that wall."

Nice one Oggy!

A later pub we visit is the *Crown* (Peopleton). The gaffer gives me a 'Whitbread Ales' water jug and writes on it 'Keep going lads.' He then said, "If any of you can solve this riddle I'll buy you all a pint. What can a blind man see and if he eats it, will die?"

He told us we've four weeks to come up with the answer. Leo ponders over this and replies, "I know the answer, it's Nothing."

The gaffer's a little cheesed off at this and said, "Nobody's got it that quick before, I'll buy you your drinks on your next visit."

What a surprise that is! Drove steadily home now finishing off a pleasant night.

Well, another year over and it's certainly been eventful – roll on next year.

The Lads 'ready to go' with Pint & Platter Map (Pg 19)

Invasion Imminent (Pg 42)

143

Ethel Hale and staff receive our cheque (Pg 53)

Behind the bar of Pub No 1,082. Yew Tree, Cauldon. May 31st 1987 (Pg 87)

Presentation night at Banks's (Pg 91)

A well-dressed barman. White Bear, Masham (Pg 99)

Hardknot Pass (Pg 109)

Me, Jacqui Knott, (Landlady) and Foxy. Pub no 1,203.
The Nutshell, Bury St Edmunds. 5th August 1987 (pg 112)

The Priest & Me. Moussey. (Pg 127)

The SAS Graves (Pg 127)

Susten Pass (Pg 130)

Charles & Stella. Pub no. 1,396. Oxford Arms, Kington. 29th November 1987 (Pg 139)

An early foggy morning and the Moon's still out (Pg 140)

Les Carter, joins in our singsong. Plough, Ford. (Pg 164)

Brian & Hazel, Licensees. Pub no. 1,625.
Crown & Sceptre, Ross On Wye. 15th May 1988 (Pg 169)

Landlady. Pub no. 1,659. New Buildings, Bulls Hill. 25th May 1988 (Pg 169)

Licensees. Pub no. 1,664. Cupid's Hill, Near Grosmont, Gwent. 28th May 1988 (Pg 170)

The man-eating roots (Pg 184)

Licensees. Pub no. 1,876. New Inn, Hadlow Down. 21st September 1988 (Pg 188)

The BATS outside Pub no. 1,900. Smith's Arms, Godmanstone. 23rd September 1988 (Pg 191)

John Goode & Glyndwr James. Rising Sun, Tirpil. (Pg 196)

Landlord, Mr Ryall. Pub no. 2,280. Hop Pole, Risbury. 1989
A.K.A. Bert's (Pg 211)

The kitchen in the Hop Pole (Pg 211)

Jack's Corner. Edmondes Arms, Cowbridge. (Pg 219)

Lost Saxon Gold (Pg 227)

Gwennap Pit (Pg 233)

The 'White Cat' stands guard over us, in the church yard, Zennor. (Pg 235)

Pub No. 2587. Sally & Rita. The Highwayman, Sourton.
A smile a day keeps your troubles away (Pg 247)

Aunt Mabel. Relaxes in her living room. Drewe Arms, (Pg 250) Drewsteignton. Pub no. 2,597.

Landlord serves our beer from the jug. Pub No. 2,616
Seven Stars, Halfway House, Shropshire. 30th July 1989 (Pg 253)

3,000th Pub Plaque Presentation (Pg 268)

The BATS with Mr Ian Walden (centre)

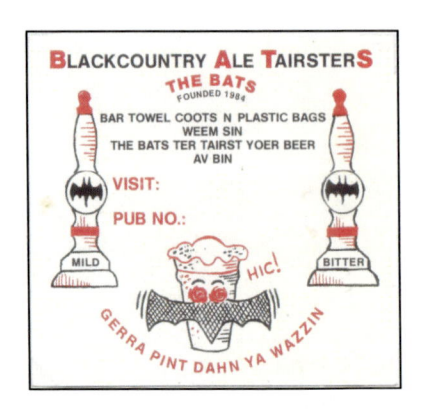

Our original pub card left in pubs, until October 2001.

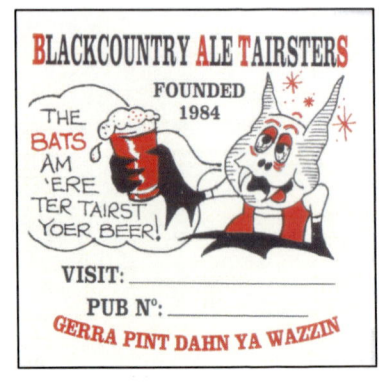

Our new designed card left in each pub from October 2001, Pub no. 10,000 to the present day

CHAPTER 9

VIVA ROSS VEGAS

January 1988, flies by as we visit pubs in Worcestershire at places such as Hartlebury, Holt Fleet and Ombersley to name just a few. Our favourite three are the *Coach and Horses* (Weatheroak Hill) where there's a good range of beers; the *Stone Manor Hotel* (Stone near Kidderminster), which was built in 1926 as a private residence. It now has twenty-three bedrooms available for bed and breakfast where a single room costs £48.50 plus £5.50 for breakfast and it stands in its own twenty-five acres of countryside; and the *Fruiterers Arms* (Uphampton) for their scrumpy cider. The first trip in February takes us to Headless Cross also in Worcestershire, where in the *Gate Hangs Well* the landlord buys us all a drink and quotes a poem about the pub.

> The Gate Hangs Well and hinders none,
> Refresh and pay then carry on,
> The Gate Hangs Well to no man's sorrow
> Drink today and pay tomorrow.

Our total of pubs visited now stands at 1,494.

It's Friday February 12th and we all meet up for a night out at a disco pub in West Bromwich called *Busby's*. Even the great pub-crawlers are due a night off. My old pals are the bouncers here and Roy Matthews and Geordie Jeff allow us all in. After a while a wench (girl) that I knew from years ago (her name is Dawn) comes over and asks me the way to the toilet. I point the way and think nothing of it.

Later the lads move on to a nearby nightclub. This wench happens to be in here too, so I ask her for a dance and we arrange to meet again. Sunday night and it's off for a good pub-crawl around Astwood Bank. It's now, during our time here, we all start noticing quiz machines appearing in lots of pubs. Last pub of the night is the *Why Not* (Astwood Bank) named after a racehorse of the 1800s. I get yapping to the relief managers Brian and Hazel. Hazel says she was a semi-professional singer and her ex-husband and son bought a gypsy caravan and last year started travelling from Scotland to China for charity. It will take them three years; I wonder if they will ever make it?

It's during the week that I arrange a date with Dawn, the wench I met last week. On our first date I take her to the casino. She's only gone and told her mother that I don't drink! If she is going to be my regular girlfriend I think I'll have to mention my hobby to her first! It's the town of Kidderminster that finishes off this month with the *Farmers Arms* being of some interest. A Scottish bloke who is a Glasgow Rangers fan runs this pub and has actual full-size Hampden Park goalposts in here. It's rumoured all Scottish people are tight-arses, but on our visit here you can't call this gaffer one – he donates £10 towards our charity fund for the Smethwick Neurosurgery unit. We show our appreciation and stop for another drink. The *Railway Train* is next. It's a bostin (great) little back street pub and is our final drink of the night. Three girls pass by and use the toilets. A few of the lads lock them in for a laugh. The licensee is a jolly old chap and he donates £5 and takes a photo of us all in the lounge. It's the first official photo of all the remaining BATS. It's been fun tonight.

We now aim to visit all the Hereford and Worcester pubs. Oggy's fifty-seventh birthday trip arrives, so it's off to Broadway in the Cotswolds to visit all the seven pubs there. Broadway is called this due to the main street being wide enough to take flocks of sheep. A new chap joins in for this weekend's tour, Jeff (the Yidd). Shaz the barmaid of our new local the *Old Crown* (Great Bridge, Tipton) joins us also, due to Fat Larry leaving the *Yew Tree* (West Bromwich) for the *Three Kilns* (Leicester). On our arrival at Broadway at 5.30 p.m. we've half an hour to amuse ourselves while waiting for opening time.

This village is absolutely lovely with all of the buildings made of beautiful golden stone. The first pub visited is the *Swan* where all of the barmaids are dressed up in beefeaters' clothes. I never asked why. Next is the *Broadway Hotel*, followed by the *Crown and Trumpet* the *Goblet's wine bar* and then the *Lygon Arms*. The latter is an upmarket hotel built in 1520 when it was known as the *White Hart*. Both King Charles I and Oliver Cromwell were past visitors to this old coaching inn. Then around 1830 General Beuchamp Lygon purchased the inn. He served under Wellington at Waterloo and from then it was called the *Lygon Arms*. A superb place to visit but a bit snobby. Why pay extortionate prices for bed and breakfast when our plastic bags do just the same job and cheaper? The *Horse and Hounds* and the *Fish* are both closed in Broadway tonight, we'll have to visit these at a later date.

Our tour continues and we visit three more pubs before reaching our planned destination, the *Plough* (Ford). On arrival at 10 p.m. we all sign the visitors' book and to our surprise Wayne, Lowey and Foxy have turned out for Oggy's birthday. Les is sitting in his normal position at the bar and I buy him a drink. We all have a big drinking session in the lounge and enjoy a good sing-song. Les isn't too happy about me and Gav having an arm wrestle and says to Gav, "See you next Tuesday."

I think it's time for bed. Everyone's either pissed as a 'Bobhowler', pissed as a 'Newt' or pissed as a 'Parrot.' Again our sleeping quarters are up above in the old barn. Gav, Leo and John are now jostling for top-spot in the throwing-up league. Jase says he needs a tin opener to get Shaz's jeans off. Shaz says he's hopeless anyway and he never does succeed.

The following morning, we have breakfast and then play 'Chase the Ace' and have a few beers until midday. Les tells us it's his sixty-eighth birthday in April and we're all invited. Travelling on to our first pub of the day the *Childswickham Inn* (Childswickham). This is the first pub ever to throw us out of the lounge due to the popularity of food in pubs. We're told to drink in the bar room. The fifth and final one of the day is the *New Inn* (Cropthorne). An Irish chap in here tells us about when he carried a one hundredweight sack of coal over twenty-six miles and got in the record books. On his last attempt he collapsed after twenty-two miles and almost died. He's now trying to grow the largest crop of potatoes off one plant. Well, that's a bit of a turn around isn't it? It's off home now and not one of our most outstanding tours but still quite memorable. It's still March and in Kidderminster we meet two wenches (girls) in the *Coopers Arms*. Joanne and Lisa live by the *Old Bear* (Kidderminster) and are barmaids in the *Fox* (Chaddesley Corbett). They tell us they know all the pubs in the town so we follow them. In our last one of the night the *Crown* (Hoobrook), Leo arranges a date in the week with one of them. Meanwhile Oggy said to them, "Is it right to say the yolk of an egg are white? Or the yolk of an egg is white?"

"The yolk of an egg is white," they reply.

"Wrong, it's yellow," loffs (laughs) Oggy.

They agree on a time and a place to meet up with them next week and we shoot off to Dudley for fish and chips. The *Broadwaters* (Kidderminster) the following week is where Joanne and Lisa meet us again. Leo is blanking them out, as his date with one of them during the week didn't go to plan. They take us round all our remaining five pubs left in the town. I draw them a map of the *Old Crown* in Great Bridge and tell them they are welcome to come and pay us a visit at anytime. We thank them for all their help and leave for home. I doubt if we'll ever see them again.

Finally it's Sunday 27th March and the clocks go forward one hour. The *Plough and Harrow* (Drakes Broughton) starts tonight's session. Oggy throws some of his loose change in the tray of the fruit machine and shouts out, "Look what I've won!"

Jase hears this and put his money in the fruit machine. He loses his money before he even spins the wheel, as it's out of order! Jase is still puzzled at how Oggy won his money on a machine that's broken. The second alehouse is the *Old Oak* (Drakes Broughton), where Oggy tells us of when years ago he went sheep rustling with his two mates Soapy and Little Rich. He says they were on their hands and knees on a moonless night bleating like sheep when the farmer came out with his gun and they legged it. Trying another field they managed to grab some sheep and put them in their hired van. "We only got a few miles down the road when we ran out of petrol and we had to let them go," he said. "Then, by the time Soapy had walked to get some petrol, it was light, so we ended up coming home with a bag of apples and plums we had scrumped off some farmer's trees."

Our next pub is the *Anchor* (Wyre Piddle). This has riverside gardens and moorings. A poem on the wall reads:

There's Upton Snodsbury,
Peopleton and Crowle;
North Piddle, Wyre Piddle
And Piddle in the Hole.

We completed a few more pubs, headed home and had a stop off at Frankley services arriving home at 1 a.m.

Well, I'm still seeing Dawn and she and her mom both know about my hobby. I said to her, "As long as yoe ay gooin' [you are not going] to try and stop me visiting pubs we can continue to see each other."

She accepts this, but is curious and would like to know what we get up to.

What better introduction can she get than her first beer run to the *Plough* (Ford) for Les's sixty-eighth birthday on Saturday April 2nd. Thirteen turn up for this trip, including three wenches, Shaz, Jayne and Jase's new girlfriend named Sharon. Leaving at 5 p.m. we visit eight pubs before arriving at the *Plough* at 10 p.m. Upon entering, we give Les his large birthday card signed by all of us. Our first pint is the S.B.A. Donnington's bitter, which is excellent! Drewy starts hitting the scrumpy cider that has enough live bait in it to feed a shoal of fish. He throws a miniature Loch Ness monster in the bin. It was enjoying a swim in his drink. Out of the blue, Foxy and Lowey, who have been in the other room, join us. There's a Cockney folk group singing in the bar room and we have our own sing-song in the lounge. A couple of hours of merriment pass and Jeff (the Yidd) and Lowey both pass out.

Gav, Drewy and me carry them, one by one, up the steps to the old barn. Usually we have this to ourselves but tonight the folk singers have laid down their sleeping bags in here. I go back to the bar while Gav and Drewy grab Lowey's legs and spin him round. The only problem in doing this is, Lowey starts chucking up like a farmer's muck spreader all over the folk singers sleeping bags. It's a great night tonight as we carry on drinking until Les closes his bar at 1.30 a.m. When we all get in the barn the folk singers are already settled down. The trouble is, our lot are really noisy. So they decide to get up and sleep in their cars. Oggy also sleeps outside on the bench in the beer garden. Drewy and Mark argue over which one is having the spare pillow and Mark ends up with a black eye. Leo keeps turning the lights on and off, so I throw my shoe at him and this seems to do the trick. Eventually it goes quiet and we're all off in the land of nod.

It's 8.30 a.m. when we rise with the barn smelling like a Hippo's harem. The landlady Ann does her normal call of, "Breakfast's ready."

A full turnout fails for this morning's fittle (food). The effect of last night is still keeping a few of them asleep. With our bellies full, some play cards and the lovers, John and Jayne, Dawn and me sit round the old stone log fire having a slow couple of pints to pass the time until midday opening time. Again we thanked our hosts for the memorable evening we had and paid Ann our breakfast money. Our journey continues to the two Broadway pubs not open on our last visit, the *Horse and Hound* and the *Fish*. Both have recently opened after a refurbishment and are busy serving meals. There's a saft thing we're all doing at the moment. Some cars have an alarm key fob that turns the car alarm on and off. We pretend we've all got one and when whoever points it at you, you have to jump up. John tries it out on me and I jump up, hit my head on the low-beamed ceiling and get a grade A-sized egg on my noggen. This puts a stop to this silly game. The fifth and last pub to finish off our trip is the *Old Mill* (Elmley Castle).

On the way back home we stop at a country shop. Two women riders on horseback are slowly approaching the cars. John turns to Jayne and tells her not to sound the horn in case it startles the horses. Jayne then jumps out of the car to fetch something out of the shop.

John thinks she's taking too long and leans over and sounds the horn, completely forgetting the horses that are now just passing the cars. This causes one of the horses to rear up and throw its rider. It then gallops off down the country road with the unseated rider running after it and the mounted one finally catching it. Well done John, none of us can believe he did this. Both of the riders come back and give us a right bollocking for being so stupid. Jayne now exits the shop unaware that anything has happened. I think we'd better drive home quick, arriving back at base after a somewhat eventful trip.

We're really getting stuck into these two counties now and we're off again to the *Crown Inn* (Whitchurch near Ross on Wye). Dating back to the sixteenth century, originally serving the Horse Drawn Royal Mail Coaches. The inn has five bedrooms, a restaurant, a skittle alley and poolroom. The *Royal Arms* (Llangrove) is next, we're told it's the only pub sign in England with five Heraldic signs on it; all the others have four! The pub itself has a dartboard, pool table and Guinness memorabilia on the walls and a two-foot chocolate rabbit on the bar. All the pubs in the Symonds Yat area are now ready for visiting. Quick drinks are had in the *Old Court Hotel*, the *Wye Knott Inn* and the *Paddocks Hotel*. From the *Olde Ferrie Inne,* our sixth pub of the day you can catch the 'Ancient Ferry Crossing' that was introduced 200 years ago. It's a small boat attached to a cable spanning the river and it costs 40p to get over to the other side. Once there, a short walk will take you to the *Royal Hotel,* erected as a hunting lodge about 1876 and converted to a hotel in the 1920s and the *Saracens Head Hotel* where Russ, Jan and Mike welcome you to this small hotel. The gaffer who's a West Ham fan said, "Is that enough for your charity?" as he shoves a £20 note in my hand.

I'm flabbergasted. It's the biggest donation we've ever had and my mouth has opened wide enough to swallow the River Wye. I love it around here; it's beautiful. You can even hire a canoe and row down the river or visit the nearby 'Maze'.

With closing time upon us again we have a few hours to kill and Ross-on-Wye is our destination. Here we buy fish and chips for £1.30 and listen to the football results Ipswich 1 v 1 West Bromwich Albion.

At least Albion scored a goal this week. Our time is spent walking in a park, playing cricket with a piece of wood as the bat and stones as the ball and then strolling around the town with its impressive sandstone Market House and the old prison 'lock up' building. Jase bangs the old knocker on the old studded door of this prison and shouts, "Is there anybody there?"

We all jump out of our skin as the door opens and a woman replied, "Yes, can I help?"

Well, we decided to scarper at this and didn't bother waiting for the pubs to open in this town and drove to the *Kerne Bridge Inn* (Kerne Bridge). I got out of the car to walk to the pub door and I saw two large Alsatian dogs running towards me, I leg it back to the car jump in and lock the doors. Leaving the other lads outside where Leo shouts, "Hilly, open the door, we'll all end up as dog meat!"

"Every man for himself," I say.

Dogs are not my favourite animals but these two turn out to be rather friendly pets in the end. The next pub is the *Castle View Hotel* (Kerne Bridge) where we sit and watch the very last episode of *Crossroads* on the telly. Three more pubs are visited at Goodrich and Walford. Here, at our fourteenth pub of the day, the *Walford House Hotel,* I was just going to get the gaffer, who is a large overweight chap, to sign my book when he slips off his stool and gets stuck between the wall and the bar. I tried hard not to laugh but couldn't help myself, so I went into the lounge and got the barman to sign it. At the following inn, the *Crown* (Howle Hill) which dates back to 1857, we're told that a ninety-year-old landlady keeps an unspoilt pub nearby at Bull's Hill called the *New Buildings*. I'm really looking forward to this visit as our drive takes us uphill in pitch darkness. Then, suddenly, we spot an unusual concrete gnome sitting on a wall, staring at us with his beady cat-looking eyes. It frightened the bloody daylights out of us! My sphincter muscle was flapping like a kit of pigeons flying off. Opposite this though is the *New Buildings* and it's closed tonight. A visit here is certainly booked for a future trip but during the afternoon when it will be light. The penultimate pub of the night is the *Hunston Manor Hotel* (Weston Penyard). Gav and me walk into the bar and the landlady yells, "Get out or I will call the police!"

The chap on the piano stops playing and the people in the room go quiet.

She comes over to us and thinks we are two heavies sent to smash up her pub. We tell her who we are and she then calms down and explains to us that last week fourteen local lads came in, all had a steak meal and refused to pay and walked out. Well, let's move on to the last pub of our tour, the *Weston Cross Inn* (Weston Cross). This is more like it, as the licensees Barrie and Jacqueline ask us if we're hungry. Of course our answer is, "Yes!"

What hospitality as two large plates of chips, a big noggin of cheese, pickled onions and bread is brought over for us. In return I buy Jacqueline her favourite drink, whisky and milk. I tell her of our visit to the last place and what had happened. Barrie says, "The reason the lads didn't pay for their steak meals was because they were rubbish."

A fabulous finish to another interesting pub adventure. We say our goodbyes and travel homeward.

Over the next few weeks, we travel around Worcestershire to the towns of Tenbury Well, Malvern and Lower Broadheath (birthplace of the composer Elgar). A couple of notable pubs of interest are the *Pembroke House* (Tenbury Wells), a nice old crooked black and white half-timbered building with beer barrel tables and brasses around the room and the *New Inn* (Clifton-on-Teme) set in twelve acres of farmland. The landlady has an unusual collection of plastic dildos – some 10 inches long – including the batteries.

It's now Saturday 14th May and all the pubs in Ross-on-Wye are our targets for this weekend. John (Bungle) now has a different car, a Ford Escort two door X-reg. We arrive at 5.30 p.m. It's a little early for the pubs to open so a few of the lads have a game of football by the river. I sit in my car and I put on my Elvis Presley tape. *Viva Las Vegas*, which we soon adapted the lyrics to Viva 'Ross' Vegas! It's opening time; the *Swan Hotel* is our first drink of the day. It's a family-run hotel that was originally a coaching inn. Our second pub is the *Kings Head Hotel* with its wood-panel walls, old fireplace and a 'Well' sunk in the floor and covered with glass. A single room is £29.00. Next is the *Rosswyn Hotel,* this dates from the fifteenth century, followed by the *Kings Arms* nicknamed Benson's after the licensee's thirty-seven years at this pub. Then into the *Crown and Sceptre.* Here the licensees Brian and Hazel offer us a breakfast for £1 tomorrow morning. Four more pubs are visited the *Horse and Jockey*, the *King Charles II,* the *Eagle* where Leo and John throw up in the bog and *Jacqueline's lounge and steak bar.* Now for the *Royal Hotel,* built in 1837 the hotel once played host to Queen Victoria, Queen Mary and Charles Dickens and a single room is £50. Along the side of the river is the *Hope and Anchor*, which is very busy and popular with the young. The *Man of Ross* is visited where you can buy a hangover cure called 'Underbergs' this is sold in a leather belt. Enough of town pubs and we now head for the country to the *New Inn* (St Owens Cross), a sixteenth century inn, then the *Broad Oak* (Garway) with it's stuffed fox by the fireside, a stuffed pike at the back of the bar and a rabbit's head on the wall.

Finally our pub-crawl for today comes to an end at the *Garway Moon* (Garway). This is where we can relax, some of the lads play a game of pool. I yap to a woman named Chris Goodwyn who tells me she has appeared on the television programme *Heart of the Country* talking about herding goats. All of us enjoy a large quantity of ale and large plates of chips before leaving at midnight. Coming out of here I spot in the moonlight the silhouette of the tit on top of a police car hiding in the country lane behind the hedges. We've no intention tonight of driving our motors anywhere as there's a large common opposite the pub and it looks a great place to kip. So we get out our sleeping clobber and walk across the common and bed down by some goalposts. During the night I'm woken by the sound of dogs and a jeep with it's headlights on full heading towards us. I have no time to get out of my sleeping bag, all I manage to do is kneel up and wave my torch. The jeep swerves away from us and disappears with the dogs following him into the night. Another lucky escape for the BATS. We could have been roadkill.

At the break of dawn a bloody Cuckoo now wakes me. Cuckoo, Cuckoo! The flying feathered fiend must be interested in laying her egg in my pillow. Eventually I get up at 8 a.m. and wake the others up for a kick-about with the football I brought along. I then cool off with a walk in the woods. With a beautiful carpet of bluebells covering the ground, I have a piddle. It's now time for our breakfast at the *Crown and Sceptre*. On our arrival we all sit on the wooden bench by the Market House until Brian the gaffer opens up at 10 a.m. He sits us down and taking one look at Oggy, he said, "What was the ground like when you got up this morning?"

Could Oggy be a zombie?

Just in case, Brian puts a large brown paper bag over his head. This saves us all from having to stare at such a bad facial hangover.

We all enjoy our fittle (food) and Brian opens the bar up for our first pint of the day. Oggy falls in love (in his dreams) with Tracy the barmaid, who I think is Brian's daughter. Is there a possibility she could end up being Frankenstein's bride?

Ta-rah Brian, Ta-rah Hazel and Tracy as we leave and walk down to the *Barrel*. I went in first and shot straight back out, a massive black Great Dane came bounding towards me. I let the others in and then I follow behind. With another five fairly disappointing pubs visited in Ross-on-Wye our merry mob journey home for a bit of a rest.

After a couple of weeks visiting mediocre pubs our second trip to the Ross-on-Wye area begins on Saturday 28th May 1988. Ten of us are on this tour including two wenches, Dawn and Jayne. This journey takes us 2¼ hours due to traffic jams on the M5 before reaching our first pub, the *Plough Inn* (Tudorville), a working men's pub with long wooden benches and solid wood tables. This is a friendly place where we yap to three old blokes and a woman who the locals call 'three tit Wyn: The landlady gives me a newspaper cutting: showing caricatures of the pubs Skittle Team. The fourth pub is going to be the one we tried to find a few weeks back where the ninety-year-old landlady runs the *New Buildings* (Bull's Hill). I really hope it is open this time.

Yes, on arriving, the door is open and this time, passing the beady-eyed gnome didn't scare me. All ten of us quietly enter this fascinating pub. The landlady herself is behind the bar, with three regulars sitting by the small stone fire with a mirror above it covered in old postcards and photographs. The walls are covered in old floral discoloured wallpaper, there's an old cupboard with lots of old wartime photos on it and the woodwork is all painted in a mustard colour. The landlady isn't too well today and struggles adding up the cost of all our beers. So one of her old regulars did the honour and he also signs my book for her. I can't quite read his signature, but it's something like Mrs Bundy. It's been great meeting her, so we all finish off our pint of Whitbread and travel on.

More pubs are visited, then we have our afternoon break in Ross Park. Some of the lads play football and I sit on the grass and watch. Who's got a first aid kit? Mark hurts his hand, Gav trips up and twists his ankle and Jeff (the Yidd) is gasping for air in between puffing away on his fag. The game comes to an end as the ball flies over a wall. It's opening time and I nip in the *Crown and Sceptre* to see if Brian will cook us all a breakfast tomorrow morning. The answer is yes and he says he'll throw a dinner in as well for £5 each. This sounds a good deal to me so I book us all in. Our next licensed premises is the *Pengethley Manor Hotel* (Harewood End) followed by the *Bridge* (Kentchurch). In the *Bridge* the pop group Curiosity Killed the Cat arrive. We're told the lead singer got married today. We leave here and end up getting lost. I'm glad we did, as we spot a really old pub the *Cupids Hill Inn* just over the border in Gwent near Grosmont. This is another unique and strange pub. It's like someone's kitchen from the 1960s. It has a fluorescent ceiling light, a large table in the middle of the small room with wood chairs, old beige floral wallpaper and a bar with shelves at the back. It only sells bottled beers and scrumpy cider out of the barrel. The elderly landlady JJ Godding signs my book and I take her photo. This is a classic boozer – you don't see many like this.

We journey on to the *Temple Bar* and the *Dog Inn* both in Ewyas Harald, finishing at the *Neville Arms* (Abbeydore). The boozing BATS now down quite a few ales. Gav says, "I've had enough beer to fill Oggy's bath."

"That's a rarity, the last time any liquid went in his bath was when he emptied water from his fishpond and put forty newts in it," I replied.

"Ar, that wor (wasn't) funny. When I got home they had all climbed out and was all up the bathroom and kitchen walls," frowned Oggy.

Drewy now passes out and we carry him to his car. Jackie and Pete the licensees call closing time at midnight. This pub is out in the country and it's now raining. We find a field close by and put our plastic bags down under some trees for more shelter. At four in the morning Gav gives up trying to sleep in the rain and goes in the car with Drewy. The rest all hang on until the morning.

When we do wake up, the sun is shining and we can see what attractive countryside we are in. Our sleeping bags are soaking so they are all put over the nearby fence to dry out a little and it's off for our pre-booked breakfast. On entering the *Crown and Sceptre* Brian this time looks at Oggy and said, "You shouldn't be allowed out in the light," and gives him a piece of cardboard to cover his face. All took in the best of fun! After breakfast and a couple of early pints apiece, our pub-crawl continues to the *White Lion Hotel* (Wilton). The gaffer tells Mark, John Bungle and Jeff (the Yidd) to take off their leather jackets and all of us must take off our beer towel coats before he would serve us. Well it's the first time this has ever happened. The hotel was built circa 1600 and the beer garden overlooks the River Wye and the old stone bridge. A single room costs £18. Over the road from this place is the *Wilton Court Hotel*. The sixteenth century courtroom has been preserved and is now the lounge bar. A chap plays the piano and we drink our beer in the nice beer garden. Third pub of the afternoon is the *Yew Tree* (Peterstow) where the licensees Dick and Jackie tell us they had heard we were in the area and, if they'd known, we could have slept in their caravan last night. It's a bit late for that, I thought. We all nip down the road now for a quick one in the *Red Lion* (Peterstow), then it's back to the *Crown and Sceptre* for our beef dinners. Jeff (the Yidd) uses his loose change up on the pub phone to talk to his missus. He doesn't get through so instead of putting some more money in he says he'll send her a letter instead, it's cheaper. "I wouldn't say he's a Jew he's just a careful Christian," says Oggy.

Another smashing weekend break comes to an end. During the week, alas, it's also the end of my weight-training partner of four years and big boozing pal John Bungle. This is due to all the Mondays he's been missing at work because he's too pissed to get up from the previous night's exertions. A real disappointment, he's a best mate, but the adventure must go on.

CHAPTER 10

UNDER THE MOON OF LOVE

Over the next few weeks we visit a number of interesting pubs one of which is the *Boot Inn* (Orleton). This is a smart black and white half-timbered pub with a nice beer garden and I meet a chap who's a member of the SNAGS (Social Nocturnal Anglers and Gamblers Society). Our 1,682nd pub is the *Sun Inn* (Leintwardine). Miss Flossie Lane, who was born at the pub in 1914, is the owner. I recently had a Herefordshire beer and cider guide given to me, it says "nice old lady who appreciates a log brought for her fire." She only clocked us all getting out of the cars and came out of the pub and told us to clear off. At that we nipped down the road into the *Lion Hotel*. In here we decide to take our beer towel coats off and walk back over to the *Sun Inn* one by one. It works, as she serves us all with our drinks from the small serving hatch. We sit in one of England's rare pub interiors, a small square basic old-fashioned room. It has three old wooden tables, wooden benches, beige and orange floral wallpaper, lime green woodwork with a lime green painted small brick fireplace and a red-brick floor. On the mantelpiece is a small wooden box with four shelves and there is an old clock on the wall. I put our calling card on one of the shelves after we've all finished our drink and went up to the old lady to get my book signed. Somehow she recognises us and she comes from around the serving hatch and runs us out of the door. I'd like to know what we have done? One day I'll have to come back when she's long gone and get my book signed. A great old pub though.

Another pub is the *Mortimer's Cross* (Mortimer's Cross). This has accommodation and facilities for camping and caravans. The décor has pictures of fighter planes and skydivers on the walls and also a big aeroplane propeller. I get yapping to a chap who tells us the gaffer's a skydiver. The gaffer turns out to be a miserable bloke and Oggy says to us, "It's a pity his parachute opened."

It's here at Mortimer's Cross that the site of the last decisive battle of the War of the Roses occurred in 1461. It was this battle which won the Crown of England for the Yorkist leader, Edward IV.

We move to the *Royal Oak* (Bredon) where the gaffer tells us he knew a bloke who worked on Ocker Hill power station, (near where we live) but he fell off. At the *Gay Dog* (Baughton), the village where Nigel Mansell the Grand Prix racing driver was born, we're told his grandparents own the pub.

For my 32nd birthday, we visit two newly built Banks's pubs in Staffordshire. The *Winding Wheel* (Cannock) gets its name because it stands near to the site of the old 'Number Four' pit, which was an active coal mine until the 1920s and where the winding wheel controlled the movement of cages in the pit shafts. The *Samson Blewitt* (Cannock) gets its name from a local man of note. Born in 1864 in the Black Country town of Wednesbury he then moved and became a farmer at Pye Green in 1886. Later he was a coal merchant and ran the local taxi service for soldiers stationed on Cannock Chase during the First World War. Samson's father was a beer retailer and grocer and later built Blewitt Street in Hednesford and part of the Goodyear factory near Wolverhampton. Both licensees had signed my book before in 1985.

Back in Herefordshire the following week, in Bromyard, we were sitting in a pub and I said to Leo, "I've forgot the name of this pub mate can you nip outside and see what the sign says?"

He goes out and comes back in. "It's called the car-park at the rear," he joked.

This old pal of mine is getting wuss (worse) by the wik (week).

It is called the *Queens Arms* and Barry, the gaffer, tells us if we're in this area again we can all sleep in his spare room above his pub for nothing.

The *Rose and Lion* (Bromyard) is another pub worth a visit just to listen to the local old character's telling their stories. It's a lovely drink too. While walking back to the cars one young chap shouts over to Gav and said, "Fancy a blow-job for a £1?"

Gav's annoyed at this and runs the cheeky little twat down the road.

This beer run finishes off the month of June.

It's Sunday July 3rd 1988. Drewy returns after his holiday abroad. He's spent twenty days in a West German prison after getting nicked at the England v Republic of Ireland game at the European Championship in Stuttgart. We stop local and visit pubs in West Bromwich tonight. In the last pub, Mark has a coke with ice and lemon. This is due to his mom telling him if he comes home drunk again she will kill him. Three weeks pass, visiting seventeen additional pubs. Whilst in one of these pubs, the *Cross Keys* (Malvern Link) a bloke comes in and takes his wig off, as it's been raining and puts it on the coat hangers to dry. We've all got a week off work so in our holidays we're going to tour Herefordshire. Our cars are ready for action and so are we. It's Saturday July 23rd. The weather is dire today, it's really ommering (hammering) it down driving through the country lanes and it's flooding some of the roads. We sample ales in seven pubs during the day. With the rain still pouring down I phone up Charles and Stella at the *Oxford Arms Hotel* (Kington). Hopefully they will put us up in their hotel. They say it's okay and will sort something out for us.

We arrive at 10.15 p.m. at the *Oxford Arms Hotel* and the rain has finally stopped. There's a wedding reception in the back room and the happy couple ask us to join them, as there are only half a dozen folk that have turned up. The large table is full of food and we're told to help ourselves. The evening's entertainment is records being played on an old gramophone. This is a smashing end to a somewhat dreary day.

Leo is now drinking pints of snakebites, Drewy is on the port and Dawn is trying to keep up with the rest of us drinking scrumpy cider. Leo talks to one of the local lads, while Drewy snogs with this lad's missus in the hallway. Dawn tries teaching Mark how to 'bop' to Showaddywaddy's old hit single *'Under the Moon of Love.'* I think I'll try my own version of this hit single later on. It's 1 a.m. When we hear a large crash. Drewy's collapsed headfirst in the large mayonnaise bowl. Gav and I first wipe his face then carry him upstairs to the room that the landlord is kindly letting us have for nothing. I fancy sleeping outside, now the sky is clear and the stars are out. So Dawn and me settle down on the beer garden. I said to Dawn, "If you look up at the sky you can occasionally see the odd moving star slowly making its way across."

"They all look like they're moving to me," she replied. Bang goes my idea of a perfect night under the moon of love. Dawn's had seven pints of scrumpy and throws up and flakes out. You could say she's totally scrumped!

Stella wakes us up for our breakfast. Dawn is still being sick and nobody can find Drewy. Eventually he's found laid out in another of the hotel rooms. Around the breakfast table we loff (laugh) and joke about the great time we had last night. While sitting by the window two little chaps start cheeking Drewy so he pulls the sash window down and shuts one of them in it. Drewy then gets a felt pen and tries writing Black Country on his forehead. He's not the greatest of spellers and he's still pissed. Eventually the little chap pulls free and runs off, with the word Black Country minus the 'O' on his forehead. Oggy meanwhile is shouting over to the cleaner asking her when the hotel opens for drinks. She carries on cleaning to Oggy's annoyance, so he repeats himself and still no reply. Stella the landlady then came in and said, "She can't hear you, she's deaf."

Good old Oggy, he's forever putting his foot in it. Last night we had a really good time and again we thank Charlie and Stella for their hospitality. What a fabulous couple.

Moving on, we drive now to the village of Pembridge and its three pubs. This is possibly my favourite little village to date. You can imagine yourself travelling down the main street in an old horse and carriage. The village is on the black and white trail due to most of the building being made of black timber framing with white plaster or brickwork. We have a walk to a spooky old type church building possibly a bell tower in the local graveyard while waiting for opening time. The first drink of the day is in the *New Inn*. Built in 1311, it's another superb black and white timber-framed building situated in the market square. Accommodation is available and a single room is £12 and a double £19.75. Phil and Jan Fox are the licensees of our next pub the *Red Lion*. There's a pool table in here and two dartboards with lots of farm tools and animal traps on the walls. They also do accommodation and a single room is £10. At present the most popular pub name in Great Britain is the *Red Lion* with more than 600. It owes its popularity to two powerful men: John of Gaunt (1340-99), the Duke of Lancaster and fourth son of Edward III, his emblem was the red lion and James I of England and VI of Scotland (1566-1625). In 1603, when James I became king, he commanded that the heraldic red lion of his native Scotland be prominently displayed in public. Third and final pub in the village is the *Pembridge Inn,* which was called the *Greyhound.* Mark finds a bag of stick-on face spots and warts in the toilet and comes out with them all stuck over his face. He now looks like he's got a bad case of the pox and the locals keep their distance. The last two pubs, the *White Swan* and the *Cross Inn* are in the pleasant village of Eardisland where the River Arrow slowly flows by. A very scenic tour.

With us all having a day's rest, we're off out again on Tuesday morning July 26th. Our sixth pub of the afternoon is the *Pandy Inn* (Dorstone), the oldest pub in Herefordshire. Built by Richard de Brito in 1185, originally to house his workers while building Dorstone Church. Licensed in 1603, it's also another pub old Oliver Cromwell is known to have frequented. I'm told the pub gets its name from part of a machine that was used to stretch cloth. Pandy also means 'mill' in Welsh. There's a stuffed fox and stuffed stoat in glass cases here. Leo says, "The kennels are a bit small for them ay they?"

We all have a nice drink of scrumpy while playing pool in the best pub of the afternoon. The pubs don't open until 6 p.m., so our journey continues and takes us into the wonderful little town of Hay-on-Wye. If you can't read it's no good coming to this town as there's loads of shops selling books. At least this passes a couple of hours.

On the way to visiting our ninth pub of the day we have to cross the Whitney Toll Bridge. This costs us 30p. This is to get to the *Rhydspence Inn* (Whitney-on-Wye). The stream at the rear of this pub is the border separating England from Wales. Peter Glover is the landlord of this 1984 Egon Ronay Pub of the Year. Limited accommodation is available plus traditional ales. This lovely old pub is certainly worth popping in for a pint and a meal. The fourteenth and final public house today is the *Ancient Camp Inn* (Ruckhall Common). A hard to find pub by the riverside and a good place to kip. It's been totally messed up inside by a 1985 renovation. The landlord is arrogant, the pub has no atmosphere and we don't like this place. We leave and find a good place to get our heads down. Mr Moanalot (the landlord) comes out of his pub and tells us to move on. I can't be bothered to argue with such a miserable git so we decide to drive to a more suitable site. A mile down the road we find an excellent spot near some radar domes. These domes are lit up beautifully against the night sky and a quiet night's sleep is had by all.

We wake up to a lovely sunny Wednesday morning. It's a good job we didn't drive across this field any further because we'd have dropped down a ditch. We pack up our gear and drive into Hereford. This is where we find a café near Hereford football ground for a breakfast. Then it's opening time and the day's drinking starts in the *Old Harp (Hereford)*. This is a dump of a pub with buckets on the floor collecting water from a leaky roof. There's no paper on the walls and the bogs are riffy. The gaffer remembers us from the *Prince Albert* (Manchester) and the *George* (Moxley) near Bilston in the Black Country. Banks's have recently bought this boozer and they intend to refurbish it. Our next three pubs are the *Three Horseshoes* (Thruxton), the *Red Lion* (Kilpeck) and the *Black Swan* (Much Dewchurch), this is where Leo does his goldfish impression outside the pub window. Then we move on to the *Tump Inn* (Wormelow) an eighteenth century inn named after an ancient burial tomb, which is said to have been built in the fourth century. Next is the *Fountain*

(Orcop) and the last one on our tour is the *Harewood End* (Harewood End). In here the landlady's language is wuss (worse) than ours and she puts a tea towel over her husband's head because he's flaked out across the seats due to a very late night's drinking session. Sadly another adventure comes to an end after the dinner-time closing hours. We'll be back tomorrow!

Thursday 28th July and off we go again on our pub-crawl. Today the *Tram Inn* (Eardisley) is visited. Inside is an ornament made of a piece of tram track, which ran from Brecon to Eardisley in 1820. Next is the *New Inn* (Eardisley). This was called the *Mountie* after a crackpot of a gaffer who knew a Canadian couple and he used to put plant pots on the bar thinking they were customers. Mick and Carolyn Baxter are the licensees now and B&B for a single room is £10. Mick said, "If you've nowhere to stop tonight, come back here."

So, six pubs later we're back. We all go in the bar room and yap to the gaffer and a bloke called 'Willie the Wisp' an old chap who talks to us about boxing. Oggy tells him the best 'boxer' in the world comes from West Bromwich. The bewildered Willie then asks Oggy what his name is."George Webb."

"I've never heard of him," replied Willie.

Oggy then said, "When he puts ya down yoe never get up."

"Why?"

"He's our local undertaker!" Oggy even had us fooled on this one.

Mick brings over three large bowls of chips and bought us two pints each. We stagger out of here at 2 a.m. Mick offers us the option of sleeping in his lounge or the beer garden. It's a nice night so we go outside. During the night all we hear are ducks, chickens, horses and dogs. You name it we hear it. On waking up in the morning a bloke comes over from his tent and said, "You lot are quite mad sleeping like you do just lying on the grass."

This bloke isn't all there either. He tells us his name is Alec and he's a Rhodesian. He's wearing a big hat and buckskin coat and he's riding a horse around Herefordshire to find work. Mick calls us in for a bacon and egg sandwich. This is hospitality at its best, but our time here comes to an end and we must journey on.

We travel on into the village of Weobley. This is another superb (black and white) village a little more upmarket than our normal destinations. Three pubs are here, *Ye Olde Salutation,* the *Red Lion Hotel,* and our favourite one the *Unicorn Hotel.* Our last two pubs of today are both Whitbread-owned pubs the *Crown Inn* (Dilwyn) and the *Lamb Inn* (Stoke Prior) – this is a local farmers' pub that was once a vicarage. Drewy tells us why he doesn't like farmers. When he was twelve years old, a farmer caught Drewy and his mate throwing apples at his beehives so the farmer grabbed Drewy and stuck his head in one of the beehives. He now calls all farmers shit-flingers. So completes a lovely week off work. Mark now decides he's had enough and calls it a day. Well, there goes another good mate and certainly a comical character.

With August now upon us, the *Talbot* (Knightwick) starts the month off. Jeff (the Yidd) says, "This pub has a damn big fireplace," and he's right about this.

The pub is situated on the banks of the River Teme. Bed and breakfast is available and there's darts and pool in the bar. It's a cracking pub that serves meals too.

A night out is due. It's August 13th and it's off to Herefordshire again. Our third pub today is the *Cornewall Arms* (Clodock). This is at the side of a graveyard. There's one keg beer available and the rest is bottled cider. Inside, it has no bar counter only a small serving hatch and games called 'Devil among the Tailors' and 'Quoits'. A stone floor, old wooden seats and settees. I'm told by the landlady, J.M. Williams who signs my book, that there's a chap buried in the graveyard with his coffin upright. This is because his wife said he could never keep out of the pub and at least this way he wouldn't be able to open the coffin lid. It's a rather unusual pub and so is the next one, the *Carpenters Arms* (Walterstone). It's nicknamed '*the Glue Pot'* because once you're in here you are stuck here. In this pub there's an old fireplace, a small serving bar and an Alsatian called Brandy. Touring around this area is amazing. It's like being on a wildlife expedition.

Down the dark and unlit narrow roads we almost run over dogs, cows, sheep, frogs, rabbits and various other mammals.

It's a twenty-minute drive before we arrive at an isolated pub called the *Bull's Head* (Craswell). This is a must visit pub. If you are after a real unspoilt pub, this is it. There's a tiny serving hatch, stone floor, wooden seats, an old cast fireplace, darts and table skittles known as 'Devil among the Tailors'. You also receive a warm welcome off the landlady, Mrs B. A. Lewis. Our travels today have taken us into some really classic pubs and everybody should visit the three I have mentioned. The next pub on our itinerary is the *Sun Inn* (St Margaret's, Vowchurch). On entering this pub the décor is like someone's living room. It's set in the depths of the English countryside between the Golden Valley and the Black Mountains with marvellous views of the surrounding area. Richard and Pat Hornby are the licensees. The rumours are there's a pub that serves overtime nearby so why hang about? Let's go.

On approaching our last pub of the day we cross a small bridge to the pub appropriately called the *Bridge Inn* (Michaelchurch Escley). This is an attractive stone-built thirteenth-century inn, which lies at the foot of the Black Mountains, alongside the Escley brook. Darts and pool are in a separate room. The bar room is packed with folk tonight (they must have heard of the overtime drinking). To the rear of the pub is a licensed caravan and camping site. Peter and Jill Newing are the proprietors. A local lad sells tickets for £2 to Leo, Dawn and me for a plastic Duck Race on August 27th. The winning duck gets £100. We're all enjoying our excellent pints of Robinson's bitter. Drewy's eyes are now beginning to shut. He says, "I hate beer that doesn't get you drunk but meks yer eyes shut."

A fine statement and only five minutes later he passes out. I now go and see Pete the gaffer to arrange a breakfast and somewhere to sleep if possible. He tells me he's been expecting us. The gaffer from the *Pandy Inn* told him about us last week. Our £2.25 each for a breakfast is arranged and paid for in advance. As it's 1 a.m. we decide to get our heads down. Outside it is still raining. We all have to climb over a four-foot high fence to get in a field and tonight's sleep is definitely inside our plastic bags.

It's still raining as we wake up in the morning and notice a sign on the fence saying "Beware of the Bullocks!" Luckily we never see any! We now stroll over to the pub for our breakfast but we have half an hour before it's ready. Over by the brook is a tree with a rope tied to one of its branches. Drewy tries swinging over this brook on the rope and he leans backwards and hits his head on the bank and falls in. Gav grabs the rope for his turn and totally misjudges it too and he ends up to his knees in the brook. Thankfully it's now time for our food. After our breakfast it's time to leave, as we are all slightly knackered after our grand day out yesterday. We only manage four dinner-time pubs before returning home.

During the week there's been a couple of newspaper articles about the most haunted village and graveyard in England and the most dangerous pub in Great Britain. Between us we have decided not to travel to Europe this year. Instead we are going to hire a minibus and go on a 'Sup South Session'. We intend to sleep in the most haunted graveyard in Kent and then continue into Wales to the most dangerous pub.

A very important date now arrives. It is Saturday 27th August 1988. This is the start of 'all-day' drinking in Great Britain and longer opening hours for the first time since 1915.

CHAPTER 11

THE SUP SOUTH SESSION

It's Tuesday 20th September 1988. The 'Sup South Session' is finally here. The hire of our minibus costs £184 for the week and we fill the tank with £22.65 worth of fuel. After almost four years of travelling and drinking in pubs, six BATS are left. They are all on this trip. (Oggy, Drewy, Leo, Gav, Jase and myself). Wayne comes too as our guest drinker. We're all looking forward to this run. For some reason, Drewy has left a spike on one of the seats and poor old Oggy happens to sit on it and it sticks in his arse. We set off now on a long drive to our first pub, the *Ostrich* (Colnbrook). This isn't that far from Heathrow Airport. We've started here because of the macabre history of the place. Years ago, when guests and travellers spent the night here a landlord called Jarman and his wife made a special bed fixed with a trapdoor. While asleep a total of sixty customers lost their lives, as the trapdoor opened plunging them to their deaths into a cauldron of boiling beer in the kitchen beneath. This is a superb old pub but it's full of yuppies (young upwardly mobile professionals). We didn't get a very friendly welcome off the landlord either, so we didn't stop long. Our next pub is over the road and up a bit to the *George,* another yuppie pub. The gaffer in here wouldn't serve us with our beer towel coats on, so we left without having a drink. We don't class this as a visit and I don't think we'll bother going back in a hurry. We only manage one other pub, the *Horsley* (East Horsley) and I don't think these have heard of the all-day opening times, as it shuts at 2.30 p.m.

After a somewhat disastrous start to our trip we drive on,

eventually stopping off in a forest lay-by. This area had been badly damaged by the horrendous hurricane-force winds that this part of the country experienced last year. There are lots of large uprooted trees, but alongside them numerous small ones have been replanted. We find a great spot to warm a few cans of stew up on our stove. While I sit on a log I notice that the roots of these fallen trees look like alien man-eating monsters, as they loom menacingly above me. Eventually we reach the village of Plaxtol with its three pubs. None of them are open yet so Gav, Wayne and Jase play 'stretch' with a knife on the village green. The game of 'stretch involves two people taking it in turns to throw the knife in the ground near one of your opponent's feet. He then stretches with his leg until his foot touches the knife. If he can do this, it's his turn to make you stretch. The winner is the one who outstretches his opponent.

Yippee, a pub opens to quench our thirst. This is in the *Papermakers Arms* a Fremlins boozer. The *Rorty Crankle Inn* is where we have our next drink. This name is Anglo-Saxon and means 'Happy Corner.' This has a small pleasant lounge with lots of cards hanging above the bar with 'Happy Corner' written in over sixty languages. It's dark outside now and just a little out of the village centre is our last pub the *Golding Hop*. Opposite the pub on the car-park Wayne shuts Oggy's fingers in the minibus door and he claims to have lost two fingers. Luckily he's only cut and bruised them. While we all walk across to the pub Oggy, who's still blowing his fingers, doesn't notice a grass slope leading off the car-park and falls down it into the road. This time he hurts his hip and hobbles in the pub. The gaffer in the pub gives him a plaster for his fingers. The bitter is served straight from the wood and there's home-brewed cider too.

We leave now for the village of Pluckley in Kent – reputedly the most haunted village in England. Our first pub in the village is the *Black Horse*. We receive a lovely welcome off the gaffer and he says we can sleep in his pub tonight. I explain to him that we've come all this way to sleep in the graveyard. I thank him for his offer. Oggy the ex-REME trained soldier attached to the airborne in his National Service days, pipes up and replies, "There's absolutely no chance of me sleeping in it, not what's happened to me today. I've had a spike up my arse, my fingers shut in the door and I've hurt my hip falling down that bank."

Well, that's one down. Then the ex-T.A cadet joins in, "I think I'll keep yoe company in the minibus too," said Wayne.

Two down, five to go.

The gaffer then gives me a poem written by a chap called Eddie Moore about this pub being haunted. The last three verses are:

Across the table sat a man
And we began to chat
About the weather and the rain,
About just this and that.

Our conversation turned to ghosts
And were they true or false.
And what and when and where they were
Came into it, of course.

"I don't believe in them," I said
"I don't believe at all."
The man said nothing, just got up
And walked out – through the wall.

Black Horse special coffees are available. With a touch of spirits!

The St Nicholas church and the graveyard are right next to this pub, but before we get our heads down we visit the other two pubs in area. The *Dering Arms* is about one mile down the road by the railway station and has an unusual exterior. It also does accommodation. This was once a hunting lodge. Our last one of the night is a drive back towards Pluckley to the *Blacksmith's Arms*. It was previously called *Ghosts* and prior to that the *Spectre*. Your hosts here are Bill and Josie Woodward and again we have an offer of sleeping here.

We return to the *Black Horse,* park up for the night and go in for an overtime drinking session. Well, what a day! We are last out the pub and say our goodbyes before departing for tonight's spooky sleep.

Five of us grab our sleeping clobber and find a suitable spot by some gravestones. It's certainly an eerie night and just like in the old movies a mist descends. I'm almost in the land of nod when on the hour the church clock strikes once, an hour later twice and then it's thrice. I'm not sleeping too well so I grab Gav's 'Benny' hat, pull it off his head and throw it six feet away, I quickly turn over pretending to be asleep. "Who's that, who's done that?" screams Gav.

"Not me Gav." I replied.

"Somebody has, my hat's all over theer by that gravestone."

"It must be a ghost Gav, go back to sleep."

Gav decides to move and gets his sleeping bag stuck in some wire netting that's wrapped around a tree. Who did this?

I now try to get to sleep, but all I can hear are woodlice munching through the bark of a tree that my head is touching. I think the whole population of bugs and slugs are paying me a visit tonight and they're scaling the gravestone I'm sleeping next to. There goes that bloody church clock again. Bong, bong, bong, bong. It's four in the morning and I eventually fall asleep until the eighth bong wakes me. What a rough night I've had.

I'm driving today, so it's back to the minibus and onto the M20 where we stop in a café for bacon and a cup of tea. The toilets here are riffy. I fill the minibus with petrol and our journey continues. We head to Greatstone-on-Sea to fill in the time until today's boozers open. On arrival there's some large concrete bow and dome-shaped 'listening devices' we want to see. One is 200ft long and 25ft high the others are smaller. These were built in 1928 to reflect the sound of enemy aircraft. An early form of radar. They turned out to be useless as the aircraft could be spotted quicker with the naked eye. The so-called garden of England is somewhat of a disaster area down this way. On our left, for miles, is a large concrete sea defence wall and on our right, rubble. Passing Dymchurch a sign reads 'A children's paradise.'

"It's a bog hole," says Leo summing things up nicely.

The lads clock a grotesque thing at a bus stop. It's some fat punk wench wearing a miniskirt. The lads can't stop laughing, the cruel bastards. Mind you, she is rough. Never in the world of pig's pudding was this a woman. We pass 'Paradise Caravan Park' and have another good laugh. We decide to follow a coach of German Fraüleins thinking it might be going somewhere special. It goes to Dungeness nuclear power station. The security man stops me and asks me where we're going and my foot slips off the pedal and I almost squash him. I decide to turn the minibus round now and head for our morning rest in New Romney. The pubs still aren't open so Gav, Leo, Jase and Wayne each buy a water pistol. This could be the start of a very wet week. This town is one of five towns known as the Cinque Ports (pronounced 'sink'). The other four Cinque towns are Sandwich, Dover, Hythe and Hastings. All banded together by Edward I in 1278 to defend the English Channel. Winchelsea and Rye joined them later.

The first pub opens and the ale trail starts at the *Cinque Port Arms* (New Romney). Wayne tries his water pistol out on Oggy, so Oggy throws Leo's beer all over him. Most of it goes up the lounge wall. Leo is somewhat upset about this. Our adventure then takes us into the *Smugglers Arms* further down the coast at Pett Level. This is right by the sea. The gaffer tells me a story about when he made a contraption called a 'Lug Pump.' He told one of his locals it was a new method for digging up lug-worms. So the local chap took it down to the beach and tried it out. The only problem was the gaffer only made it for a joke and when the local chap got back to the pub everybody curled up with laughter. He said the chap has never lived it down since and has reverted back to the easier method of using a fork. He also gives me an old match striker. We get back in the minibus and as I drive off, all the bags fall out the back due to Oggy leaving the back doors open. After a short delay, it's off to Hastings for the afternoon.

Arriving in Hastings our first drink is in the *Royal Albion,* (Up the Baggies) then we all eat our fish and chips with a pint on the benches outside the *Cutter.* The eighth pub today is the *Jenny Lind*, named after an old actress and singer whose real name was Madame Goldschmidt. She was born in Sweden and died in Malvern. Our next pub in the town is the *First in Last Out*. The gaffer is just shutting his pub but lets us in. He brews his own beer on the premises and it's known as the FILO (First in last out) Brewery. The gaffer's name is Mike and he shows us around his microbrewery. This is the first one we have ever been round and he lets us taste his two brews called 'Old Crofters' 1040° original gravity and the 'Cardinal' 1048° original gravity. Our last drink in town is in the *Cinque Port Arms* where we have a pint of Fremlins. Liz and Andrew Lipscombe run the pub. The beach at Hastings is all bibbles (pebbles) and it's here where the lads decide to have a water pistol fight to the amusement of passing locals. There are also lots of tall fishermen's huts, used for hanging and drying their nets in. These pong quite a bit. Near these is the start of the East Hill lift, where for a few bob a carriage takes you up to the top of the cliff on a single rail. We travel on to the *Crown* (Blackboys) East Sussex. This is located in the heart of the Sussex Weald where Frank and Pauline Pulley welcome you to this mainly food-orientated pub with a blazing log fire. The fourteenth century *Blackboys Inn* (Blackboys) is next. It's a lovely old pub with a pond outside. The gaffer, Patrick Russell, is as saft as a bottle of pop – he only goes and fills the lads' water pistols up. The friendly attractive barmaid is called Astrud and it takes a while before all the lads will leave her alone and move on to the next pub.

By chance we then drop on a superb unspoilt little pub called the *New Inn* (Hadlow Down). An elderly brother and sister run this place. Our beer is served from three eighteen-gallon stainless steel barrels that are stillaged on top of the bar counter. At the back of the bar are shelves full of bottles and four small green porcelain casks serving spirits. The landlord tells me there's a possibility the developers might move in, in the near future and demolish this pub. I hope not. We then move on to the *Farmers Arms* (Scaynes Hill) where the proprietors are Chas and Lorraine Regan and the *Sloop Inn* (Scaynes Hill) a Beards of Lewes house where your hosts are David and Marilyn Mills. The fifteenth-century *Three Crowns* (Wisborough Green) the licensees are Brian and Sandie Yeo. The final alehouse tonight is the *Bat and Ball* (Newpound). This is where we finish off on pints of Guinness. The landlord allows us to sleep on his field outside by a fishpond. It's a nice night as we bed down on top of our plastic bags, but during the early hours it tips down with rain. How uncomfortable is this? We all have to wake up and crawl inside the bags to keep dry. Not an easy job when you are all half-plastered.

It's misty when we wake up on this Wednesday morning the 21st September. Most of us have a go at feeding the hundreds of goldfish with stale bread and apples. The apples are off the trees in the pub's beer garden. We find a café for breakfast at 8.25 a.m. With our appetites satisfied we drive to Minstead, listening to the music from 1959 and 1980 on Radio One's Golden Hour. On arrival in this village we still have half an hour before opening. The 'gang of four' water-pistol boys spend their time chasing cats and squirting water at them. I'm off to the nearby churchyard to find the grave of Arthur Conan Doyle author of the Sherlock Holmes books. On the way, I bump into an old chap who resembles Albert Steptoe out of an old television series from the sixties and early seventies called *Steptoe and Son*. He says he knew Arthur when he was a child. I have a long chat with this knowledgeable bloke. He tells me his name is A. J. Paice and he wrote a book called *Love for Elizabeth*. He then says that he had been a prisoner of war and had brought his friend, who he hadn't seen in forty years, on a small tour of this area.

"Thanks for the stories," I replied and said my goodbye to a smashing old chap.

Drewy now joins me and between us we locate the author's grave. His inscription reads as follows:

Steel true
Blade straight
Arthur Conan Doyle
Knight
Patriot, Physician and man of letters
22 May 1859 – 7 July 1930

When we get back to the minibus I discuss with the lads about going on a trip sometime in the near future to Hound Tor in Devon. This had been the setting for a version of the film *Hound of the Baskervilles*, a screen adaptation of one of Arthur Conan Doyle's most famous novels, starring Peter Cushing. It falls on deaf ears for the moment. Anyway the *Trusty Servant* (Minstead) is now open and the most interesting part of this visit is its pub sign. It has a ten-line poem all about the name of the pub.

We leave here for Swanage and get stuck in traffic. Caused by what looked like a massive black pudding being transported to somewhere with a police escort. Actually it was a 220-feet long black cylindrical container made at Babcock's in Oldbury, West Midlands about two miles from where we live. Eventually we are free to travel through Bournemouth to Sandbanks to catch a ferry to Swanage. This costs us £2.10 one way and the crossing takes about five minutes. We're all a bit thirsty and need a wazzin wash, so our first port of call is the *Ferry Boat Inn* (Swanage). I have a bottle of Newquay Steam beer. This beer has a rather unusual bottle with a flip top. The beer garden is by a small stream. Our next nine pubs are all in Swanage. The *Crow's Nest, Grand Hotel, White Swan, Purbeck Hotel, Anchor, Red Lion, Ship, White Horse* and the *Peveril Inn*. Before we leave for the *St Peter's Finger* (Lytchett Minster) our bellies are filled with fish and chips.

We arrive at the aforementioned pub for a pint of Tanglefoot and a game of pool. Three more country pubs are visited before we go in the *Royal Oak* (Cerne Abbas). Barry and Chris are the licensees and they tell me there's two more pubs in the village. Next is the *Red Lion* run by your hosts Chris and Jill Grey. They give Gav an ashtray and Drewy an optic. The last pub in the village is the *New Inn,* a busy pub where the strongest bottled beer in Great Britain is sold for £1.50. 'Thomas Hardy' strong ale. Drewy, Leo and myself buy some. These, we are told, will keep for twenty-five years and I intend to do so. The village of Cerne Abbas is famous for the large chalk-carved fertility giant in the hillside with a prick as big as King Kong. Oggy said, "I know who's got the biggest prick in West Bromwich."

"Who?" replies Leo.

"Me! There he is," he says pointing at me.

"Cheers Dad," I said.

"No problem, son."

We continue on our journey. There's another pub not too far away that also claims to be the smallest in England, so we aim to find it. We get lost and end up in the *New Compasses* (Charminster) to ask for directions. We are told we've come past it. It must have been that small we had missed it. We jump back in the minibus and all of us, except the driver, are totally arseholed. A few arguments occur due to us not being able to find this smallest pub and it's a rare occasion because I lose my temper, and my self-control. Eventually we give up and most of us can't take any more beer anyway, so a nice spot is found on a piece of grass beside a small river. I've drunk between seventeen and twenty pints today and I've vowed not to have this much ever again. I'm so paralytic I fall asleep as soon as my head hits the pillow.

At 7 a.m. in the morning on Friday 23rd September a bloke wakes us up, along with a few ducks from the River Cerne which is ten feet away. We are soaked due to the vast amount of rain that fell during the night. To our astonishment, the pub we were looking for last night is only yards away from where we are. It's called the *Smith's Arms* (Godmanstone) and the bloke who woke us up is the gaffer. He asks us if we would like to come in and have a cup of tea after he has taken his daughter to school in Bournemouth. An offer we can't refuse. On his return, we go into this fantastic little stone-built building with a single-storey thatched roof. Inside this small rectangular room (which measures 29ft 6inches long x 11ft 6inches wide) are wooden pews, solid wooden tables, a stone-walled fire, brass plates on the walls, a dartboard and a wagon-wheel ceiling light. The gaffer's name is John Foster who took over the pub in 1981 with his wife Linda. He had been a national hunt jockey for Falke Walwyn but he had injured his neck and had to retire. Souvenirs are on sale including bookmarkers, T-shirts, mugs, tankards and postcards. I buy myself a tankard and postcards.

This pub was originally a blacksmith's shop. King Charles II stopped here to have his horse shod, but when he asked for a drink the blacksmith replied, "I have no licence, sire."

So there and then he was granted one. The building dates from the fifteenth century. After spending time here drying off we say our farewell to a smashing gaffer and a pub certainly worth a revisit.

There's a café back at Charminster so that's where we head. I tried eating my breakfast but to no avail, as I'm now sick in the toilets. I do manage a wash and shave – the first one of the week. The lads fill up their water pistols for the umpteenth time. Our adventure continues to the lovely village of Broadhembury and its pub the *Drewe Arms*. A cracking old unspoilt pub with accommodation, Singer sewing machine tables and a lovely beer garden. Les and Eileen are the licensees. Another entry in the record books is the shortest named pub. This is just called *'X'* but on our arrival we find it's reverted to its previous name the *Merry Harriers* (Westcott). I'm sick again. This expedition of ours is full of surprises as we drop on the village of Bickleigh. A beautiful area where you have to cross over the fourteenth-century stone bridge on the road to Tiverton, to the *Fisherman's Cot* with its attractive thatched roof. This is the first of two pubs in the village and it is superbly situated on the banks of the River Exe. Accommodation is available. A single is £30 and a double is £40. The décor inside is modern and the walls are full of various framed items such as coins, fishing hooks, insects, scorpion's etc. The second one in Bickleigh is the *Trout Inn* another thatched pub by the waterside. It's a large open-plan pub with an older traditional style décor and again with accommodation.

It's a decent drive now and I need a short stop for a breath of fresh air. I'm still feeling a little rough. In our next pub the *Jack Russell* (Swimbridge) I have a glass of milk to put a lining back in my stomach before I drink my beer. From here it's about a twenty-mile drive into Woolacombe. Where we visit the *Jubilee Inn* and we warm our tins of soup up in the car-park. Ilfracombe is next on our agenda and on the way here we all hang our sleeping bags out of the minibus windows to dry them out for tonight's kip. The *Sandpiper* (Ilfracombe) is visited. Whilst in this town, in the local joke shop I purchase a green skeleton face mask with long black hair and Oggy buys a Sooty puppet for his grandson. Meanwhile the water-pistol boys squirt three local wenches with their guns and get called "Dutch wankers." Will somebody volunteer to stick these water pistols where the crabs don't crawl?

A unique and world famous seventeenth-century inn is next at Combe Martin. This is the *Pack o' Cards*, built by Squire George Ley to commemorate his luck at gambling. He built this pub in the form of a castle erected from playing cards; hence four floors (the four suites of the pack); thirteen doors on each floor (for each denomination) and fifty-two windows (one for each card). It also houses the famous Press Gang Table in which customers would hide to avoid capture by Navy Press Gangs. An informative little booklet is worth buying because it tells you the complete history of this fascinating pub. The *Pack o' Cards* will 'suit' you well – you'll be sure of a 'good deal'. The landlady tells us all about the mysterious beast of Exmoor. We drive on to the highest pub on Exmoor at 1,340feet above sea level the *Culbone Stables* (Porlock Hill). Here we relax for a while as a couple of the lads play pool, Wayne has plaice and chips, Jase uses the pub phone to talk to his missus and the rest of us watch *The Two Ronnies* on the telly.

The *Dunkery Beacon* (Wooton Courtenay) and the *Rest and be Thankful* (Wheddon Cross) are our next two pubs before the final one of the day, the *Royal Oak* (Winsford). This is a thatched pub where the locals, who are mainly yuppies, go shooting quail and things. Gav said to them, "We go shooting."

"What calibre do you use?" replied one of the yuppies.

At that Gav, Leo, Jase and Wayne pull out their water pistols hold them a loft and all say, "This one!"

I don't think this amuses them very much but I couldn't stop laughing. The pub does accommodation, but at £60 for a single, I'm glad I've got my plastic bag to sleep in. The gaffer is a friendly chap who tells me his brother runs the Exmoor Park. I pick up a leaflet in here and it tells you there's a famous stone river crossing nearby so I think this will be a quiet place to doss down tonight. On leaving this village you have to drive through a ford in the road. This is a first. Now we can head for the stone crossings called the Tarr Steps.

A slight problem occurs and upon leaving the village we get lost. Eventually we have to settle down in a field on Exmoor. None of our sleeping bags are dry so there's only four of us deciding to sleep outside and the others stop in the minibus. I put on my green monster mask to frighten the lads tonight but it doesn't work as they think it's Oggy messing about. It's so uncomfortable getting into my wet bag and now the wind starts to really pick up. This crisp sharp wind rips into us. Drewy and Gav go back in the van while Oggy and myself brave the elements. I'm woken during the night by grunting and blowing at the back of my neck. I'm too scared to turn round so I just pull the plastic over my head and hope whatever it is goes away. Thankfully it did. Was it the Exmoor beast?

On waking up, the force of the wind had filled Oggy's plastic bag with air and he'd rolled down a small bank. A couple of the lads rescue him, as he's now becoming shrink-wrapped. Gav commented that he is a bag of wind anyway! It's only now that we can appreciate our surroundings. There are trees, open fields, ferns, sheep and wild ponies. We're now ready to move on to find the elusive Tarr Steps. I'm soaking and I don't think I've fully dried out for days as we now pull away. If we don't find them now I'm not particularly bothered, but we do and it's a few hundred yards walk from the car-park. The walk is certainly worth the effort as large flat stones roughly six feet long, three feet wide and one-foot thick span the river and they are really safe to stroll across. I take a small stone as a souvenir.

Minehead is our destination for breakfast. There's a fair amount of driving to do today as our main aim is to visit the most dangerous pub in Great Britain. But first, Wayne, who's driving today, takes the A39 on a long drive to Thornbury to a new Banks's pub. On the way we get stuck in a traffic jam. When the minibus is stationary, which is at regular intervals, I put on my mask and I wind the window down wishing a good morning to the passing pedestrians. This makes them jump a bit and it's quite funny seeing the expressions on their faces. Meanwhile Oggy is out of the opposite window with his Sooty glove puppet on his hand greeting passing motorists. We are following a coach along this road and a little kid is looking at us from out of the rear window. To amuse myself I put on my monster mask again. This frightens the little kid and he tells his mom. But before she could turn round I'd taken it off. I did this several times then his mother must have got fed up with his constant whinging and gave him a clip round the earhole. I wonder if she ever did believe him?

Finally we reach our first pub of the day the *Knot of Rope* (Thornbury). The Banks's mild is lovely so we have four pints each. This pub, until recently, was called the *Exchange*. Our journey then continues towards the Severn Bridge where the crossing costs 50p. It's a nerve-racking drive across as the wind is gale force and the minibus is swaying from side to side. We had to make this before 8 p.m. tonight as the bridge closes for maintenance work. Our tour stops at Tintern, where there's only one pub open all day, the *Rose and Crown*. I give a local chap a game of darts in here and I finish in twelve darts. I play him again and almost brush him. At this he gets quite upset and said, "What a waste of money, I paid £20 for these darts and they are no good." He storms off and plays cribbage with his mates. Tintern Abbey is down the road, so we decide to pay it a visit only to discover a tyre on our minibus has a puncture. It takes Wayne half an hour to change the wheel. The *Moon and Sixpence* opened at 6 p.m. so we go in here instead. A small stream runs through the bar room. A 6lb trout once lived in the stream and it's now stuffed and is living on the mantelpiece in a glass case. The Banks's mild has lived too long and ends up down the bog! Bed and breakfast is £10. Also in Tintern, and a little harder to find, is the *Cherry Tree*. This is a nice find. There's one small room that either smells old or it suffers from rising damp. Hancock's beer is served straight out of the barrel. Guns decorate the brick walls.

It's a long and hard drive to our next alehouse the *Wingfield* (Llanbradach) then the *Capel Hotel* (Gilfach). The most dangerous pub in Great Britain, our main objective, is not too far away, the *Troedrhiwfuch Inn* in Glamorgan's Rhymney Valley. This pub is beneath a moving mountain and could be engulfed at any time. Our notes tell us the licensees Phil and Olga Chivers found this pub boarded up as they drove through the deserted village while on holiday and decided to re-open it. We are all looking forward to our visit here and after 892 miles we reach our goal to find it is closed, derelict and with no glass in the windows. It's a ghost village and it seems like we're stuck in the middle of nowhere. With nothing else planned for tonight and morale low we all agree we're 'manic depressives'. The weather tonight is terrible. It's now raining and the wind hasn't died down all day. For the first time ever, I don't think I can hack another night in a wet sleeping bag. The lads discuss moving on to a pub we passed about a mile back on the A469, the *Rising Sun* (Tirphil). This sounds a great idea to me as it's getting late. Wayne puts his foot down and we're off.

Yes! It's open, so in we go and at last we have a pint. It's a friendly old locals' pub. I get chatting to the landlord Glyn James. He's a jolly character and we receive a really warm welcome. He tells me about his early nuclear warning device. He said, "Every village and town in the country has one, usually it's located in the police stations, but as this village hasn't got one – they use my pub."

This I find really interesting. He continued, "It consists of a short transmission of the warning signal followed by the giving of a code word and the Ministry of Defence checks my device every six months."

I now start yapping to a bloke in his late fifties and he tells me he's a professor of Psychology at Cardiff University. His name is John Goode. We get on really well and I explain the predicament we're in tonight, having to sleep in our wet sleeping bags if we find somewhere to sleep. The professor said, "The village I live in has three houses, two pubs and a church and I've also got a caravan in my garden. You can sleep there if you like."

This is great news so I round up the lads and we say good night to our host Glyn James. We vow to come and see him again. The professor's local pub serves overtime too. We've decided his nickname is now the 'Prof'.

Wayne follows the 'Prof' through windy and isolated roads to the village of Bedwellty. The Prof's local is the *Church Inn*. The bar room is rough and rowdy so we go in the quieter lounge where the Prof's mates are. One of his friends owns the local greyhound track in the village and tells me it's been going sixty-seven years. The Whitbread Welsh bitter is going down a treat. Then Gav jokingly said to one of the elderly locals, "Do you know how you got the name Welsh? I do… when the Saxons and Vikings raided England you welshed out of a fight and ran to the hills."

On overhearing this, a massive Welsh chap comes over and said, "Who told you that, boyo?"

Gav sheepishly points to Oggy and said, "He did!"

It's a good job he saw the funny side of it.

The banter and jokes we've all been having with the locals has made this one of the best nights of our trip. It's 2 a.m. and it's time we said our farewells to the new friends we've made in this pub.

The Prof shows us his caravan and Oggy, Drewy, Jase and me grab a bed each. The other three sleep in the minibus. My kingdom for a bed! This is just what I need. During the night Oggy needs a dump and opens the wardrobe door thinking it's the bog. I have to jump out of bed and show him the way outside, as there isn't a toilet in the caravan. I think he ended up cementing two bricks together! I have a sound few hours sleep and I don't wake up until 9.30 a.m.

It's Sunday 25th September and the last day of our epic tour. The Prof invites us into his house for a cup of tea and to meet his charming wife Anita. The greyhound track happens to be at the back of his house so I take a quick look and then I have a walk around this small village. There are some smashing views from the graveyard across the valleys. Our host now escorts us to a café at Aberbargoed for a £1.35 full Welsh breakfast. This is just what we all need. There's an old mining works here and it still has a winding wheel. The Prof and myself exchange addresses and we intend to keep in touch. I thank him for all he has done for us and wish him well. He then leaves and we continue our adventure.

It's a pleasant drive (and it's not raining) to our first pub of the new day the *Red Lion Hotel* (Llangynidr). This is an ivy-covered fifteenth-century inn in the Brecon Beacons. It's busy serving meals.

Bed and breakfast is £40 for a double room with shower. We sit outside on the benches. This is the first time Oggy notices the split in the arse of his trousers. "How long have I been walking round like this?" he asked us.

"Three days," was the reply.

Moving on, we now visit the *Vine Tree* (Llangattock), the *White Hart* (near Crickhowell) and the *Dragon's Head* (Llangenny). This is where the water pistols make their next appearance. I was hoping they had lost these. Our next pub is the 'Oldest Pub in Wales'. The *Skirrid Inn* (Llanfihangel Crucorney). This shuts at 2 p.m. until the evening session and we only just make this one. It's now a good old place to visit but many years ago over 1,800 hangings took place in here from the beam above the stairs. You can still see the rope mark visible in the beam today. The inn is said to date from 1100AD. It was originally called the *Skirrid Mountain Hotel*.

Well, it's arrived. The final pub on our epic and eventful tour, a Whitbread house the *Rising Sun* (Pandy). This we assume shuts at 3 p.m. There's only us in this pub so we decide to celebrate the end of our journey in style. Drewy tries some concoction: a pint of Guinness and Lucozade. It's bloody horrible. Oggy starts hitting the top shelf, the rest of us just down pint after pint as Ann the barmaid tells us it's open all day. I buy some jars of honey for £1.50 each, all locally made. I'm starting to get hungry so I nip out to the minibus, I get the stove out and warm up a tin of stewed steak mixed with a tin of Irish stew. My mouth is watering at the sight of it bubbling away. Then this nasty looking Doberman runs towards me so I jump in the minibus and this lousy wammel eats all my saucepan of food. Ggrrrrrrr! Eventually, with his belly full he stops gawping at me and disappears, so I stroll back in the pub, have a bag of crisps and a sulk. I soon liven up when I'm back on the beer. Our merriment continues until 5.15 p.m. This is when we leave, after a fabulous afternoon drinking session. Sadly our epic and enjoyable journey ends.

We arrive home at 7.00 p.m. after completing 1,016 miles and seventy-one pubs.

CHAPTER 12

2,000 NOT OUT

Over the next few weeks we concentrate on visiting the pubs in Worcestershire. A couple are worth a visit including the *Three Kings* (Hanley Castle). A traditional fifteenth-century inn, with an old interior and a room called Nell's lounge bar. Your hosts are George, Sheila, Sue and Dave Roberts. Bed and breakfast is available plus real ales. The other is the *Malvern Hills Hotel* (Wynds Point), a smart hotel with a smart lounge with wood-panelled walls and fifteen rooms available for accommodation. From most of the rooms there are superb views over the western slopes of the Malvern Hills and rural Herefordshire. Leo is fascinated by the barmaid and tells me she's got big Malvern's. Nicely spotted my old pal.

We have to finish the city of Worcester now. A few pubs worthy of a mention are the *Alma* with its tiled picture of the Crimean War and a Coalbrookedale fire made near Ironbridge; the *Park Tavern* has a humorous Irish landlord who tells me he only works part-time here and the other part-timer is his wife. I ask him for a souvenir of the pub and he gives me a baby's rattle. A new Bank's pub is visited, the *Oak and Apple*; there's an annual 'Conker Knockout' at the *Lamplighter*. But best of all is the *Jolly Roger* a brewpub. Three ales are available and we try them all. The first is called 'Severn Bore' and then we have the 'Quaff bitter': both are superb. The third is called 'Small Brewers Revenge' and is claimed to be the world's strongest draught beer at 1134 original gravity.

It's Saturday 12th November 1988 and another milestone is

reached. Our 2,000th pub. This is the sixth of Mad O'Rourke's pubs the *'Cradley Sausage Works'* (Cradley Heath). It's a bit of a reunion tonight as a dozen of us turn out for this little celebration. Bangers and Mash are consumed by a few of us with various flavour sausages. Gav's in love with a wench called Andrea and is spending most of his time in the beer garden talking sweet nothings. I called out to Gav and said, "It's a bit nippy out theer mate."

"My heart will keep me warm," he replies.

God strewth, this is putting me off my sausages. He's already told me they have something in common. They both smoke. In one of the pamphlets I pick up there's a sentence about the pub, that's quite informative if you understand the humour of Mad O'Rourke. He claims in his usual mad cap manner, that the name sausage refers to the people of central England who the Celts called 'Saussanach' which means 'He who carries his dinner in a pig's bladder'. How little things have changed. It continues to say sausage exports collapsed causing the depression of 1926 (the "Wall's" Street crash). Well, enough about this, as we move on completing a pleasant evening in our local the *Old Crown*.

Evesham pubs are next where two of particular interest is the *Evesham Hotel* and the *Green Dragon*. Built in 1540 as a Tudor Manor and modernised in 1810, the *Evesham Hotel* stands in 2½ acres of gardens. The *Green Dragon* is a 16th century coaching inn. Whose interior has original oak beams, with Cotswold stone fireplaces surrounded by brass and copper ware. Both pubs do accommodation. This run takes us into the Christmas period.

Bromsgrove is next and this town opens up the year for our travels, it's January 1989. A delightful pub to start off the year is *Ye Olde Black Cross*. This is said to date from the 14th century and was licensed in A.D.1640. The pub is associated with Oliver Cromwell, whose commanding officer at the Battle of Worcester used it as his headquarters. It's now a new recruit joins the BATS, his name is Maskell. He lasts a month completing all the Redditch pubs before dropping out! Our very last tour of Worcestershire ends in Droitwich visiting the French chateau-styled building called the *Chateau Impney* *hot*el. It stands out like a sore thumb from the roadside and I can't wait to see the interior décor. The hotel is a unique and brilliant example of design, artistry and elegance. There's a doorman who lets us in this hotel where accommodation is expensive at £74.95 for a single room and a double is £79.95. It may be smart from the outside but the inside I find slightly disappointing. The lounge room has white artex walls with red velvet seats; there's also a modern extension built on the side. Then the *Old Cock* is paid a visit. This was licensed in 1712, the tenth year of the reign of Queen Anne, it has three real ales on: Hook Norton, Wadsworth and Pedigree. We are slowly getting the taste for all these different bitters on offer. Finally we finish at a revisit pub the *Gardeners Arms*. Mel and Viv are the licensees and we stop for a drink over. They ask us if we want to build a raft and join in the annual raft race in June. All in aid of the restoration of the historic Droitwich barge canal. This sounds too energetic to me so I think we'll give this a miss as we will be wasting valuable drinking time. Now all we have left are the last few tours into Herefordshire to complete all the pubs in both counties.

Leominster, pronounced Lemster is the first town this year to be visited in Herefordshire. The *Hop Pole* is where I sit and listen to the gobbledegook between Gav and Leo. Both of them are playing pool and Gav said to Leo, "Where's the light for the dart table?"

"I don't know, but do you want any chalk for the snooker board?" replies Leo.

With just over four years travelling to different pubs I think the effects of drinking alcohol is hitting them hard. At the *Talbot Hotel* (a combination of buildings, dating from the fifteenth century to the present century) the gaffer tells us that Leominster, during mediaeval times, became an important wool market town and the parish church features an ancient ducking stool last used in 1809. In the *Black Swan Hotel*, Gav yaps to a bloke with a dog and fancies the two ugly wenches with him. I'll stick with the dog. Our next boozer is the *Royal Oak Hotel* an old coaching house with eighteen bedrooms at reasonable rates, a single room is £25.50 and a double £38.00. The lounge bar has original oak panelling, a wealth of beams, two open fires and there is also a cellar bar. The *Bell* is next where a chap rather wuss (worse) for wear comes up to Gav and says, "Can I wipe my glass on your beer towel coat?"

Gav shows him his fist and replied, "I'll wipe this on your nose."

Not the friendliest welcome we've ever had but we carry on supping in the last pub of the night, the *Chequers Inn*. This is a black and white half-timbered pub built about 1480 to serve the wool markets. We get served with pints of Ansell's bitter by the licensees Bill and Brenda Phillips who allow us to drink over until 11.30 p.m. It's been a good run tonight and our journey home takes one hour and ten minutes.

During the next couple of weeks we finish off Leominster and various country pubs. The *Nag's Head* (Canon Pyon) is a nice old pub; the *Plough* (Canon Pyon) is where the lads go on a suicide mission with Gav and Oggy having seven pints and five whiskies each and Drewy and Leo pass out on the whisky and vodka. Another lovely place is the *New Priory Hotel* (Stretton Sugwas). Ken Benjamin has recently purchased this. He likes to be known as Benj and runs this hotel with his daughter. It is set in its own 3½ acres of land with gardens and terraces. The accommodation is excellent value £20 for a single and £35 for a double. Benj is a great bloke and donates £20 for our charity and tells us to come back soon.

Enough money is now raised to present our cheque for £500 to Moxley Hospital. So today Saturday 4th March we have the pleasure of meeting the Health Authority officials Margaret Bliss, Karen Dowman and Bryan Cotterill to hand over our cheque at our local the *Old Crown*. Our local Black Country Bugle newspaper covers this celebration under the heading *BATS Sup Up For Charity*.

The following day before we venture out on our first trip into Tewkesbury, I have to meet Drewy outside the Hawthorns football ground. Both of us have been to the game where the final score is West Bromwich Albion 2 v 1 Leeds United. Drewy happens to be a Leeds fan and I'm Albion so Drewy hands over our little wager and I'm £5 richer. It's only recently we have come to the decision to take it in turns driving and it's Gav's turn tonight in his new car.

We arrive at Tewkesbury and go in the *Bell Hotel*. A chap from Yorkshire said to Gav, "Call yourself an ale taster. You're drinking orange juice."

"Yoe come and drive mate and I'll show ya how to drink," snarls Gav.

What a way to start the night off. The next pub on our itinerary is the *Royal Hop Pole Hotel*, which Charles Dickens mentions in his book *The Pickwick Papers* (chapter 50) it says that, "At the *Hop Pole* at Tewkesbury they stopped to dine."

Gav is still wound up about the comment made to him in the last pub and walks out of this place. We all think he's gone to fetch the car but on coming out of here we can't find him. We carry on to our eighth pub of the night, the *Tudor House Hotel*. This is steeped in history. A chimney in the Mayor's Parlour conceals a priest's hole and axe marks reputedly made by Cromwell's soldiers can be seen on the old oak door leading to the Secret Garden. We're all panicking a little now, as Gav still hasn't turned up. On leaving this hotel he's nowhere in sight and as we walk across the road some local yobs in their car drive straight at us so I have go at kicking it. The only problem is the police saw me do it and ask if my mom taught me about the Green Cross Code.

Well, that's a telling off isn't it? At last we spot Gav. He's calmed down now and he's scoffing a bag of chips. We do two more pubs in this town, before finishing at the *Lower Lode Hotel* (Forthampton). This is a fifteenth century riverside inn, with accommodation, caravans and moorings. I finish off on two pints of Old Rosie cider and I'm totally rat-arsed. On arriving home I'm carried upstairs to my flat, where I'm sick. Work the next day is a no go!

During the week the officials at Moxley Hospital invite us all along for a get together. The only problem is, only three of us can make it and the food they put on for us is huge. We do our best to eat as much as possible and the rest is given out to the patients. This was a lovely gesture and we have a wonderful evening. The following

Sunday, Tewkesbury is finished off. Our last pub of the night on Sunday March 19th is the *Swan* (Hereford). The licensees are Lee and Val Knight. Lee buys us all a pint of Guinness, a whisky and a jug of Weston's scrumpy cider. He says we can sleep in his pigeon pen if we want and tells us a tale about one of his locals that went fishing and thought he had caught something. Lee says he did, he hooked his own ear! It's a true story. Honest. On the way home from this pub Gav gets out at the bank in Stourport to get some money out of the hole-in-the-wall. A police car slowly drives past and ends up stopping us two miles away for a spot check and they give Drewy the breathalyser. He's our driver tonight so he passes with flying colours. It makes a change tonight and it's Leo's turn to spew up.

During the following week all five members of the BATS meet up in the *Old Crown* over a few pints of Banks's. It's all about the need for a new challenge to keep us going, because Herefordshire will be completed in a few weeks. Oggy comes up with the idea of travelling around the entire coastline of Great Britain and to have a drink in every county and region in England, Scotland and Wales. This is going to be a mammoth task and needs dedication. Drewy, Leo and myself agree it could be one hell of an adventure. However, following our discussion and totally out of the blue, Gav decides he doesn't want to take his turn driving again and facing the hardship which will be involved in trying to complete our new mission. He says he's had enough. He calls time on his pub-crawl and after many fabulous and hilarious times together he will really be missed.

It's Saturday 25th March and we remember Benj the gaffer of the *New Priory Hotel* and his offer. So, it's off to the city of Hereford for a four-day tour. It's a great start to our day in Hereford as the landlady in the *Game Cock*, Jeanette tells us we can come back tomorrow dinner-time for a free Sunday dinner. It's somewhat spoilt in the next boozer the *Newmarket* when a chap keeps following us around the room saying, "Private conversation, private conversation." Then he slaps his mouth with his hand and starts singing, *I'm leaning on the lamp-post at the corner of the street,* an old George Formby record. Trust us to bump into the local nutter.

I park the car at this pub and we now journey on foot around the city.

The *Wellington* is honoured by our presence, then so is *Saxty's* bar where if you want to read a book you need a trampoline, because the bookshelves are up to the ceiling. Three more pubs are visited. The *Imperial Hotel*, a Berni Inn; the *Bowling Green* mainly bikers in here and the *Three Crowns* run by Andy and Liz Herd who tell us it's due to close on May 12th and be converted into shops. The *Hereford Times* newspaper reporter Alison Hughes arrives for our next pub the *Queens Arms* and does an article about us entitled *Pub Crawling for Charity*. We're enjoying our time in the city and the *Green Dragon Hotel* is the next to be recorded in our notes. The present facade of this building, with its swirl-cast iron balcony, was erected in 1857. Now for a visit to the *Spread Eagle*, *Orange Tree*, *Black Lion* and the *Saracens Head*. The latter named pub is right at the side of the river. This is a run-down pub so we don't stop long. We're all clammed (hungry) so we nip over to the nearby fish and chip shop. We sit on the bank of the river eating our chips and watch a copper go by. I saw him earlier, around the city and it feels like he's keeping an eye on us.

Hereford is certainly a place to come and see the sights and drink beer and even more beer in the numerous alehouses. The Cathedral has a Chained Library including an eighth century Gospel and the Mappa Mundi, a map of the world drawn in about 1290. There's also a Cider Museum. It's also the city for visiting our next nine pubs. During these visits I've parked my car at the *Hop Pole*. On coming out of our twenty-second pub today, the *British Oak* I notice a copper hiding behind a shop entrance on a walkie-talkie. We jump in my car and I said to the lads, "I bet that copper has phoned up a patrol car to follow us."

No sooner had I said this than, 200 yards behind me at the traffic lights, I spot a police car. There's a sharp turning into the back of a supermarket delivery car-park so I take it and they go sailing past. I have a word with the lads and I decide to drive on and give myself up or they will follow us all night.

So back on the main road I go and half a mile down the road I see they have parked up and I pull in front of them and stop. The police woman and her male accomplice now get out their car and come over to me she says, "Are you lost?"

"No, I'm looking for the Grapes pub," I replied.

"Have you just arrived in Hereford?" she asks.

"No, we've been in 22 pubs in the city today."

"You've been drinking then?" she said.

"No, I'm driving."

"So you won't mind blowing in the breathalyser then?"

At this I'm put into the back of the patrol car and I take the test. When I pass she says I'm not blowing in it properly and I have to do it once more and again I pass. This seems to upset them, so she says she'll find something wrong with my car. As she walks around my car the lads who are all blottoed begin to get annoyed and start shouting at her. They are told to shut up but it's hard to keep them quiet. I then ask her why we were being followed. It turns out that we have out of town car number plates. At this I'm allowed to drive on. Eventually we find the *Grapes* and it's being supported on the outside by scaffolding as the building is falling down. It's a Whitbread pub full of bikers and Oggy yaps to them about his Suzuki 750-cc kettle he rides and his old 1948 B.S.A gold star. There's one last pub before we reach our destination the *Starting Gate*.

At 10 p.m. we thankfully arrive at the *New Priory Hotel*. The landlord Benj serves us our drinks and we sit and relax after an exhausting day. To our great surprise three old members turn up and join in the fun, Wayne, Lowey and Jase. It's great to see them again. I get yapping to a chap who lives next door to this hotel – he's also called Wayne and he says we can all sleep in his flatlet. The supping continues until the early hours and finally we call it a day. The local lad Wayne shows us the way into his flatlet and Jase grabs the settee the rest of us doss down on the floor. Lowey never made it and collapsed in the car outside. Local lad Wayne said, "Whatever you do, don't break my wife's pot plant."

During the night Jase is throwing up in the bog, in the kitchen sink and then on Wayne's pillow. The whiff of sick starts Leo off and now it's his turn to chuck up. Drewy staggers over everyone to have a piss and falls over. He gets up again and falls the other way. The day's drinking has paralysed all the BATS.

In the morning I'm first to wake and notice that the pot plant hasn't quite made it through the night. I look around for something to mend it with and I find a roll of sellotape in a drawer. When Drewy fell over he bost (broke) one of the large leaves off it. I wake Drewy up and he puts a small cuddly toy under the leaf to hold it in position and sellotapes it up. He's just in time as local lad Wayne brings us all a cup of tea and biscuits in. This lad deserves a medal putting us up overnight and we wish him all the best in the future, because our breakfast in the hotel is now ready. After a somewhat mediocre meal we all say our goodbyes to everyone including Wayne, Lowey and Jase who are off home.

The day starts off again in Hereford. We visit the *Three Elms*, *Greyhound Dog*, *Crown*, *Ship*, *Belmont* and the *Moat House*, before our free Sunday turkey dinner at the *Game Cock*. Jeanette the landlady has kept her word so we go and buy her a large box of chocolates. All the pubs are now shut for the afternoon so we buy a newspaper and sit at the side of the riverbank on a lovely sunny day listening to the birds singing, the church bells ringing and watching a cat have a shit.

Don the gaffer opens up the *Golden Fleece* our first pub of the night. Then we move on to the *Barrels* pub. This was formerly called the *Lamb Hotel*. This place brews its own Wye Valley beers and the landlord is Peter Amor. Next door to the *Barrels* pub is the *Sun* where there are barrels of cider on top of the bar. Next a smart hotel is visited. The *Castle Pool Hotel* is situated close to the Cathedral. The house dates back to 1850 and was for a time the residence of the Bishop of Hereford. There are twenty-seven comfortable bedrooms in this country-style hotel where a single room is £36 and a double room £50. The lovely beer garden overlooks a large pool and you are served from the patio bar. Then it's off to our next pub, the *Bricklayers Arms* where a copper comes in, looks at us and then leaves. Are they keeping an eye on us?

Three more pubs are visited and this completes our ale session today. We then drive a few miles to Checkley Common near a place called Old Hill House. This is out in a secluded wooded area and we bed down for the night. At the break of dawn it's like waking up in pets' corner. I think the cowboys from *Rawhide* have brought their whole herd of cattle out to graze; the noise the cows are making is deafening and *Ben Hur* has brought his horses along to add to the noise. Kermit has made his mark too as a couple of large frogs come hopping and croaking over my pillow and the total population of wood pigeons must have arrived and found it an appropriate place to congregate. To top it all there are numerous pheasants roaming around our plastic bags making a racket like an old steam train. Anyone fancy pheasant for breakfast?

Eventually, I get up at 8 a.m. and I'm covered in slugs. I go for a walk and carve my initials on a wooden stump. Back at the car everyone is up and we're all packed away and journey back into Hereford for breakfast. I nip in the bookies to put a bet on and when I get back to the car I realise I've left my keys in their toilets, so I run back in and luckily someone has handed them in. The day's drinking starts, smack on opening time. Later in the afternoon, we find the *Antelope* an ex-Navy bloke runs it at the moment, called Paul with his wife Mary. They are here for a few weeks as relief managers for Whitbread. They invite us to finish off our pub-crawl tonight at the other pub they run in the village of Munstone. At the 9th pub of the day the *Sawyers Rest* the old ex-landlady educates me on how to cook a pheasant. I could have done with this lesson this morning! Our next pub is the *Heart of Oak*. This pub has four dartboards and four pool tables. Alan and Jenny the licensees give me a small poetry and advice book. One verse reads:

Call frequently
Drink moderately
Pay honourable
Be good company
Part friendly
Go home quietly

The eighteenth pub and final one today is owned by Whitbread, the *Rose Gardens* (Munstone); the one Paul and Mary at the *Antelope* told us about earlier in the day. Both of them are in here and we receive a warm welcome and the offer to sleep in their shed in the beer garden. This will certainly come in handy as we can all now settle down for a good drink of beer. They hand out song sheets to everyone in the pub and an old lady starts playing the piano and we all have an old fashioned singsong. Again we've dropped on an overtime-drinking pub and by the time we come out of here we are all pie-eyed and our legs are like buckled wheels. We decide not to sleep in the shed and just doss down on the grass. But during the night it tips down and Leo succumbs to the cover the shed provides.

It's 9.30 a.m. on Tuesday 29th March when we wake up. Toasted sandwiches and cups of tea are kindly given us by our hosts in the pub. It's our last day today and more Hereford pubs are visited. The *Oxford Arms,* a 17th century inn, the *Entertainer* then the *Moorfield* all three are Whitbread houses. Finally *Chasers* bar completes all the licensed alehouses in Hereford. The gaffer of this place is a scouser and informs us he kept a pub in Tipton for a while called the *Tipton Tavern.* This is only a half-mile from my flat. He tells us he couldn't understand the dialect when he first took over there and recalls an incident when a chap ordered a whisky and asked him for wairta (the Black Country word for water). He said he'd told him to fetch it himself, as we don't supply waiters! He had almost had his earhole thumped for saying this. The last two pubs, to end our enjoyable but exhausting trip, are the *Bell* (Tillington) another Whitbread pub run by Jackie and Glenn Williams who said we could have slept in their barn last night and finally the *Royal Oak* (Burghill). This has a lovely, untouched interior with old beams, an old clock, a dartboard and the noggen juice called scrumpy cider. This adventure has taken us 236 miles to complete sixty-two pubs.

During early April we visit pubs like the *New Inn* (Knightingfield) a basic living-room design interior with the game of quoits. The *Alma* (Linton) another of our Whitbread pubs is visited as is the *Crown and Anchor* (Lugwardine) a super old pub with darts, quoits and poolroom. Now we must conquer the dozen pubs in the ancient market town of

Ledbury. Drewy turns up for our journey here on crutches. He's only gone and fallen eight feet off some scaffolding at work. This is beer dedication for you. Our first pub in this delightful town is the *Feathers Hotel* built in 1565. There's a black and white exterior to this old Elizabethan coaching inn. It has eleven bedrooms, a single room is £40 and a double is £60. An open log fire, and cosy furniture feature in this hotel. John Fuggle helped make Herefordshire famous with his world-renowned hops and *The Fuggles room* has lots of hops hanging off the old beams.

The other pubs in order of drinking are the *Bull* a long narrow room with a pool table at the end. The *Prince of Wales* is situated down the narrow cobbled Church Lane, and has a Scottish theme with Black Watch emblems on the walls, tartan curtains and a miserable Scottish gaffer. The *White Hart* is where Drewy hops to this pub and falls up the step. This is a dump and there's no air in here due to all the locals filling the room with fag smoke. The *Seven Stars Hotel* has accommodation and two steps on entry, Drewy's okay with these. The *Horseshoe*, there's six steps into this one and we have to help Drewy up them. This is a fourteenth-century Grade II listed pub. Next is the *Plough Hotel* a traditional town pub with a skittle alley, pub games and Bed and Breakfast is £14 for a single room. The *Brewery Inn* a Victorian-style pub with many Grade I listed features. The *Royal Oak Hotel* is an old coaching inn with a skittle alley, ballroom and accommodation. *Ye Olde Talbot Hotel,* formerly an old coaching house, is a Grade II listed timber-framed inn built in 1596. Lastly is the *Full Pitcher* a large family pub. The twelfth pub the *Ring of Bells* is a terrace-style pub, which is closed at the moment for refurbishment but opens soon.

Sunday April 16th sees our old mate, Jeff (the Yidd) make a guest appearance for our journey to a new Mad O'Rourke's pub in Worcester called the *Little Sauce Factory*. This has blue and white wall tiles and a tiled map of the world on the ceiling with shelves of Worcester sauce bottles and scrubbed wooden tables. This one completes all our pubs in Worcestershire again.

CHAPTER 13

THE FINAL FLAGON

Another mission is undertaken as we continue visiting the pubs of Herefordshire. It's Saturday 22nd April and it's an early start on a bright sunny day. Drewy picks up Oggy, Leo, Dawn and me and we travel to our first alehouse of the day; the *Barneby Arms Hotel* (Bredenbury), then the *Lemster Ore* (Docklow) followed by the *Wheelbarrow Castle* (Stoke Prior). The fourth pub is a great find, it's the *Hop Pole* (Risbury). I've never seen one like this before. It's unique. From the outside it looks nothing like a pub. It has the name of the licensee above the cottage-style building and has an adjoining old barn. All that's left of the pub name on the shed is --- --- E Inn, the rest of the letters have fallen off. On entering there's a small square bar room with a dartboard, five old coach seats, two wooden tables and the walls are covered with dotted wallpaper and has a Page 3 topless girl calendar hanging on it. The tiny bar has no beer pulls or fonts, just a wall unit at the back with four shelves of beer bottles. I shout out for service and the elderly landlord with his white beard comes in from his kitchen and serves us with bottled beers only. His name is Mr A. G. Ryall and he signs my book. The adjoining kitchen is full of junk and his washing is piled up on the table. We stop for another bottle of beer, a chat with the gaffer and a game of darts. I'm really chuffed we have a hobby like this because this type of pub is going to disappear soon and it's given me the privilege of experiencing a few of these fabulous unspoilt buildings.

We are forced to spend our afternoon in Leominster since all the country pubs have shut for the afternoon. The *Black Horse* is revisited, as it's open all day. Later we have fish and chips. As we continue our journey, our thirst is quenched in another six nice old country pubs before arriving at our final one, which is hard to find in the dark, the *Three Horseshoes* (Little Cowarne). It's a busy place where an old chap is playing the organ and his mate is singing along to it. I said to the landlady, (whose name I think is Linda) "Do you know where we can get a breakfast in the morning?"

"Yes, here and if you need somewhere to sleep you can use the field in our paddock," she replied.

This is brilliant so we decide to stop for the night and get in some serious ale tasting. It's Flowers IPA and it's a cracking drink. I'm told to watch out for a local chap called 'Shitters' because he tries getting off with everybody's missus. I yap to an ex-merchant seaman who now breeds rabbits for the supermarkets and is known locally as 'Steve the Buck'. It's 1 a.m. Another chap called Steve, who's had too many beers, drops his trousers to reveal a pair of woman's lips tattooed on his backside. Steve (could this be Shitters?) ends up chatting to Dawn while I end up listening to his mate Guss about fire fighting in the Navy. It's almost 2 a.m. now and we're the last ones left in the bar so it's time to end the day's drinking and head off to the paddock where we settle down for the evening.

A really quiet night's sleep is had until 7 a.m. when it starts to rain. We give it a couple more hours before we go in the pub for our breakfast. I send Dawn in first because 'Lady' the Alsatian and guardian of the pub is sitting at the entrance and I'm not too keen on the way she's looking at me. I'm glad I did as it starts barking at Dawn who came running out of the pub. The landlady calmed it down and we follow her for breakfast. It cost us the colossal sum of £1.20 each and it's a real filling one too. We all have three hours of warmth by the old log fire and a game of cards. The pubs are now open so it's farewell to this welcoming old pub and off to the *Wheelwrights Arms* (Pencombe). The gaffer has read about us recently in the Hereford Times newspaper. Leo doesn't fancy a pint so has two halves instead! The *Green Drago*n is our second pub of the day and 'Pinto' is the gaffer of this place and there's a good range of real ales. While we're here we watch as one of the local lads named James fills up a four-pint jug five times for his old mates' pint pots. They're bigger piss-heads than we are. It's St George's Day today and when we mention this to Pinto, he gives us a four-pint jug for free. Our time is spent happily quaffing our Timothy Taylor's Landlord bitter and we all have a good laugh in this pub. The *Chase* (Bishops Frome) is just down the road and is a total contrast. There are only half-a-dozen folk in and the pub is dead quiet. Our last pub of the weekend is the *Majors Arms,* a short drive away. I'm told this was an old cider house and parts of it date back to the 16th century. The view from the beer garden up here is smashing. It's been a marvellous little tour around this old English county and I'll be sorry when it ends.

It's Saturday April 29th 1989 and it's our very last run into Herefordshire. The same drinkers from last week descend on this beautiful county for the final time. In drinking order we visit the *Wheatsheaf* (Fromes Hill), the *Bell* (Bosbury), the *Oak* (Staplow) and the re-opened *Ring of Bells* (Ledbury). The *Farmers Arms* (Wellington Heath) is next. Wellington Heath is a unique village, known as the independent state of Monkey Island since it was formed at 1307 hours on Friday 6th January 1989. This village, in defiance, has declared itself independent in protest at the government's announcement in summer 1988, that British citizens are to lose their traditional passports for the boring red European ones. The monkey islanders have produced various items for sale, including passports, flags, currency and a coat of arms. There is also a toll barrier to check visitors' passports. All this is a humourous idea to raise money for local charities. Cheques can also be made out to 'Monkey Island'. A deadly warning is written in the Monkey Islanders' Ministry of Defence list. It says: "The defence computer and infra-red scanners were fully operational by 1310 hours and our Marconi high-decibel Tom Jones Detectors were in situ and operating on a 250 miles radius with the locked in Shirley Bassey Laser programmed for immediate retaliation." So the British government must listen, you have been warned!

Our journey continues to the *British Lion* (Kings Caple). This is a must visit pub. Once you pass all the chickens running about outside you enter an unspoilt bar room with an old iron stove in the middle with a pipe coming out of it and going through the ceiling. There is a dartboard and poolroom and B&B is an unbelievable £7.50 for a single room. The licensees are Drena and Owen Walker. They also have a camping and caravan site and a nice beer garden. Drewy reads a notice on the wall and finds it hilarious. It says:

> She offered her honour
> He honoured her offer
> All night long it was
> Honour and offer.

We leave this smashing old pub for the *New Harp* (Hoarwithy). Here we have a game of darts and pool. Better still is a visit to St Catherine's Church, which is a short walk away. It's of Italian design and was the life's work of the Reverend William Poole the vicar for nearly fifty years. Due to afternoon closing we drive into Ross-on-Wye to see if Brian and Hazel at the *Crown and Sceptre* will cook us a breakfast in the morning. We arrive at 4 p.m. and Brian said there's no problem and of course he'll accommodate our needs. Tracy the barmaid has left. She's pregnant. Meanwhile Oggy falls in love with one of two women who are out enjoying themselves because their husbands have gone to Cork in Ireland to play rugby. Their names are Ann and Sheila. Oggy and Ann exchange phone numbers. Once we get in this pub it's hard to get out and it's three hours before we make a move. This time it's to the *Plough* (Little Dewchurch) where they are building an extension to the pub. Then it's a drive to the *Brockhampton Court Hotel* (Brockhampton). This is a grand nineteenth-century country mansion built in a Gothic style and set in six acres of its own gardens and grounds. The bar is furnished with elegant wood panelling and a superb carved wood fireplace. There are twenty-six bedrooms and B&B is £27.50 per person. Clay pigeon shooting is available and situated in delightful wooded surroundings costing £17.50 for an afternoon shoot. It's a bit of a snobby place, though.

Three more pubs are visited until we arrive at the *Moon* (Mordiford). I get yapping to the landlord who tells us we can sleep on his campsite at the back of the pub. This is great news so we decide to make this our last pub of the day and get stuck into some excessive drinking. We're really enjoying ourselves in the lounge bar when the gaffer's missus comes over asks us to drink up. "But the gaffer said we could sleep here tonight," replied Leo.

This falls on deaf ears. We've been drinking all day and there's no way we can gulp our beer down that quick. She comes over again and this time she said, "If you don't drink up I'll tip them down the sink." Then she grabs my beer and I have to stand up and grab it back. She then sends one of her locals in who is drinking in the bar room and he shouts, "Are you lot taking the piss!"

Nobody takes one blind bit of notice of this twit and all Oggy does is laugh.

"You should get him out of here, he's trying to cause trouble," I explained to this hateful woman.

"It's you lot I want out of here."

What's the point? I can't be arsed to speak to this woman or her wimp of a husband, so we leave.

Our night now is somewhat in disarray and we must find somewhere to doss down. It's as black as charcoal driving down these country lanes. Leo suddenly spots a cutting in some woods called Haugh Woods. This will have to do. Drewy's passed out in the car so he's best left in there while we find a decent spot to rest our heads. Inbetween two trees there is a flat piece of long grass. This will do and our sleeping stuff is laid out. Dawn goes for a widdle in the woods and sinks in mud up to her ankles in this soggy wooded area. At daybreak, after an uncomfortable few hours kip, I wonder how we haven't been eaten alive. We're surrounded by mass armies of big red ants climbing up the trunk of every tree in sight. I'm only grateful that we pulled the plastic bags over our heads. At last it's time to get up and we travel into Ross on Wye for breakfast at the *Crown and Sceptre*.

It's Sunday 30th April and there are only three pubs left to finish Herefordshire. On entering the *Crown and Sceptre,* Brian the landlord said to Oggy, "I see they've taken the stake out of your heart then."

"Morning Brian," replied Oggy.

With our breakfast consumed we have two pints apiece to wash it down. Brian brings Oggy a pig's trotter."What's that for?" said Oggy.

"To match your head," replied Brian.

It's a good job we understand his humour and it's all taken in the right spirit. We say our last goodbyes to Brian and Hazel because our time spent in this county comes to an end today and another adventure will begin.

First stop of the day is the *Walwyn Arms* (Much Marcle). A Whitbread owned pub with skittle alley and poolroom. We leave here to visit the local churchyard not far from the *Walwyn Arms*. The reason for this is that there is a magnificent old yew tree in the churchyard and inside its massive trunk is an arched wooden seat for eight people. I find this absolutely amazing and I'm glad we have made the slight detour to see it. Back to the main road and turn right takes us to our next pub the *Royal Oak* (Much Marcle). The gaffer Chris Hall talks to Oggy about his collection of eleven motorbikes, which includes two rare ones. This place also has a skittle alley and has camping and caravan facilities.

Well, this is it, our final pub in all of Worcestershire and Herefordshire, the *Slip Tavern* (Much Marcle). This pub is named after the famous land-slip of 1575 when Marcle Hill moved some 400 yards over three days burying a chapel and a herd of cattle. If you ever go jay walking around the Car Park watch out for a six feet drop into a small stream. It's fittle time as the lads tuck into a meal and go on a celebration session, downing pints, shorts and seven Gaelic coffees each. Gilbert and Beryl Jeanes are the licensees. Dawn and myself sit outside in the beautiful beer garden. This pub is a wonderful ending to our travels, but it's not quite over yet!

A chap comes over to us after hearing of our exploits and said, "Have you ever been round a proper cider factory?"

"Ar, mate quite a few," replied Leo.

"You've not been around one as big as Weston's I bet?" he says.

"If you follow me I think you will be amazed."

We might as well, so off we go. I think he says his name is Mike Ross. It's only down the road to this place and what a place it is! But before our tour he takes us in the small bar area for a sample of Weston's cider. This is named after Henry Weston who moved here in 1878. Off we go for a glimpse around this cider factory. This is quite a shock to us all and he's right – it's huge. It's like stepping back in time as he shows us the old cider-making machine and tells us that this was a farm built in 1611 and it started brewing cider in 1880. We continue our guided walk and on the 15th and 16th of July this year, the brewery will be represented at the 'Much Marcle Steam Rally' by its very own traction engine called Old Rosie. This is also the name to one of their strong ciders. Mike uncovers this marvellous machine and what a fantastic piece of engineering it is. Moving on to the gigantic vats made of two-inch thick English oak-butt and joint with cast iron strips around their girths. Mike says there are seventy-three of these altogether and the largest, called Squeak, holds 42,107 gallons.

The vats all have names like Oval, Darby and Wembley. Mike points out the name next to the Wembley vat. "It's called Hereford United and it's next to the Wembley one because that's as near as they will ever get to it."

I know nothing of how cider is made or stored so I hope Mike isn't making up stories. He tells us that the reason for the skylights being situated in the roof is it's the only way they can get the ladders into the vats when they need cleaning. Mike now shows us the more modern vats, which have metal strips around the girths. If they need either more or less tension, tightening the bolts can alter the strips. I'm finding the visit fascinating and Mike carries on explaining. Now, we go outside and there's a 1947 H. Weston and Sons delivery van and also a 150-year-old 'Bull Cart', the only one left in the world, which was used to take bulls to market. On the opposite side of the yard was an 1890 cider-making cart. Our tour continues across the forecourt to what from a distance looks like a bike shed. It turns out to be an extremely rare seventeenth-century bull lifter. Mike goes on to explain, "This is where the bull would walk in and be lifted by chains off the ground so its hooves could be inspected."

We personally think it's a BAT trap for lifting Oggy. A great contraption that we could use for getting his toenails clipped!

All of this walking has made us thirsty so Mike suggests a tasting session back in the small bar area. As we stroll back, there's an unusually shaped round house, made up of five trees with a small entrance where you duck under and, once inside, there are a couple of benches to sit on. This is amazing. We don't stop long here though as the thought of tasting some real scrumpy cider is getting the better of us. Back in the bar Mike shows us all the different ciders available. We all try the Vat 53, Top Line, Country cider, the Vintage, the Centenary Vintage, Extra Dry, a perry (made from pears) and finally we all buy a final flagon of Old Rosie. I can't think of a better way of finishing off every single pub in Herefordshire and Worcestershire. The hospitality we've received off Mike Ross has been a fitting tribute to our journey around these two great counties. In exchange, we all put some money in his wife's donkey sanctuary box and bid him good health and all the best in the future.

While driving home we discuss Oggy's idea of travelling around the entire coastline of mainland Great Britain. I said to all the lads, "Am we up for this challenge or what?"

"No problem mate, I'm ready," replied Leo.

"Without a doubt," says Oggy.

Drewy pipes up. "Doe leave me out, I'm coming n'all (as well)."

Well, it seems we are going ahead with this massive adventure but we'll give it a few weeks before we start so we can save some money. After our interesting and enjoyable trip we arrive home having competed 203 miles. Our tally of pubs stands at 2,308.

CHAPTER 14

OFFSPRING OF OFFA

Before our next adventure begins we spend three weeks travelling round Gloucestershire pubs. We visit the *Coalhouse* (Apperley). The River Severn flows past this pub and there is mooring for boats and a free ferry service during floods. 'Coalhouse steak on a stone' is licensees Barbara and Alan Butt's speciality dish. Next is the *Gloucester Old Spot* (Piffs Elm). This is named after a breed of pig. Inside here is a small cosy bar with a large copper jam boiler in the centre of the room. It also has an old grandfather clock; hops hang from the ceiling and there's lots of brass and copperware about the room. The *Boat* (Ashleworth) is a fairly difficult pub to find. Follow the sign to Ashleworth Quay and it lies at the end of a dead-end lane where parking is very limited. The River Severn runs past this lovely old pub. The Jelf families have been at the *Boat* for well over 300 years and on our visit the landlady Irene Jelf signs my book. She was actually born here in February 1916. For many years the pub was regularly flooded, until in 1981 when a flood defence bank was built.

At last, it's Saturday 27th May. It's a lovely sunny day as we start our three-day journey on the 'Welsh Wales Run'. It takes us three hours before we reach our first pub due to the volume of traffic on the roads. This is the *Red Lion* (Bonvilston), followed by a redbrick and stone-built pub the *Edmondes Arms* (Cowbridge). This is where the pub dog has his picture painted on a large red board outside the pub called 'Jack's Corner', because this is where he sits all the time to watch the world go by. I actually get a photo of him in his rightful position. The *Eastgate* (Cowbridge) is next, where a sign says 'Beware of the wife, the dog's okay'. The fourth pub is the *Master Brewer* (Cowbridge) known locally as the pink palace. Another five more pubs are visited in Cowbridge before travelling on to six other pubs: the *Pelican Inn* (Ogmore by Sea), the *Cornelly Arms* (Cornelly), the *Angel Inn* (Maudlam), the *Old House* (Llangynwyd) and the final two of the day the *Corner House* (Llangynuyd) and the *King Alfred* (Maesteg).

It's only 10 p.m. but we have to finish early tonight because my vision is going funny. I've got a migraine coming on and I haven't brought my tablets along. This is the first time this has happened to me while on a pub-crawl. We immediately have to find somewhere for me to sleep, as usually I've got twenty minutes before I'm sick and have a blinding headache that will put me out of action for twenty-four hours. If we find somewhere to sleep in time I might get away with it. Drewy drives to a campsite at Llanmadoc and this is where I intend to stop for the rest of the night. The lads also decide to call it a day and bed down too. I flake out straight away and I don't wake up at all until 5 a.m. I must have just caught my migraine in time, as I feel all right this morning. We all pack away our sleeping stuff and leave promptly because otherwise we might have to pay someone for the overnight camping we've just had.

With lots of time to spare on this Sunday morning, Drewy takes us on a sight-seeing tour past Kidwelly Castle and then to a fabulous place he calls the 'Lily Lakes' at Bosherton. What a peaceful and tranquil place this is. To appreciate the full effect of the thousands of water lilies that float on top of the lake, there's a narrow footbridge that you can walk across. After a while taking in this scenery, we go back to the cars and drive to St Govan's Chapel. I can't think of a better way to spend our time waiting for the pubs to open than this. It's a small disused old stone chapel overlooking the sea. To get to it you have to walk down many steep slippery stone steps. It's said that if you can count the exact number of steps going down to this chapel, on the way back up your count will be different. I have a go walking down, but after dozens of these steps I lose count and give up. I think next time I come I'll bring a calculator with me. It's a spooky little place inside this chapel and outside there are a few more steps to what looks like a Stone Age dog kennel. Watch out for the loose rocks and large boulders though. One slip and you could end up on your arse or bash your head in.

I'm really enjoying exploring this part of Wales as we travel on into Pembroke. There's still an hour before opening time so we pay £1.20 each into Pembroke Castle. One of the towers in this castle is called the Henry VII Tower and is reputed to be the birthplace in 1457 of Harri Tudur, the Welshman who became King Henry VII. This is definitely worth the money to get in but it helps if you're a scaffolder with the amount of climbing needed to get to the top of the Great Keep. But your effort is rewarded, as the view across the river and rooftops is spectacular. We climb down from the Keep and go underground into a large, rock-like cave. Drewy – who is a scaffolder – somehow manages to climb the stone wall in here up to a stone window ledge to prove his fitness. I just watch to prove mine! Oggy, meanwhile, is walking around the vintage cars and motorbikes on the castle courtyard. Well, with my wazzin as dry as Oggy's bath, we've had enough of historical places. The pubs are open, it's noon.

The first pub today is the *Moat House* (Pembroke). The gaffer David Clinch tells us the pub is actually built on the old moat of the castle and the rear wall of the pub is part of the original wall of the castle. Next is *Cromwell's* (Pembroke) followed by the *Hope Inn* (Pembridge) where you can eat a sandwich called 'Porky in a cabbage patch'. Three more pubs are visited in this town before we leave for the *Denant Mill Inn* (Dreenhill). This pub is nicely situated in a so-called 'lost world' valley. The gaffer's an Asian chap called Sydney, he's from Cambridge. The building dates back to the sixteenth century, when it was a purpose-built corn mill. The large waterwheel is the last surviving 'inside' water wheel left in Wales. A cosy television lounge adjoins the wheel. B&B at this pub for a single room is £12. Back in the motor we drive on to the *Masons Arms* (Dreenhill) where the first thing on our agenda is something to eat. We all have a ploughman's lunch except Oggy who asks for two ploughman's lunches. After he eats the first one he now asks the landlady for the other one. "You've had the two of them on the one plate," she said.

"Hang on a minute, the one I had was the same size as the one's the others had," replied an irate Oggy.

"Yes, but the cheese was thicker," was the answer off the landlady.

We all find this a total rip-off so decide to leave.

Then she says we haven't paid the full amount and wants another £4.80 of us. We have paid, but we don't intend to argue over it so Leo pays it again. The licensees of this pub have no hope of making a go in the pub trade so we leave without saying anything. Again dinner-time closing time forces us to go sight-seeing. Our journey takes us to Broad Haven where we sit and relax on a grass bank by the beach and we have forty winks in the glorious sunshine. After an hour or so we move on to another superb place called Solva. Somebody's pulled the plug out here this afternoon and all the small boats are stranded on the bottom of the seabed because the tide's gone out. We travel on to the smallest city in Great Britain 'St David's'. Here we have a tour around the cathedral – with its deafening bells ringing out – and then go into the abbey. It's close to opening time so we wait by the old cross in the middle of the square for the first pub to open. This is the *Old Cross Hotel* (St David's). Originally an eighteenth century house it was completely modernised and extended in 1959. Oggy and Drewy have a meal in here. Rainbow Trout costing £12 a head.

We now move on to the *Farmers Arms* (St David's) followed by *The Globe Inn* and *Black Fox Bar* (Upper Fishguard). The next one is the *Ship* (Lower Fishguard) which is a nautical gem with its low ceiling, nets hanging off the beams, old lantern lights, wood-cladded walls; barrel tables and fishermen memorabilia around the room. It's a short drive to the *Dinas Arms Hotel* (Lower Fishguard). Inside here is the jaw of a large swordfish on the wall. We continue our travels into an unusual pub called the *Dyffryn Arms* (Pontfaen). To get here we have to drive down small country lanes. An elderly lady keeps this pub and doesn't like you asking for a shandy. If you do ask you won't get one. The pub has a plain living room-style interior with a small serving hatch, a tiled floor, beige wallpaper, green-painted woodwork and a small wood settle. We leave this lovely unspoilt old pub and it's

10.15 p.m. before we arrive at our last pub of the night, the *Sailors Safety* near Dinas.

This pub is packed with local youths and drunks – we join the drunks. A cockney chap runs this pub and he serves overtime too. It's a nautical theme interior again with fishing memorabilia; nets and old wood tables. The gaffer buys us a drink and offers us the chance to sleep in his minibus. No thanks, as Oggy and me go outside at 2 a.m. to put all of our sleeping bags out on the beer garden overlooking the nearby sea. Watch out for hedgehogs! Then it's back in the pub for more beers. Drewy starts downing double whiskies when suddenly we hear a bang. I turn around and find Drewy passed out on the table. The gaffer comes over and jokingly says, "I said you could sleep in the minibus, not on my tables."

Leo and I carry Drewy out the pub and put him in his sleeping bag, before we go back in the pub for more drinks. The serving of alcohol goes on until 5 a.m. when the gaffer finally bangs his pub window from the outside with a pint glass and shouts, "It's a police raid everybody out!" This does the trick and eventually he calls closing time.

With two hours of lying on the grass it's not been much of a kip as we wake up at 7 a.m. on a damp morning. What sleep I did get wasn't spent listening to the tide coming in. We're not far away from the sea and ending up in Davy Jones's locker is not what I have planned. There's a large anchor outside this pub and a large snail crawling over Leo's forehead. Drewy's eyes this morning belong on top of cocktail sticks. Come to think of it so do mine. We push on and follow the coastline for breakfast at the railway station in Aberystwyth. Following our breakfast it's a long drive to Porthmadog. We arrive too early for a drink so we pop into Portmeirion. This is where they made the 1960s cult television show *The Prisoner*. The entrance fee is £1.95 each. This is the fantasy creation of Sir Clough Williams-Ellis who began work on this Italian theme village in 1925. Leo stands on top of a fish pond wall and shouts, "I am not a number, I'm a free fish!" to the astonishment of several tourists.

It's certainly an unusual place and I take a bit of stone as a souvenir. Drewy takes the bog roll out of the toilet for emergency reasons.

At last it's opening time so we shoot off in our motor. We get caught up in a traffic jam leading into Portmadog. Caused by a chap collecting 5p off every car driver at the private toll. Today's opening drink is in the *Ship & Castle* (Portmadog). We sit and listen to the locals talking away in Welsh. We then walk to our next pub the *Australia Arms* (Porthmadog). A short drive is then taken to three more pubs; the *Golden Fleece* (Tremadog), the *Union* (Tremadog) and the *Royal Madoc Hotel* (Tremadog). The *Goat* (Bryncir) is next and the gaffer tells us various celebrities have stopped off here including Ken Dodd. Also in the village is the *Bryncir Arms*. The gaffer here is a Brummie who had kept the *Roller's Arms* (Coseley) and his Black Country spaken (speaking) kids will now have to learn Welsh. Our next visit is to the *Quarryman's Arms* (Llanllyfni). The locals all speak Welsh and there's a large collection of quarrymen's tools on the walls. The *Alexandra Hotel* (Caernarfon) is where we stop for another beer. Again Welsh is spoken and I don't listen to them too much in here as the cricket is on the telly.

It's a drive now towards Anglesey and on to a very long named village called:

Llanfairpwllgwyngyllgogerychwyrndrobwllllantysiliogogogoch.

This means 'St Mary's church in a hollow by the white hazel close to the rapid whirlpool by the red cave of St Tysilio'. Here we visit two pubs the *Penrhos Arms* and the *Ty Gwyn Hotel*. Whilst in the latter named pub the local piss-taker tries his patter out on Oggy and insults him. The bloke meets his match though as Oggy replies, "I like sitting by yoe mate. Yoe mek me look handsome."

He doesn't stop there, as again Oggy hits back and says,

"You'll be all right mate in your right place, but it ay bin dug yet."

He then goes on to tell us everything he's done in his life and said there's a raft race taking place down the road. I couldn't help saying, "It's a wonder yoe ay in it mate, yoe've done everything else."

Well, this passes half an hour and by this time we're all laughing and joking, we eventually shake hands and leave.

Our next destination is the town of Beaumaris. Its name means 'beautiful marsh' and there's a smashing old castle here surrounded by a moat. This was the last of eight castles built in North Wales by Edward I. On arrival we go in the *White Lion Hotel* and after a relaxing drink in the pub we continue our adventure arriving at the *Bryn Tyrch Hotel* (Capel Carig). This hotel is set amid the magnificent scenery of the Snowdonia National Park. Accommodation is available and the proprietor is Rita Davis. Next, our thirst is satisfied at the *White Horse Inn* (Capel Garmon). Oggy gets a wooty (sulk) on him in here because the gaffer asked if we had visited 2,394 pubs today.

Oggy thinks this gaffer's being stupid and on leaving this pub he told him that we were going to visit another 1,000 pubs before 10 o' clock.

One more is visited. The *Foelas Arms Hotel* (Pentrefoglas). Then we're off to the 'Highest' pub in Wales the *Sportsmans Arms* (Bylcau, Denbigh Moor). We have a singalong to Level 42's hit single *'We're on the road to nowhere',* and going down the road to this pub it seems like we were. This pub is stuck out in the wilds. We all expected a traditional unspoilt pub but to our disappointment it's full of mealies (diners). But there is a dartboard and pool table. The gaffer's a decent bloke and buys us a pint apiece. Some chap shouts to Oggy, "Watch the beer towels!"

This is relating to our beer towel coats we've got on.

Oggy, who still hasn't cheered up any, asks him if knows something more original.

We drive on to the *Queens Head* (Cerrigydrudion), the *Goat* (Maerdy) and the *Bull* (Llangollen). In the latter pub Oggy yaps to a local wench and some of the local lads are getting upset at this, so we have a quick drink apiece and leave. We have one more pub on our list. The *Ponsonby Arms* (Llangollen) and this ends our travels around Wales. All in all it's been a good trip and we arrive home at midnight.

After last week's run we start visiting Gloucestershire pubs again. Continuing our tour around this county we visit an interesting pub, the *Royal Oak* (Greeton). The gaffer Bob Willison gives me a clocking-in card – the sort used by factory workers to clock in. I put it in the clock for proof of our visit and I get it stamped 4.18 p.m. The actual time is 10.15 p.m. The clock's stopped. There are a few more pubs of interest. The *Royal Oak* (Prestbury), where the gaffer gives us a white crock jug each. These are used for drinking cider and this gift upsets his locals because they never get anything given them and they've always thought the gaffer was a tight git. The *Plough* (Prestbury) is opposite the church. It has a thatched roof and the beer is served out of barrels behind the bar. It has a small cosy lounge and an old grandfather clock. We're told the *Plaisterer's Arms* (Winchcombe) is the only pub in England allowed to fly the coat of arms for the Plaisterers (Plasterers). It's also the only one spelt with the letter (I) in it after James I visited this pub and spelt it the Scottish way. This is mainly a pub for bikers with a group called the 'Dark Horses' playing here tomorrow night.

It's my thirty-third birthday in two days time and I fancy going somewhere different. So this Sunday 18th June 1989 my old pal Drewy drives to Oxfordshire and Buckinghamshire. We arrive at our first pub the *Jolly Weavers* (Banbury). Oggy yaps to a bloke at the bar about his National Service days. He tells him about when two American servicemen who were stationed in Banbury got beat-up and died. The local bloke said his dad remembers that incident too. Another chap in here walks over to us and thinks we are Dutchmen. Later on in the *Angel* (Bicester) we again get mistaken for Dutch. Well, we have been known to talk double-Dutch but our Black Country accent is certainly stumping them tonight. Wearing our wooden clogs didn't help either. We finish tonight's pubs in Buckingham. Nine pubs have been visited and we haven't had one good drink. A bit of a dumpy tour and we've travelled 174 miles to find that out.

The BATS are ready for their next weekend out and Dawn's tagging along too. It's Saturday 24th June 1989. We're off to the county of Shropshire. We visit thirteen pubs today with the most memorable one being the *Stables Inn* (Craven Arms). This is opposite the cattle market and we are told that until September 1988 one half of the pub was a fish and chip shop and the other half an antique shop. Leo said, "That's why I can smell chips in here and Oggy must be the antique."

Two good pubs where you can pitch your caravan or tent are the *Kangaroo* (Aston-on-Clun) and the *Engine and Tender* (Broome). Then there's a lovely old fifteenth-century listed building called the *Sun Inn* (Clun). This is owned, lived in and run by Keith and Bunny Small.

The thirteenth and last pub is the *Red Lion* (Llanfair Waterdine). This pub is in the middle of the Teme Valley and the River Teme runs just below the garden and is the border of England and Wales. The *Red Lion* has a lounge bar and taproom both heavily beamed with inglenook fireplaces. B& B is available. Your hosts are Diane and Ben Owen and they organise a breakfast for all of us. Leaving this welcoming pub we cross the road and bed down for the night on a comfy flat piece of grass.

We rise in the morning to the rays of the sun and in beautiful surroundings. Ben the landlord calls us in for our breakfast. After eating this I have a walk over to the river where I see lots of trout at least two feet long. The view in the distance is magnificent with hills and wild untouched countryside. The pub is host to at least twelve nesting house martins. Not far from here is Offa's Dyke, an old earthwork built by the Anglo-Saxon King Offa in the eighth century to repel the invading Welsh. This ran from the River Dee in North Wales to the River Wye in the south. The Offa's Dyke National Trail is 177 miles long. I've never seen this before so I must make an effort to find it. It's a real bumpy road but eventually we find this ancient earthwork. To get to it we have to jump over a fence. Dawn loses her gold earring posing for a photo on top of this bonk (bank) so if anyone finds it in the future, let me know. The large earthen mounds are now covered in grass and you would never think that it was ever a form of defence. Today it is only a defence for the numerous sheep that shelter from the wind. Leo and myself take a bit of rock as a souvenir. I've got a few historical pieces of rock or stone in my collection and this will help to build it up a little quicker. This is a place I shall never forget. You just have to let your imagination drift back to the days of the Saxons. We are, after all, offspring of Offa.

We take a steady ride into Bishops Castle. On arrival be prepared to walk up a steep High Street or down depending where you park your car. There are seven pubs in this town. We start at the top of the hill in the most famous of these, the *Three Tuns,* which brews its own beer. The *Castle Hotel,* the *Black Lion,* the *Crown and Anchor Vaults* and the *Kings Head* follow this. Then it's a short walk to the *Boars Head.* This was granted its first full license in 1642, but the building pre-dates this. Your hosts are Ann and Peter Smith and B&B is £12.50 for a single room. The final pub in the town is at the bottom of the hill, the *Six Bells,* an ex-Davenports alehouse. Moving on, we enter the *Powis Arms* (Lydbury North). They have no cider, no Old Rosie, no Guinness. Only Ansell's keg beer and this is vile. Dawn says the bogs are riffy and there's a fat Doberman dog roaming round scrounging salty scratchings off any local who will kindly feed it. Our last pub for this weekend's tour is the *Sun* (Corfton). This is a cracking old pub with a decent drink of Wood's Parish bitter and an old bar room where we play pool. A great pub to finish in before our drive home.

I was wondering where in Shropshire they brew Wood's Parish bitter and during the week I find out. Obviously, a trip is organised straight away to the *Plough* (Wistanstow). On arrival we find the pub a real let-down. There are signs saying, 'shirts must be worn' and 'no children under the age of fourteen after so-and-so hour.' The lounge is mainly a restaurant and the gaffer's not too jolly either. It's a good job the beer was okay.

In my local *Express* and *Star* newspaper I spot an article about a chap called Michael Knights, of the Burton Heritage Brewery Museum. He will lead a three-hour pub-crawl on Saturday 8th July around Lichfield in Staffordshire. I cut his picture out of the paper and I hope to meet him because this is going to be our next adventure. The meeting point for this tour around Lichfield is the *King's Head.* In here I meet up with Michael Knights and I get him to autograph his picture.

It's jam-packed all around this town tonight and I find out the reason why. It happens to be the town's yearly festival. We follow Mr Knights to the *George Hotel*, which he tells us is an early eighteenth-century building. There's too much talking about the history of Lichfield for our liking so we shoot off to the *Earl of Lichfield* nicknamed the *Drum* and to the *Scales Inn,* an old M&B pub with a barbecue in the passageway. In the following pub, the *George IV* we bump into Michael Knight's crew. He gives me his number to ring him up for a free visit to the Burton Heritage Museum. Meanwhile Oggy and Leo have fallen in love with two local wenches and have disappeared. One hour later after visiting the *Prince of Wales,* the *Fountain* and the *Greyhound* they finally turn up on their own. This town is really buzzing and there are quite a lot of women about. I'll have to behave and keep my eyes on something else because Dawn's keeping her eyes on me. The final boozer before heading home is the *Duke of Wellington.* A chap in here called Alec tells me Lichfield was known as the 3 P's years ago: Priests, Pubs and Prostitutes.

Shropshire beckons again for the next couple of weeks. The *Ragleth Inn* (Little Stretton), nestling at the foot of the Long Mynd mountain (which rises to almost 1,700ft) dates back to 1663. It has two bars, a restaurant with oak beams, inglenook fireplaces and antiques. The beer garden has a rare tulip tree. Outside, in an adjacent field is a large ten feet high rotten tree trunk that resembles the shape of a dog's bone. Leo wonders how big the dog is!

In another pub, the *Green Dragon* (Little Stretton), I meet a chap called Joe Lawless. He's the editor of the CAMRA *Cheshire Ales* book. We have a chat about CAMRA and one day, when I've got time on my hands, I will look into this organisation more deeply. But until then I'm still supping. Joe says I can have this book if I buy him half a pint of Woods Parish bitter. I oblige.

At the *Swan* (Aston Munslow) the conversation was quite varied. I walk in and yap to some friendly old chaps who tell me that their mate named Fred Jordan (who is a folk singer) has just had the BBC visit him and they're chuffed to bits about this. Oggy walks in and the gaffer shouts to him, "You come to taste my beer then?"

Oggy gets his beer and replied, "Ar, but I didn't expect to pay £1.05 a pint for it!"

At this the pub goes quiet. I order my beer and the gaffer asks who the cheeky bloke is.

I tell him that Oggy's on the dole and can't afford too much. "Well, it's about time he got a job then," the gaffer commented.

On the other side of the room Leo chats up this local wench. Oggy again can't keep his gob shut and shouts over to them, "I wouldn't mess with him cocker, he's at the VD clinic next week!"

With 2,489 pubs done and dusted we discuss what to do when we reach our 3,000th pub. This we want to be something special. I have an idea. So, with my camera I go and take shots of the *Bottle and Glass* pub in the Black Country Museum. I work as a maintenance engineer, so I've decided I'll make a scale model wall plaque of the pub out of various types of metals. I get down to work on this project as soon as I can. Working ten-hour nights comes in very handy indeed. Between jobs, I've estimated this model will take me approximately six months to complete. This means I'll be running around like a blue-arsed fly, looking for copper, brass and anything else that will make this a unique piece of work. Will it be a challenge too far? I hope not because presenting my work of art to the museum would make the 3,000th pub memorable indeed.

CHAPTER 15

WE ARE EMMETS

It's Saturday 22nd July, and we have decided to go on a seven-day trip around the Cornish coastline. Our tour doesn't start on time due to Oggy not being ready. He's stopped up half the night to watch Mike Tyson win his heavyweight fight in ninety-four seconds. Eventually we start our journey and Oggy immediately starts on his allotment sandwiches. I think he's got all the vegetables available to the human race on these and he's making a right mess in the car. After a trip of 156 miles we need a break so we stop at our first pub the *Castle Hotel*. This is situated in the picturesque coastal village of Porlock. Inside are two pool tables and dartboard. B&B is £13.50 per person. Not far away is the *Anchor Hotel & Ship Inn* (Porlock Weir). This pub is a combination of the nineteenth-century *Anchor Hotel* and the sixteenth-century *Ship Inn*. Make sure your car is in tiptop condition around this area because you have to negotiate a road with a gradient of 1-in-4 called Porlock Hill. We continue our travels to our 2,500th pub the *Rising Sun Hotel* (Lynmouth). An historic fourteenth-century thatched smuggler's inn with an oak-panelled dining room and bar. Accommodation is available and the hotel overlooks the harbour.

It's a smashing hot summer's day as we drive on towards Cornwall. We stop at our next pub the *Hoops Inn* (Horns Cross). A thatched pub with massive white cob walls that stands 500 feet above sea level, it is believed to date from the thirteenth-century. Onto the last pub in Devon called the *West Country Inn* (near the border with Cornwall), where there's a boar's head on the wall. It was killed on 9th

December 1924. Hooray! We've crossed the border into Cornwall. The *Crooklets* (Bude) is visited. It's in Bude, where we have horrible fish and chips. The appropriately named pub, the *King Arthur's Arms* (Tintagel) is next. We nip down to see the castle ruins. Tradition says Tintagel was the seat of King Arthur and his knights, but it's not up to much and we're told the ruins only date from about the twelfth century. So off we go to a busy pub, the *Port William Inn* (Trebarwith Strand). It's hard to park your motor here but it is worth it if you can because you can sit outside on the benches that overlook the sea. Adjacent to this pub is a six-berth caravan for hire. We think about spending the night here but it's too early in the day to commit.

Our ale adventure takes us into the *Bettle and Chisel* (Delabole) and then on to the *Port Gaverne Hotel* (Port Gaverne). This is an early seventeenth-century inn and is situated on a cove half a mile from Port Isaac. Freddie and Midge Ross are in their twenty-first year as resident proprietors of this hotel. Our eleventh pub visit of the day is the *Cornish Arms* (Pendoggett). I have a lovely postcard of the pub given to me that shows the outside walls covered in ivy. I ask why all the ivy has now gone and I'm told it is due to the roots of the ivy working their way into the brickwork and beginning to pull the walls down. The outside appearance now looks completely different from the postcard. We drive to three more pubs the *Mariners* (Rock), the *Bridge of Wool* (Wadebidge) and the *Old Custom House* (Padstow). Slowing down a little, we arrive at the *Harlyn Inn* (Harlyn Bay). What a lively pub this is and it's packed out with young women! One of them buys me a brandy. We can't stop too long we've got a mission to complete, but don't get roaming off across the beach at Harlyn at night because there's dangerous sands about. Heading off to our next port of call we find the *Falcon Inn* (St Mawgen). This pub is a sixteenth-century inn situated in the wooded vale of Lanherne and opposite the church. We consider kipping in the graveyard but it's too open and in view of passing pedestrians. Then two pubs in St Columb are visited before finally relaxing at our 17th alehouse of the day the *Pen-y-Morfa Inn* (St Mawgan). This is a modern country hotel with an outdoor swimming pool. But better still there's a lovely field to sleep on and we're told we can if we want. One of the licensees tells us to knock the door in the morning for a breakfast. What a stroke of luck this is, so we jump the small wall and, on a warm quiet night and after all the day's drinking, we all nod off.

On a sunny Sunday morning we're woken up by the sound of dozens of caw-cawing crows. Bloody things! Mind you, the view as I wake up is magnificent and I make a sketch of this and send it to Dawn by post. Well, it is something to do while we wait for our breakfast. At 9.30 a.m. the door opens and our breakfast is well worth the money. Today's run starts at the *Tudor House* (Newquay). Our second pub is the *Seagull* (Crantock), followed by the *Old Albion* (Crantock). This one is a thatched roof sixteenth-century building and named after HMS Albion. (Up the Baggies!) We meet a family in here from our street back home who are all having a meal. It's amazing what folk you can bump into. Again our tour must move on and this time it's to another thatched boozer that sells its own hand made pottery, the low-beamed pub called the *Treguth* (Holywell).

It's a drive into Perranporth (which takes its name from St Piran, the patron saint of tin miners) and into the *Perranporth Inn*. The next supping house is the *Green Parrot*, where a sign on the wall reads, 'It's not how deep you fish, it's how you wriggle your worm.' The *Tywarnhayle Inn* follows. Oggy and Leo sit on the wall overlooking the Perran beach, watching all the girls go by. Leo spots massive tits sitting on a horse. Drewy and myself decide to go for a swim in the sea. I take a bar of soap and the idea is to have a wash in it. The only problem is I can't get the soap to lather up. We enjoy the swim anyway and then walk over to the public toilets to dry off and have a swill in the sinks. While I'm here I use the bog and I overhear two Cornish locals yapping to each other about all the 'emmets' invading Cornwall and drinking all their water. I can't make out exactly what this conversation is about and think nothing of it.

We fancy a trip to the Gwennap Pit, an historical amphitheatre we've heard about. This is where the founder of Methodism, John Wesley (1703-91) preached. This is a fabulous thing to see and it's while sitting down admiring this pit that a coach-load of English tourists arrive and we overhear a Cornish woman with her two kids say, "Come on kids, the 'emmets' have arrived, they drink all our water and we have to go on rations."

I'm curious now and I have to go over and ask her what she means. She tells me all English are 'emmets.' It means ants! "Well, yoe'm English," I replied.

"No, I'm Cornish," she quickly stated.

What a load of crap, I'm a Black Country bloke but I'm still English. So after all his preaching to the people of Cornwall, poor old John Wesley was an emmet. Leo jigs about yelling like a town crier:

We are emmets! We are emmets!

Back to the pit. This is a very large circled whirlpool-type design with 13 circles of grass steps down to the bottom. If you walk around the circumference, people say it's a mile by the time you reach the bottom. I have a go and upon finishing I sit down and cross my legs as they no longer want to work. Coming back up though is easy because I just step up to the top in one straight line. All this walking has made my wazzin call out for hopped water!

It finally gets its wish in the *Miners Arms* (Mithian). The date of 1577 is carved into one of the ceilings. Is this the date it was built? It has a few paintings from the Elizabethan era on the walls and in the small spooky cellar room is a large landscape painting of copper and tin mines. I'm told a chap painted these in the 1950s. We journey on into St Agnes to *Bad Harry's* and the *Peterville Inn*. The other pub in the village is on the way to the beach and is called the *Driftwood Spars*. Inside this pub is a breathalyser machine that costs 50p a go. With a plastic straw you have to blow into the machine. This records the units of alcohol on your breath. Thirty-five units are the limit. Mine registers at 103, Leo's at 114 and Oggy's is ninety-one. Drewy's is zero as he's driving today. After a bag of cheese and onion crisps mine drops down to 91. Leo's next go is quite funny. He's blowing really hard for a while and he's turning white and nothing is happening. Oggy starts laughing and tells him he hasn't put the 50p in.

Leaving St Agnes we arrive at the *Bucket of Blood* (Phillack).

This got its name from when the Innkeeper some 200 years ago went to his deep well (the only source of water for the inn) and drawing a bucket from the well, pulled up not water, but blood. A search found a badly mutilated corpse. Somewhere around the reign of King George III the name changed to the *New Inn* and it wasn't until 1980 that it changed back to its original name. The pub itself has a very low ceiling and a nice-looking barmaid. A few miles further south we reach the town of St Ives. This is a smashing and bustling place but everywhere is packed including the three pubs we visit, the *Lifeboat*, the *Castle* and the *Union*. The chance of a good night's kip around here is none.

We take the road south again for a few miles arriving at the *Tinners Arms* (Zennor). This is an isolated pub situated by a twelfth-century church. Zennor is a tiny ancient stone village with lots of history. The 'Mermaid's Chair' in the church is thought to be 600 years old. According to local legend, the Mermaid of Zennor for generations tempted unwary lads to follow her to a watery grave. It's also the place the author D. H. Lawrence came in 1916 with his German wife during the First World War, but they were ordered to leave on suspicion of being spies. The village, due to the cholera epidemic in Cornwall (1832-1849), also has a 'Plague Stone'. The depression in the centre of the stone was filled with vinegar. Money that changed hands between villagers and outsiders would be placed in the vinegar and thus be disinfected. Well, the pub itself isn't much to write about. We just manage a last drink before the strict gaffer calls time at 10.30 p.m. As there's no chance of an overtime drink we get our sleeping clobber out and settle down in the graveyard. I'm certainly expecting a quiet night but a yapping Yorkshire terrier interrupts it along with lots of bo-bo flies (our new word for midges), the smell of cow shit and a purring white cat. Drewy says that if he'd got a can of red paint he'd paint the cross of St George on it. The white cat stands guard looking over us all night.

I wake up at 7.30 a.m. on a lovely Monday morning and I spy with my little eye something beginning with 'C'. The white cat is still there but by the time I wake the others, it's gone. We follow the coast road towards the little town of St Just. On the way Leo spots two cows having a fight and said, "So that's how they churn the milk to make yoghurt."

Just before reaching St Just we take a minor road to the headland site of Pendeen Lighthouse. Leo nicknames this lighthouse Stumpy due to it being a short, phallic-shaped building. It's only a short drive now to our destination, the delightful granite-built town of St Just. No pubs are open for beer at the moment, but the *Commercial Hot*el is open for breakfast. Sitting in the modern clean conservatory we all eat our fittle (food). After a drink of ale we leave for the nearby *Star Inn*. Real Ale from the wood is their speciality so we have a pint of St Austell bitter. It's a lovely interior with a piano and the wood-plank walls are decorated with a display case of stones and rocks and a replica of a large old ship. Accommodation is also available. Moving on to another in the town, we go in the *Wellington*. I get yapping to an old bloke at the bar about pubs. He tells me the local nickname for the *Star Inn* is the Wacky Backy or the Happy Valley. The fourth pub in town is the *Kings Arms*. The local bikers use this pub and again beer is served out of barrels. I now nip out to the shop to buy me some 'After-sun Cream' because I've got sunburnt from yesterday's swim in the sea. I'm as red as a baboon's bum. Our final visit in St Just, before heading further south, is the *Miners Arms*. A chap in the bar tells me about the 'Wink.'

He said, "People in the old days wasn't allowed to ask for a drink of spirits, but a 'Wink' to the landlord and you could get one."

I've not heard of this before and I don't really understand why this was. No matter, it's conversation isn't it?

He also tells me about a white cat that haunts the churchyard in Zennor. I can't believe this. He must be pulling my pisser.

Leaving this pleasant town, our journey continues to the seventeenth-century *Old Success Inn* (Sennen Cove). King Arthur is said to have defeated the Danes at Sennen in the great battle of Vellan-Drucher. No, I've never heard of it either but it's nice to learn about things. Beside the pub is Whitesand Bay's excellent beach where there's a cracking view out to sea. Our next two pubs are the *Radjel*

Inn (Pendeen) and the *Trewellard Hotel* (Trewellard). In this *hotel*, Leo falls in love with the barmaid who's from Bromsgrove. She refuses to tell him her name, but he said he'd like to give her one anyway and he can't take his eyes off the lumps in her T-shirt. The landlord tells us this place is haunted. Leo said, "It's not now mate, Oggy's frightened it off."

The barmaid then says to Leo that her name is Sarah Jane Hodgkinson Bottomley. Leo doesn't believe a word of it, and we leave. Mind you, with a name like that, I think I'd need two tongues to say it! After getting back on course we arrive at the *First and Last Inn* (Sennen) for a pint of Wadworth 6X. We're all getting rather clammed (hungry) and decide that in the next pub we'll have something to eat. The *Wreckers Inn* (Sennen) is the one we come to first. This is situated in thirty-three acres of its own grounds set in the majestic splendour of the Land's End Peninsula. Our meals of steak pie and chips satisfy our appetites and are swilled down with a pint apiece.

It's only three quarters of a mile to Land's End and it's £4 to get in. I turn the car around and reverse down the road until Leo notices a gated field. Oggy jumps out and opens the gate. I then drive across this bumpy field and park up out of sight of prying eyes. The only obstacle we have to conquer now is a small wall. This is easily done and we all get in for nothing. Our walk takes us to the tourist signpost where you can have your photo taken with the name of the town you live in and how many miles it is from Land's End. Obviously this costs money and ours is better spent on beer. We do however take our own photos with the date reading 24th July 1989 and 874 miles to John O' Groats. Nearby is the *State House Hotel,* the first and last hotel in England. A double room per person costs from £30 to £45 per day. It says in the brochure a glimpse from the windows or a view from the all-glass observatory restaurant and you are instantly confronted with that great panorama of land, sea and sky that is the very essence of this historic and awe-inspiring coastline. It's all a bit posh and too clean and you must wear a shirt. So we get our drink and sit on the rocks outside overlooking the sea. Leo falls in love with Long John Silver, the one-legged seagull, as it hops over to him as he tries to feed it crisps. I jump the wall back to the car and the others open the gate for me. The ticket collector spots us and shouts us back. Alas, the car carries on and Land's End becomes a memory.

Not too many miles away along the coastal road is the *Logan Rock Inn* (Treen); an old, unspoilt pub and a National Trust property. Peter and Anita George are the proprietors. Nearby is a secluded beach and the famous Logan Rock, a rocking stone weighing over sixty tons from which the pub derives its name. The pub sign is double headed. On one side it shows a chap beginning to push one of the stones off Logan Rock onto the beach below and on the opposite it shows him succeeding. This is because, according to Cornish folklore, in 1824, a Naval Lieutenant shoved a stone off in that year and at his own expense was forced by the locals to replace it. We leave this pub behind us now, heading for the Merry Maidens. This is a stone circle with around seventeen stones, each roughly three feet high and making up a circle of about fifty feet in diameter. I pose for a photograph sitting on one of the stones. Drewy said they should rename them after me the Merry Bachelor. Well, so much for our visit to a bit of English history. I need a wazzin wash.

From this historical site we carry on and have a quick drink in the *St Buryan Inn* (St Buryan), the *Lamorna Cove* (Lamorna) and the *Lamorna Wink* (Lamorna). The quaint little harbour village of Mousehole (pronounced something like Mowzel) is next. Here we visit the *Ship Inn*. The gaffer gives me my drink in a woman's glass – the ones with a glass stem. This is awkward to hold so I ask him for a straight glass. He says, "Why, isn't it macho enough for you?"

Then he spills most of my drink over the bar counter. I personally think this bloke needs a smack of the gob so we drink up, leave this rat-hole and say our goodbye to Mousehole. We continue our journey into the *Falmouth Packet* (Rosudgeon) and then on to the *Harbour Inn* (Porthleven). Also, in the small village of Porthleven and right by the sea overlooking the harbour is *the Ship Inn*. This is a smashing pub where we have a loff (laugh) with the Brummie barmaid and down pints of Beamish stout. I'm told there's a pub almost on the beach about five miles back along the A394 at Praa Sands. This could be an ideal spot to rest our heads for the night.

After taking the road to Praa Sands we go in the *Welloe Rock Inn*. It's as they say, the inn just out of the sea. They are not far wrong either. The pub is more of a caravan site's clubroom and is only a few yards from the sea. Our drinking session finishes in here at 12.30 a.m. Sleeping on the beach is a no-go as we're not sure how far the tide will come in tonight and the thought of drowning in salt water puts us all off the idea. We leave this place and drive for a couple of miles and find an isolated farmer's field to sleep in. But after lying in the long grass we're being attacked by too many bo-bo flies (midges) and again we are forced to drive on. Eventually we find a picnic area just off the main A394 road and whatever happens we decide that this is it for tonight. I open the back door and on doing so Leo, who has now passed out, falls backwards out of the car. His head hits the floor and his legs are still in the car. This revives him a little and all we got out of Leo was, "Did my parachute open?"

I wake up frequently through the night because of the noise the passing traffic makes. Finally we all get up at 9.10 a.m. It's Tuesday 25th July and yet again it's a fabulous sunny morning. The first thing I notice when I opened my eyes this morning is one of the wheel nuts is missing off my car. Leo is still pissed and starts singing, "Three nuts on our wagon and we're still rolling along."

I then make the mistake of asking him where his sunglasses are. What a plonker I am, as I now have to drive five miles back to the field we first tried to sleep in last night because he thinks he's left them there. He had as well. We go into Penzance for our breakfast and to buy a wheel nut.

Leaving this town behind, it's off to one of only four home-brew pubs left in Great Britain in the 1970s, the *Blue Anchor* (Helston). This pub started life as a monks' Rest House circa 1400, when the monasteries were dissolved it became a village tavern. Spingo is the name of their brew so we all have a pint each. The manager's name is Mr A. D. Brown and he shows us around his pub. There's a skittle alley out back that was originally built in the eighteenth century. In 1880, a man living in Chapel Opening, after a row with his wife, hung himself from a beam by the entrance door. The skittle alley was used as a stable from 1930, but in 1937 it was re-floored and re-opened for play. After the War it remained in use until 1960 when it fell into disrepair and served only as a storehouse. Today it's again re-opened and you can enjoy a bostin (great) game of wood skittles. It's hard to get the gaffer to raise a smile this morning so I buy a small ceramic *Blue Anchor* plaque for my wall at home for £10. This seems to do the trick and it's certainly cheers him up. From the *Blue Anchor* and just a short walk away is the *Fitzsimmons Arms* (Helston). This is named after Bob Fitsimmons, the last English heavyweight champion of the World (1897-99) who was born in this town. The pub sign shows him in fighting pose. Inside it has recently been refurbished with the history of boxers around the room.

The road from Helston takes us to the *Halzephron Inn* (Gunwalloe). This overlooks the sea and was built in 1468. A few miles down the road is the village of Mullion and here we visit some other pubs. The *Mounts Bay Inn*, the *Old Inn* and the *Gull and Crossbones*. Our next pub is the Lizard Centre where we talk to the gaffer about historical sites. He says he knows an historical site – his 'mother-in-law.' His missus overhears him say this and isn't too happy about it. At this I think it's time to go. We arrive at the Lizard and go to England's most southerly café to buy a bag of crisps. To swill the bits of crisps out of my mouth we go in the *Top House* (The Lizard) for a drink. Just down the road from here we visit Lizard Point and the twin towers of its lighthouse, completed in 1751. It's fittle time so we stop around the Lizard and purchase fish and chips.

The only way is up from here. So it's back to the car as we continue our journey to the *New Inn* (Manaccan). A superb unspoilt thatched pub. There are no hand pulls in here and your beer comes straight out of one of the six barrels at the back of the bar. Not far away is our tenth pub of the day. Situated in a lovely setting by the river it's called the *Shipwright Arms* (Helford Village) and was built in the eighteenth century. It's hard to park by this pub and John (Reginald Molehusband) Drew tries a fifteen-point turn in the car and almost knocks two dozen breezeblocks in the river. Our route takes us to five more pubs; the *Old Courthouse* (Mawgan) which was called the *Ship* until recently; the *Black Swan* (Gweek) another pub that has recently changed its name, it was called the *Gweek*; the *Trengilly Wartha* (Nancenoy, Constantine) the pub name I'm told means 'settle above the tree, the *Queens Arms* (Constantine) where as we walk in here the gaffer shouts out, "The English are in."

"We're Welsh mate." I replied.

On the ceiling hang lots of hats. I can't see one big enough for this gaffer. The last of the five is the *Ferryboat* (Helford Passage). A chap in here says all English tourists in Cornwall who own a boat are yellow-wellied Wally's. How's bollocks sound mate! We drink up and leave.

Our planned finish for the night is in the *Red Lion* (Mawnan Smith). The main reason for finishing in this village is it has a cricket pavilion and this will be an ideal place to sleep. In the pub though we get talking to a copper named Andy. His local is the *Plough* (Grimsargh) which is near Preston and he asks us to come up for a drink one day. Oggy tells us about one of his stories when he came down here a few years back with his friend Les Griffin. He tells us that he and Les were both standing at the bar when a local wench came up to him and said, "Do you know you've got a face like Cornish granite."

"It's more like crazy paving," replied Les.

The wench then hit Griffin around the head with her handbag, said Oggy.

It's been a tiring day and supping the last drops of ale from our glasses it's off to the cricket pavilion. It starts to rain during the night but there's a slight overhang of the roof and, as we're all in one long single row underneath it, the rain just misses us.

It's Wednesday morning; it's cloudy and we're woken up early by a bunch of wild wacky wasps. It's just our luck that their nest is in the pavilion and we are under attack. Oggy jumps in the car and immediately jumps back out as they follow him in there. After a few minutes of wafting them away we quickly put our sleeping clobber in the boot and shoot off to a safer haven. This happens to be a café in

Falmouth where we get breakfast. We notice that Oggy's belly is expanding to a size never seen before. All the booze and fittle I think and even Gert Bucket would be proud! (She's the massive fat lady who appears in the *Daily Sport* newspaper).

It's not far now to the first pub on day six, the *Pandora Inn* (Restronguet Creek). This is a fabulous thatched pub down a rather steep road that overlooks a small harbour. It was called the *Ship* many years ago and the inn was renamed in memory of *HMS Pandora*, the naval ship sent to Tahiti to capture the mutineers of Captain Bligh's ship *the Bounty*. Unfortunately *HMS Pandora* struck a remote part of the Great Barrier Reef in 1791 and sank with the loss of many crew and mutineers. The captain, Captain Edwards, was court-martialled on his return and retired to Cornwall where he bought this inn. The interior has three bars, serving four real ales, flagstone floors, low-beamed ceilings and gleaming brass work. Outside is a massive anchor imbedded in the ground and lots of bloody wasps.

From this pub we carry on to Trelissick for a very short ferry crossing costing £1.40 (We're heading for St Mawes). This is fantastic value because using the road to get to St Mawes would have been a drive of over twenty miles. Back on terra firma we pick up the B3289 towards our destination and on arrival we find the *St Mawes Hotel* a seventeenth-century seafront hotel. It's been carefully modernised by Juliet and Clifford Burrows who bought it several years ago after a career with ICI in India. We find it an expensive hotel with a plain interior serving keg beer and it's hard to park the car. The *Victory Inn* (St Mawes) is our next alehouse. This pub has records going back to 1792. The welcome in here is as welcome as having a boil on your arse. The gaffer is not interested at all when I tell him what we're doing and the locals yet again bore us by going on about the English. Just a few miles away is the *New Inn* (Veryan). Hopefully here we might receive a better welcome than the last two pubs. The village is certainly welcoming. It has five tiny, whitewashed, circular cottages all with a cross on top, which date back to the early nineteenth-century. These were made round to be 'Devil-proof' – for in a house without corners, Satan has nowhere to hide. We're all hoping he isn't hiding in the pub disguised as the gaffer. Happily he's not and we receive a friendly welcome from the licensees John and Sarah Dandy. Accommodation is available in this cosy pub with stone walls and lots of small brasses on the ceiling beams. The *Ship* (Portloe) is our next visit. Oggy and I nip to the bogs for a widdle and I find a daddy-long-leg and throw it at him. This makes him widdle down his trouser leg and he doesn't see the funny side of it and calls me all the names under the sun.

A few miles round the coast from Portloe we arrive at the *Llawnroc Hotel* (Gorran Haven). Ideally situated it overlooks the picturesque village and bay of Gorran Haven. All rooms at this hotel face the sea. Three miles up the road is the fishing village of Mevagissey. Whilst here watch out for tourists as most of them walk in the quite narrow roads and could end up as hedgehogs. The first pub we come to is the *Kings Arms*. On entry a group of locals are sitting by the bar, one of them said to Oggy, "What's this gibberish on this card of yours?"

"It's proper English," replied Oggy, who has now had enough of all the 'piss taking' off some of the Cornish locals and storms out of the pub.

"What's up with him?" said another local.

"It's yoe lot going on about not being English all the time." I replied.

"Well, we're Cornishmen and British, we're not English. We were the first race on this island and we speak the proper English," mouthed the same local chap.

His astonished mate then said to him, "I'd never believe you'd admit to speaking English."

At this we leave and jump in the car and head northwards. We did intend to visit Fowey, Polperro and Looe but quite frankly we've had enough of the same old quips day after day. So we decide after today we will spend the remainder of our holiday in Devon.

We slowly work our way north stopping in the town of Liskeard. On arrival there's lots of police about due to thousands of New Age travellers arriving in the area for a pop concert. One wench we see is pushing a baby in a pushchair that looks like it's come off the tip. She has a Mohican haircut, wears Doc Marten's and definitely needs a good wash. She's almost as black as we are. To get out of their way we nip in the *White Horse* for a quick pint and as we've arrived in this town on the wrong day we make up our minds to move on. The welcome in our next pub isn't too friendly either. As we enter the *Victoria* (Pensilva), the gaffer says, "This is a drinker's pub."

I wish he'd told the beer because it's crap. A local comes up to Oggy and asks him to move, as they want to play dominoes. It doesn't seem to be our day!

Our adventure now takes us to the *Crows Nest* (Crows Nest). What a superb old pub I think, as the landlady serves us our drinks and a meal apiece. The only problem is this causes an argument between her and her husband because he thinks we're New Age Travellers and he wants us out of his pub. I explain who we are and what we're doing and this calms him down a bit. But it doesn't stop him putting a large sign outside the door saying 'No Hippies allowed!' What a day we're having! Anyway the interior of this pub has lots of horse stirrups hanging off the ceiling beams, wood settles and stone walls. There's also a painting on the wall of a local bloke, eighty-two-year-old Bill and a brass plaque where 'Shiner' sits. He's ninety and still uses the pub. On leaving the pub the gaffer comes over and apologises, which is a nice gesture.

There is now a short drive down a country road to the *Cheesewring Hotel* (Minions). This gets its name from a nearby pile of large stones that look like they have been put on top of each other. A small stone model of this is inside the pub at the back of the bar. We drive on to our next pub the *Racehorse* (North Hill), followed by the *Archer Arms* (Lewannick). It's in this pub that Oggy's belly reaches breaking point and he can't fasten his trousers. Drewy tells him it's the beer fermenting inside it and he could explode. From this pub we carry on to the *Kings Head Hotel* (Five Lanes) and then to the penultimate pub of the day the *Rising Sun* (Altarnun). We receive a friendly welcome off the gaffer Les Humphreys. His beer, 'Bateman's xxx is good and there's a campsite opposite. This could come in handy. Ye olde preacher John Wesley's cottage is near here too in the village of Trewint.

I overhear a conversation in the *Rising Sun* of a famous pub on Bodmin Moor called the *Jamaica Inn*. We can't miss this out (even though it's still in Cornwall). Being out in the wilds it could be a good place to find a quiet spot to flake out, after our eventful day. We discover it's by the main A30 road between Launceston and Bodmin so our planned quiet night is doomed. The pub is also bigger than we thought. Bed and breakfast is £20 for a single room and £35 for a double. This was the setting for Daphne du Maurier's famous novel *Jamaica Inn*. Well, there's no surprise there then. Inside, a nice-looking girl is talking to Percy, the resident pub parrot in his cage. Leo can't resist saying, "What a lovely bird."

She turns round at Leo and all he says is, "Squawk!"

What a great chat-up line that was?

The pub was an old coaching inn, built in 1547. There's an amazing collection of swords, muskets, lanterns and old brassware hanging from the beams. The parrot tells us there is also a large souvenir shop. Believe that and you'll believe anything! We enjoy our visit but sleeping here is out of the question. About two miles away, down a narrow moorland road opposite the inn, lies Dozmary Pool, where Sir Bedivere is said to have flung King Arthur's sword, to be caught by an arm rising from the depths. This is a large freshwater lake, one mile in circumference. Surely this must be quiet and when we find it, it is. But the grass is too lumpy, too long and it's boggy. Drewy suggests going back to the campsite at the *Rising Sun*, so we do. This turns out to be a great idea, but it rains all night.

We wake up on Thursday 27th July. The rain has stopped and the sun is breaking through the clouds. Today we drive to Devon. It's only 8.20 a.m. and we chuck our clobber in the boot and head to anywhere we can find where we can have a swill. Back on the A30 we head towards Okehampton and about twenty miles away we notice a campsite at Sourton. A brilliant place this is as we all have a shave, swill and skiddy (pants) change. What a relief, I thought my skiddies had fused to my bum; Leo's are ready to run off and Drewy says he'll turn his inside out. Oggy is also a little nervous; too much water and he could dissolve like an Alka Seltzer tablet. With opening time a while away we drive down the A386 and we pass a dead oss (horse) at the side of the road. If this is road kill what hit it? Lydford Gorge is our target. It's a National Trust property and on arrival it's a superb and scenic few miles walk and you have to pay £1.60 for the pleasure too. We get as far as reading the information about this walk and visit the Castle ruin instead. This happens to be next to a pub and we can all sit down and relax.

At last it's opening time and the delightful sixteenth-century *Castle Inn* (Lydford) is now paid a visit. This inn has two bars and seven double-bedrooms. A double room is £16.50 per person and a single is £25. The pub was used in the film *The Hound of the Baskervilles* under the name of *Admiral Blake* and Sir Arthur Conan Doyle's portrait is hanging on the wall. The walls are also adorned with old plates and there's a great medieval fireplace that originated in the Norman Castle. Near the bar are seven Lydford pennies hammered out in the Old Saxon mint that was situated in Lydford during the reign of Ethelred the Unready (circa 1000). It also serves excellent food and is recommended by Egon Ronay. Just a mile down the road is our second pub of the day, the *Manor Inn* (Lydford). This is situated near the waterfall (the White Lady) and the entrance to the beautiful Lydford Gorge. In here is a dartboard, pool table and B&B is available. The third pub in Lydford is the *Dartmoor Inn* a smashing sixteenth-century boozer. This inn has low ceilings, wood panelling and massive fireplaces. Accommodation is £16 per person for a double room. The landlord Paul Hyde welcomes us to his inn with a free drink apiece and we have a good chat about our exploits over the last few days. He tells us summer visitors to Devon are called 'grockles.' "We're called 'emmets' in Cornwall," I said, "and the Cornish hate being called English."

"It's funny that, aemmet is an Old English word meaning – 'ant'," he replied.

Well how about that then!

I'm again told about a white cat that haunts the churchyard in Zennor. I now think it's the lads telling the gaffer about this cat just to wind me up.

To reach our next pub, we travel back to where we had our wash this morning. It's our 2,587th pub, the *Highwayman Inn* (Sourton). This is a place that we haven't seen the likes of before. It's a magical pub that the landlord Buster has spent many years creating. To enter this unusual inn, you have to step into and out of the Okehampton to Launceston stage coach. Inside are the two biggest and friendliest smiles you'll ever see, off the landlady Rita and her daughter Sally. The interior is fascinating. The bar counters are made from great logs dragged from the Dartmoor bogs. There are granite and stone walls; great open fireplaces and a small room full of stuffed animals and birds that have either died naturally or they've been too slow to cross the road. My favourite room is the Rita Jones Locker Bar. You are taken back to the 17th century by way of an old sedan chair and oak panelling from Drake's time. The main bar door is a carved original from the old sailing ship *Diana*. Lots of lanterns hang off the ceiling beams; the tables have been hollowed out, filled with jewels and topped with glass. The only food is pasties and the local scrumpy is noggen juice. Two pints of this and I now start whistling. I chat to Sally about the pub but there's a hair on her lip that's annoying me, so I ask her if I can pull it off and when I do it's attached to her head. You cannot miss this pub out. It's an explorers' delight. Tell me a better hobby than this!

It's interesting round these parts of Devon as we now go in the thatched *Bearslake Inn* and Restaurant (Sourton). To let the cider settle down a bit we all enjoy a Devonshire Royal Cream Liqueur. It's just a short drive away to the *Fox & Hounds Hotel* (Bridestowe). This is another pub of interest and it's our first pub that is part of the 'Dartmoor letter box' scheme. The barmaid, Lillian uses a stamp about three inches square with the name of the pub on it to stamp my book. On the wall is a large mural of a hunting scene. We are told an ex-German P.O.W. painted it in 1946-7. In the games room is bar billiards, pool, games machines and darts. Good value B&B is available and there's a nice photo of the Queen on the wall. The proprietors are Frank and Sue Ward and offer us a caravan to sleep in if we're ever in the area again. It's a smashing start to Devon and I hope it continues. There is now a decent drive into Plymouth. Here we visit the *Yard Arm* which has a nautical theme and we only stop for a quick drink. Ten mile back and out in the countryside is the *Burrator Inn* (Dousland). Again I have my book stamped but this time it has a picture of the pub on it. I find this really strange. I've never seen this letter box stamping before today and if all pubs did it, what a fabulous collection of stamps I would have had. The Burrator Reservoir is close by so we pay it a visit. Is this water used to supply 'emmets' or 'grockles?' I wonder?

On our way towards Princetown we pass Dartmoor Prison. Oggy feels quite at home passing this as it reminds him of Winson Green Prison, where he once stopped for nine months' worth of bed and breakfast. We visit the *Devil's Elbow* (Princetown). This was previously known as the *Railway Hotel*. I have another stamp for my book and this time it's of the pub sign. Moving on, we arrive at the *Dartmoor Inn* (Merrivale) for yet another letter box stamp. On entry to our next pub the *Old Inn* (Widecombe in the Moor) the gaffer takes one look at us and tells us he's closed. We come out and leave our car here and walk down the road a few hundred yards to a classic stone-built old pub the *Rugglestone Inn* (Widecombe in the Moor). There's a quaint little living room-type bar to our right and the landlady serves our beers straight out of the barrel through a small serving hatch in the passageway. An old lady sitting in here tells us of the ghosts of Dartmoor. From this pub we walk back to the car and notice the *Old Inn* still looks open. This time the gaffer is shocked to see us back in here and as there are other people in the pub he cannot say he is closed. Our travels this week are beginning to take their toll. None of us want to move on to any more pubs tonight so we find a table and decide to settle here for the remainder of the night. I was clammed (hungry) and order a Swiss steak. Oggy has the same. The chef Russell McNally comes over yapping to us and wants me to send him a *Black Country Bugle* newspaper. He asks Oggy how he wants his steak cooked. "Just wipe its arse," he jokingly replied.

On overhearing our conversation with the chef, a reporter introduces herself as Elaine Hopkins. She gives me a phone number and wants me to contact South West Regional television for an interview tomorrow about our adventures. After numerous pints of Bass bitter and several Gaelic coffees each, it's midnight and there is only us left in the pub. The gaffer then counts loads of money on his bar counter. Whether he thought we were going to mug him I wouldn't know. But on leaving we tell him what a great night we've had in his pub. He then comes running out of the door and said, "Thank you lads, you've restored my faith in human nature. I thought you were trouble when you came in my pub but you've sat there all night drinking away and have behaved impeccably."

I've never felt so chuffed in all my life.

The village of Widecombe-in-the-Moor hosts an annual fair and it's still held every year on the second Tuesday in September. It's also famous for the song 'Old Uncle Tom Cobleigh,' written in about 1880 it's all about the Widecombe Fair and Tom Pearce's grey mare, which carried seven riders to Widecombe. The greymare, after her epic journey, died and now haunts the moor at night. About two miles away is Hound Tor, a stack of granite boulders, which were once believed to be the Devil's home on Dartmoor. This is where the spooky surroundings for a version of the film *The Hound of the Baskervilles* were filmed. Our aim is to sleep near to this haunting place. It will also be the end of our association with Sir Arthur Conan Doyle. Talk about scary. We've been told to watch out for a ghost on a skeleton horse and there's a chance we'll see it too. As the four of us settle down on the grass nobody wants to sleep on the ends. Oggy and me volunteer. It's during the night about 3 a.m. that I'm woken by a horse neighing and it sounds like it's only feet away from me. Could this be the Ghost on his oss? I jump up with my torch and couldn't spot a thing. It's certainly a busy night because, later, all I can hear are cows, sheep, horses and what sounds like a bull. I get up to take a photo of the sleeping sinister shape of the 'BATSkarvilles,' who are now snoring, for England. Roll on daylight!

At last it's 9.20 a.m. Friday 28th July. It's our last day of our holiday and it's time to get up. Drewy, Leo and myself leave Oggy asleep while we climb to the top of Hound Tor or should we now call it houndsnore? I have a bit of rock for a souvenir. At the top we all start howling and this stirs Oggy from his sleep. Then, out of the blue, an Alsatian runs over to Oggy and starts licking him. This puts the shits up him and upon hearing our howling, he thinks it the Hound himself. It turns out to be the park ranger's dog and he tells him off for sleeping on the moor. He continues to explain that the moor is privately owned and he shouldn't be sleeping here. He also tells him that he's lucky the snakes didn't bite him. With all the rollicking out of the way we drive back into Widecombe for an expensive crap breakfast.

Yesterday was definitely the best day of our travels. Today we're having a steady ride homeward stopping off at various pubs. After taking the road through lovely countryside by chance we drop on the *Warren House Inn* (Postbridge). This we find claims to be the third highest pub in England and not the *Kirkstone Pass* as we had thought. A sign tells you that you are 1,514 feet above sea level. Fourteen-foot higher than the Kirkstone Pass? I have an old postcard of the *Warren House Inn* saying it is 1400ft above sea level. The pubs claim to fame is that the fire has been continually burning since 1845. It looks in a pretty poor state on our arrival. The embers are only just glowing so I help it along and throw a crisp packet on it. Situated on its own, high on the moors, there are numerous photos of the pub covered in snowdrifts on the wall. One of the worst winters the inn encountered was in 1963, when it was cut off by heavy snowdrifts, some reaching twenty feet. This lasted for approximately twelve weeks and supplies had to be flown in by helicopter. I have another letter box stamp put in my book. While Oggy stands up at the bar his belly reaches breaking point and finally blows the buckle of his belt and his trousers fall down to his ankles. It's not a pretty sight! I have to ask the gaffer for a safety pin. Luckily nobody is in the pub at the moment.

A pub I've been looking forward to visiting for a long while is next. Our journey is a long but pleasant drive to the thatched *Drewe Arms* (Drewsteignton). This is the home of Mrs Mudge, known as

'Auntie Mabel' to her locals, who has lived here since 1919. It's claimed she is the oldest landlady in Great Britain. She was actually born on 4th October 1894. Her husband Ernest Mudge died aged sixty-nine, on 4th March 1951. The pub is totally unspoilt. The next door neighbour to the pub is helping out today and serves us our beer straight out of the barrel. The bar room we sit in has flaky cream-painted wooden walls and wooden seats. There's a dartboard and by the look of all the holes in the wall the locals need a bit more practice. They'll have to give me a ring; I'll come and visit again and give them some practice. I ask the next door neighbour, who is barman for the day, if Auntie Mable is in. I follow him into her living quarters and she kindly allows me to take a photo of her. I'm over the moon that I've met this special lady and I'm so excited that I buy a round of drinks. It's not often I get this excited. Outside, screwed to the wall, is a small brass plaque that says:

In fond recognition of Mabel Mudge.
Presented on the occasion of her 70th anniversary, as landlady of the Drewe Arms.
Unveiled by Sam Whitbread.
Chairman of Whitbread on June 27th 1989.

Travelling on our way after such a fantastic pub we stop off in the *Ring of Bells* (North Bovey). The gaffer pins our calling card above the door in the bar room. Next is the *Kestor Inn* (Manaton) and the last of my letter box stamps. It's also where Leo calls me over to look at the small fishpond and I bend over to have a look and my glasses fall off and swim with the fish. The *Cleave Hotel* (Lustleigh) is next. Here, you have to walk down several garden steps to the bar room. It's a quaint interior, with a wood settle by the inglenook fireplace. The final alehouse in Devon is the *Riverside Inn* (Bovey Tracey). It's mainly a restaurant pub but in the De Tracy Bar we watch the horseracing on telly. The gaffer Pat Giblett gives us a free Whitbread T-shirt and a pint each. At the battle of Bovey Heath in 1645 that old piss-head Oliver Cromwell is alleged to have led his men into one of the Bovey hostelries (the old Riverside House) and surprised Royalists gambling and drinking. The officers threw their stake money out of the window to the Roundhead troops and escaped in the ensuing scramble. No doubt old Ollie stopped for a pint or two. There have been some wonderful and unique pubs in Cornwall and Devon and now it's sadly time to leave. There is now a long drive to cut the travelling time home down by half before our next stop.

Eventually we reach the *Golden Farmer* (Cirencester) one of five pubs we want to visit in Gloucestershire today. Drewy has a steak sandwich and gets ripped off because it's tiny. We have a quick drink and leave. The *Village Pub* (Barnsley), the *Sherbourne Arms* (Aldsworth) and then the *Lamb* (Great Rissington) are our next three pubs. In the *Lamb* we get talking to a Yank couple who say they are looking for a rich Englishman for their twenty-three-year-old daughter to marry. Oggy tries his best but fails miserably. Moving on, we find the *Bell* (Willersey) where loads of jugs, mugs and tots hang off the ceiling. Our final stop before heading home is a new Mad O'Rourke's pub called the *Upton Muggery* (Upton upon Severn). We get in here at 10 p.m. It's a pub with hundreds of mugs and jugs hanging off the ceiling. We leave this pub for a local fish and chip shop. On going back to our car we find two thirteen-year-old girls sitting in our car and they won't get out. Leo said, "Yoe pair had better get out before the video nasty arrives."

All they continue to do is laugh, until Oggy arrives and pops his head in the door. This does the trick as both of them shoot out of the motor never to be seen again. Well, we arrive home at the end of our adventure, 110 pubs and 1,160 miles later at 12.30 a.m.

CHAPTER 16

3,000 CHEERS!

With our pub knowledge widened after visiting Cornwall and Devon its back to pubs in Shropshire. It's Sunday July 30th and our journey takes us to the *Stiperstones Inn* (Snailbeach). This is nicknamed the *Beeches* and from up here it offers some of the most beautiful and varied landscapes to be found in Shropshire. The area was once mined for lead; discarded shafts and abandoned engine houses can still be seen today. We travel on to the next pub the *Seven Stars* (Vrongate). You'll have to go a long way to find one quite as riffy as this. It's locally known as Old Ethel's. She signs my book and she certainly needs some help with the cleaning. There are dead flies on the shelves, tin cans everywhere: dirty walls and the bog is home to a colony of spiders and mould. It's definitely worth the visit to see such a place. Our 2,616th pub and last one of the night is a classic boozer the *Seven Stars* (Halfway House). The bar room is tiny and you couldn't swing a BAT in here. It's very basic with white walls and grey-painted wood cladding. There's two grey-painted wood settles, a large grey-painted mantelpiece, one table, a couple of stools and the Burtonwood bitter is served from a jug fetched from the living room. An elderly brother and sister run this pub, H. M. Davies signs my book and once you break the ice with them a friendly welcome is assured. When we first walked in here they told us that they thought we'd come to rob the place.

The following week our drive takes us to the *Wenlock Edge Inn* (Hilltop near Presthope) situated near to Wenlock Edge, a massive limestone ridge that runs for sixteen miles across Shropshire. What a view it is too! Moving on we nip in the *Feathers* (Brockton), set in the lovely area called Corve Dale. The *Feathers* was originally two Elizabethan cottages, built about 400 years ago. The inn brewed its own ale until the start of the twentieth century. The well, which supplied the brewing water, is still in daily use. The massive bellows, which form one of the lounge tables, were rescued from the local smithy. The inn offers customers a pretty dining room, a comfortable bar room, a games room, a sun patio and five double bedrooms. Our final ale tonight is in the old market town of Much Wenlock. We have been here before, but this time we visit the *George and Dragon.* Live folk music features regularly at this pub. On our visit there's a chap on a violin and another on a guitar. The room displays advertisement boards on the walls, jugs hang off the ceiling and there are shelves of bottles and beer trays.

Towards the end of August we try to find the *Fox Inn* (Ryton). Drewy and myself have a misunderstanding. Drewy was driving and I said to him, "Ryton, left."

Drewy gets upset and pulls the car over and stops. "Which way do yoe want me ter go?" replied Drewy.

"Left!" I said.

"Yoe just told me to go right 'n' left, yoe'll mek ya mind up," moaned Drewy.

"Drewy my old pal, when I said Ryton, that's the name of the village!" Who would be a navigator?

Our adventure continues as it takes us to the *Unicorn Inn* (Hampton Loade). This is a family-orientated pub with a camping and caravan site on the banks of the River Severn. Although the pub's okay, the reason for coming here is to cross the river on the smallish wooden ferry. Two old ladies operate this and they use an eight foot wooden pole to punt you over to the opposite side guided by a cable that spans the river. To call them into operation you have to ring a bell and pay 20p each way – the last ferry back from the pub is 9 p.m. This is a rare experience! Our next pub is rather awkward to find. It's down a dirt track about two miles from Clee Hill off the A4117, to the old stone sixteenth-century pub called the *Colliers Arms* (Hints). Watch out for the sheep on the way here. This is a typical local farmer's pub. Drewy keeps his eyes open for beehives. His boyhood memory of a farmer sticking his head in one haunts him to this day. To finish our journey off we arrive at the *Trapnell Inn* (Boraston). The gaffer Nigel told me the fire never goes out in this pub but when he shows me it he has to put logs and oil on it to get it going! He tells me the wooden door, seats and flagstones came from the demolished Arley Castle.

With September now upon us we continue touring our local pubs in West Bromwich and Wednesbury. At *Busby's* (West Bromwich) my old pals Roy Matthews, Wayne Cowley and Big Tone help in raising £126 towards our charity. At last I've been able to organise with Peter Grieve the Tenanted Trade Area Manager of Whitbread brewery a presentation night. He's keeping his promise of giving us a £1 for every Whitbread pub we visited in Hereford and Worcestershire. It's Wednesday 13th September 1989 and the presentation evening is held at the *Sherlock Holmes* (Coseley). Seven BAT members, old and new, turn up to meet Mr Grieve and three nurses from the NeoNatal Unit at Sandwell and District Hospital in West Bromwich. One nurse named Rose Dent receives the combined cheque for £500. Mr Grieve makes the mistake of giving Oggy his plastic card and his permission to order as many free drinks as we like. Everybody goes on a bender, drinking pints, shorts and babychams. Even the nurses give the vodka a bending. Oggy then asks all the locals if they want a drink too and it's two hours before Mr Grieve finds out that his booze bill is much higher than he anticipated and swiftly retrieves his card. It's been a great night for everyone and we all give Peter Grieve a very big round of applause as he now heads off home. The nurses too have to leave and it's our turn for the applause. They exit the door, wobbling slightly more than when they came in.

With September flying by the next couple of weeks are spent touring Shropshire again. The most memorable ones are the *Halfway House* near Eardington built in 1620. A smashing old pub with a small serving hatch, wood walls, wood beams and a log fire. We have a good loff (laugh) with the gaffer and when Leo tells him Oggy's ugly, he tells us it takes an ugly bull to make a pretty calf. Next pub is the *Ye Olde Punchbowl* situated on the B4364 road one mile from the centre of Bridgnorth. This 400-year-old building was first licensed in 1740. During the siege of Bridgnorth many of Cromwell's troops were billeted in this house. Adjoining the inn is a large Banqueting room, which can accommodate 150 to 180 people. Another interesting pub is the *Cumberland Hotel* (Broseley). This has a nice hallway and an interesting case of Broseley clay pipes on the wall. Leo cracks a joke in here. I had a dog with no legs and I used to call him Woodbine. I'd take him out for a drag. Say no more!

We have a change of scenery now that October has arrived. We head for the Forest of Dean in Gloucestershire. Before we reach it, we first stop off at the *Severn Bore Inn* (Ministerworth). Originally the pub was called the Bird in Hand. John, Dave and Ruth Chase are the licensees and they tell us about a tidal wave that can be viewed from the large back garden of their pub that is situated on the banks of the River Severn. It's known as the Severn Bore and can reach a height of over six feet. This surge-wave (the Bore) travels a distance of approximately twenty-five miles between Awre and Gloucester. It occurs frequently throughout the year. We continue our drive to a pub situated in a lovely setting a sixteenth-century inn called the *Royal Spring* (Lower Lydbrook). This has a beer garden with a stream and is set in wooded surroundings overlooking the Wye Valley. A set of three lime kilns dating from the early eighteenth-century are to be found next to the new car park in the quarry above the inn. A warm welcome awaits you from Verity, Julie, Heather and Tim Akester. We venture on to the highest pub in the Forest of Dean, the *Roebuck* (Ruardean Woodside). A local chap tells us he believes you are not a true Forester and cannot be a freeminer unless you are born under the sound of St Briavels church bells. He also tells us that, while travelling around these parts, not to mention 'who killed the bear'. This is something to do with a travelling circus and its performing bear that the Foresters killed, mistakenly believing it took off with a child. If I understood him more I'd have got the full story but he's very pissed. The DJ shouts out over his mike that he's now going to play an old one from the 1950s. Leo says, "There's an old one from the 1930s here mate," and points to Oggy.

Leo then goes on to tell us about a date he had with a wench last night. He says he scored a goal but wishes he'd hit the post.

It's October twenty-second and a short trip to London is planned. We leave early morning arriving at our first pub the *Albion,* (Up the Baggies) (Hammersmith) at noon. Then the *Chancellors* (Hammersmith). Our third pub is the *Dove* (Hammersmith). This is a *Guinness Book of Records* entry for having the smallest bar room (4ft 2in x 7ft 10in). It's a casual stroll along the river to get here and it's where the annual University Boat Race between Oxford and Cambridge pass under the Hammersmith Bridge. The pub is seventeenth-century and has endless associations with literature and the stage. James Thomson (who wrote 'Rule Britannia') lodged and died here. The *Dove* stands in a group of superb Georgian houses. I open the door and sit in the tiny bar room, which is a bit of a con really. The same bar counter is used to serve a much larger room. In this little bar room is a brass plate showing the level to which the pub was flooded by the highest tide recorded in 1928. We now move on to the *Three Kings* (Twickenham). The gaffer refuses to serve us for some reason so we don't count this as a visit. Down the road is the *Prince Albert* (Twickenham) a popular place where I lean against the blackboard and all of today's meals on offer at the pub are now on the back of my coat. The *Cock and Bull* (Twickenham) is next. This is where we wait one hour and twenty-five minutes for our meal and it's crap.

We leave London for Surrey. There's two hours before opening so we agree to go and look at Newark Priory. On arrival, a sign on a tree says 'Private, no walking to the Priory.' So taking no notice of this, Drewy, Leo and me jump the gate and walk over to this ruin which is now more or less a pigeon pen. We spot another sign saying 'Private river no fishing'. I had a private thought; we're not fishing. It's getting dark and it's time to drive to another pub. The *Anchor* (Ripley) starts our evening drinking session and this is followed by the *Half Moon* (Ripley). Buckinghamshire is our destination, with a drive of thirty-five minutes to the *Plough* (Winchmore Hill). This is owned by the well-known actress Barbara Windsor of the 'Carry On' movies fame. What a great signature this will be for my records! On our arrival we discover it's her night off. How disappointing is this! Never mind we must – 'Carry On'. The *Greyhound* (Aldbury) in Hertfordshire by the village pond is where we now relax with our pints. From this pub we carry on to the *Chequers* (Whipsnade) in Bedfordshire. This is past the zoo and through some gates. It's a large pub and tonight it's quiet and we have a game of pool. Our drive now takes us to the *Bedford* (Toddington). We stop here for a quick drink and head to the final one on today's trip the *Griffin* (Toddington). There's not a lot to say about this adventure. All I can say is we've travelled 333 miles and knocked up a few more pubs.

It's the last week in October and we travel down to Cheltenham. It's while in the *Railway* a chap at the bar tells me that Ann Carter – Les's missus from the *Plough* at Ford – has bone cancer. This is a shock to us all because she's our favourite landlady. We really hope she can recover from such a horrible disease. An interesting pictorial pub sign is at the *Five Alls* (Leckhampton). This is on the edge of Cheltenham town and the pub sign stands for; *I Rule for All, I Pray for All, I Plead for All, I Fight for All and I Work for All.*

With Bonfire night arriving it's off on a visit to Staffordshire and all the pubs in the town of Stone. The *Star* is an interesting pub where the lounge door opens up and you find yourself outside by the cut (canal). On the wall of this pub is a picture of the gaffer sitting in a bath; he enters the annual bath race on the nearby river. The *Mill Hotel* (Stone) is an historical one. Built in 1795 by a chap called Robert Bill. Stoney Richard Smith was born in the Mill House opposite in 1835. His brainchild was Hovis Flour. This flour was originally known as 'Smith's Patent Germ Flour'. This was considered a cumbersome title and in 1890, a competition was held to find a more appropriate name. Mr Herbert Grime, an Oxford schoolmaster, won the competition. He suggested Hovis as a contraction of the Latin 'Homonis Vis' (the strength of man). The word Hovis was registered as a trade mark in 1890. It ceased milling corn only 25 years ago and has now taken on a new lease of life with a reputation for top quality food in their restaurant. Accommodation is available with a single room costing £26 and a double £38.50; there are eleven bedrooms to choose from. The following few weeks we're back in Cheltenham, where a good many pubs are devoid of breathable air due to the thick cigarette smoke. A pint of Bass goes down well in the smallest bar in town the *Bath Tavern*. This is another pub you couldn't swing a BAT in. It's run by an old lady, Mrs Cheshire.

The year nears its end, but not before a tour we're calling the 'North Eastern Promise'. This is going to see us venture into Northumberland, Tyne and Wear, County Durham, Cleveland, North Yorkshire, Humberside and South Yorkshire. It's December 9th 1989 and we leave early at 5.30 a.m. With only one stop at the service station on the way up, we arrive at 11 a.m. at England's most northerly pub the *Meadow House* (near Berwick-upon-Tweed). Leo, after being served with his drink, is given a Scottish £10 note and refuses to except it. He gets it changed for an English £10 note. There's an unusual plastic palm tree about a foot high at the back of the bar and when it's spoken to it begins to move and shake about. We've never seen anything like this before and find it quite amusing. The *Brewers Arms* (Berwick-upon-Tweed) is next on our itinerary. Is this haunted? We hear a banging noise coming from below in the cellar. Leo puts us all at ease. He reckons it's a mouse with clogs on. Travelling on to the *Salmon* (Belford) where, on display, there's an empty whisky bottle in an old boot. This was presented to the pub for coming last in a fishing contest.

We drive on, visiting seven more pubs. They are the *Masons Arms* (Amble), the *Cresswell Arms* (Newbiggin) and the *42nd Street* (Whitley Bay). This is followed by *Wilders Bar* (Newcastle) – Carrying on we arrive at the *Ye Olde Fleece* (Gateshead), then the *Royalty* (Sunderland) – watch out for the local 'Mackems.' The seventh one is the *Woodman* (Durham) watch out for Mr Walters the local piss-head.

Our car needs a drink so we put fuel in its tank and head to Darlington for another two pubs. The first is the *Tap & Spile* (Darlington), then the *Old Dun Cow* (Darlington). In the latter pub the landlord Geoff Addy puts up saucy snapshots of the regulars' private parts on the wall. Any customer saying, "Mine's a large one" is invited to prove it. He can have his knob photographed and it joins the others on the wall. Women can join in too and on our visit, one shot of a woman's private bit is padlocked up. How she managed to get the padlock through it I'll never know! On leaving this erotic pub we take the road to our fourteenth pub of day the *White Rose* (Middlesbrough). To reach our fifteenth pub we look out for the massive ICI works. Well, you can't miss it; it's all lit up and looks like a big city. Eventually we find the *Winning Post* (Redcar).

The booze is flowing really well today as we drive on to *Rosie O'Grady's* (Saltburn-by-the-Sea), a modern pub overlooking the sea. Not far away is the *Ship* (Saltburn-by-the-Sea). A chap in here tells me of an overtime drinking pub. A few miles away we drop in the *Toad Hall Arms* (Moorsholm). I ask the gaffer if he knows anywhere we can sleep tonight and have a breakfast in the morning. No, is the answer, so off we go to the pub I've heard serves overtime.

Our nineteenth and final pub of the day is the *Jolly Sailor Inn* (Moorsholm). I work on the gaffer quick, to see if he's interested in having our company tonight. I ask him the same questions as in the previous pub and he tells us we can sleep in his barn and he'll do us a breakfast. This is great news as we can all relax supping away more ale to end an exhausting day. It's definitely an overtime pub and at 12.30 a.m. I nip outside to put all our sleeping bags in the barn. The only problem is the gaffer didn't tell me that to get into the barn the entrance is eight feet high. I try putting some tables on top of each other and chairs to climb on. This fails miserably and I fall off. It's then that I notice a disused area under the barn with no doors on so this will have to do. As it's December, we've all bought extra clothing to kip in and it's now I find out I've forgotten our plastic bags that we sleep in. It's a good job we're under cover. Back in the pub, we are all getting leg-less. We finally exit the pub at 1.30 a.m. and flake out straight away in our beds that I prepared earlier.

On a cold foggy Sunday morning, Andy Ford the gaffer wakes us up with his dog called Enton at 9.30 a.m. I'm glad we're all in the warmth of the pub because I'm freezing. Elaine, his missus, brings us our fittle (food). Andy only charges us thirty-bob (£1.50) apiece for our smashing full English breakfast and brings a pint over for us too. Oggy meanwhile has nipped off to the bog and we don't think he's quite made it, because his underpants join us for breakfast. Drewy tells us a couple of jokes. An African cannibal tribesman goes for a job. The gaffer says, "I'll start you on as long as you don't bring anyone else with you."

"Okay," replied the tribesman.

Next day he turned up to start work with a Pygmy at his side."I thought I told you not to bring anyone with you," said the furious gaffer. "I haven't, he's my dinner," smiled the tribesman.

Nice one Drewy!

His other joke is; if you are hungry in the jungle and find a dead snake and a dead Pygmy what could you eat?

"We doe know?"

"Snake and Pygmy pie!" laughed Drewy.

His jokes are gettin' wuss (worse).

What a superb pub this is and it's the licensees that make it so. Opening time isn't too far away so we say our thanks, goodbyes and tarahs and leave Moorsholm for Whitby.

What a smashing old place Whitby is. It's a town split in half by the River Esk. The first thing any visitor should do is to climb the 199 steps to St Mary's churchyard. Our first thing however is to go in the *Endeavour* (Whitby), for a cracking drink of Cameron's ale. Oggy rests here whilst the other three of us climb the 199 steps to the churchyard and Dracula's grave. This is the legendary place that old pointy teeth is reputed to have landed. There is an open stone grave and if it is Dracula's then he's got out and flew off. It's empty. At the top over the churchyard wall are the ancient ruins of Whitby Abbey. From up here there are spectacular views over the lovely harbour and the narrow streets of Whitby. Also in town is a statue of Captain Cook; he learnt his seamanship here. Back down the steps we get

Oggy up and out of the pub and journey on to the ancient fishing village of Robin Hood's Bay. Here you have to park your car on the pay and display and walk down a very steep hill. On the way down we pass Alf Roberts (Bryan Mosley) out of *Coronation Street*. If that's how we'll look coming back up, I'm certainly not looking forward to it. Old Alf is totally knackered. Most of the houses in this tiny place were built between 1650 and 1750. Building land was always severely limited and when sons and daughters were married their families built homes for them in the yards of their own houses, hence the maze of alleys and stairways. The pub we've come to visit is the *Laurel Inn*. The inn has a delightful cosy room with a log fire. Lots of beer mats are on the ceiling and the gaffer, Bob Tucker, who signs my book puts our BATS card on there too. The Theakston's ale is excellent! This unique village and the pub are both great places to come and visit. "Now for that bloody walk back up the bonk, lads," I reluctantly said.

Halfway up this hill I'm thinking somebody could make a killing if they attached a ski cable from top to bottom, gave everybody a pair of roller skates and charged a quid a time for the journey up!

The town of Scarborough is our next port of call and we all pop in the *Albion* (Up the Baggies). This is up the hill just before the castle. There's a lovely view of the town from the patio outside this pub. The gaffer tells us the next pub east of here is in Rotterdam. One of the Brontë sisters is buried in this town. We leave and journey south to the *Belle Vue* (Filey). The *Hilderthorpe* (Bridlington) follows this. The room in here is full of smoke but its wuth (worth) inhaling it as the Stone's bitter is superb. Whilst in this town we buy fish and chips and throw some out of the car for the seagulls. A big mistake! It quickly becomes a scene from Alfred Hitchcock's movie *The Birds*. Dozens of them besiege our car and we have to take drastic action and quickly shut all of the windows.

Leaving behind the Gannets we take the B1242 road towards Withernsea. We have to cancel this trip due to the dense fog and we divert towards Hull. On arrival, we all have a one-hour shut-eye to recharge our batteries. The *Mint* is our first drink in Hull. This is the city's only pub/café bar, which was originally the Midland Bank built in the 1850s. Tonight's music is from the 50s, 60s and 70s. A local chap tells me that the ship in the historical event 'Mutiny on the Bounty' was built in Hull. He continues to tell me about some excavation work going on down the road. Archaeologists think they have found the Beverley Gate, the original gate in the wall that surrounded the city. A short walk from this place, down an alleyway, is *Ye Olde White Harte*. Built in 1553 it's our 2,915th pub visit. At the top of the stairs in this pub is the largest bottle of Newcastle Brown Ale I've ever seen, it's six feet high. The first blow struck in the English Civil War is said to have started here. A plaque on the wall tells the story. In brief, Charles I asked for a drink and the gaffer closed the Beverley Gates, told him to piss off and banned him. The King got rather upset about this. What an unexpected, interesting and enjoyable time we're having around here, but sadly we must move on.

Our drive takes us into the *North Eastern* (Goole). On our entry into this pub we get a cheer off the locals and Leo says that the Darley's beer tastes like Planter's nuts. The fog is still hanging around as we drive on to our next two alehouses, the *Hare and Hounds* (Fishlake) and the *Old Anchor* (Fishlake). These are the only two pubs in the village. With both visited we journey on to the *Buffalo* (Moorends) before finishing off in the *Corner Pin* (Thorne). Darley's Brewery is next to this pub but it is now closed down. So who's brewing Darley's beers? Inside the boozer is a Leeds fan and Drewy's in his element. It's a smoky room and an overtime pub, so we stop for an extra pint. The gaffer tells us it's 11 p.m. and if we don't go out now he will shut the door and he won't open it until 4 a.m. Because we're so far away from home we have to decline his offer. I've been yapping to a local chap called Eric Hardy who scrounges a lift to his home. He asks us in for a night-cap but his missus isn't too pleased at this, so we leave and start back on our long drive home. What a journey. The fog is still really thick in places and visibility is down to yards. Eventually, with my head stuck out of the window for a better view of the road, we arrive home at 2 a.m. after an eye-straining drive and an exhausting weekend.

It's back to work and back to filing, drilling and milling my scale model of our proposed 3,000th pub. I'm reminded that I'd better arrange things with the museum director Mr Ian Walden. I hope he finds this of interest as my model is near completion. Off I go to explain my idea to him and after our meeting he's very enthusiastic. Thank God for that!

Saturday December 30th arrives and it's our last 'day out' of the year. Due to me having a migraine on our last trip to South Wales we're going back to West Glamorgan. Dawn joins us on this trip. The 2½ hour journey is spent singing along to songs such as *I've just come down from the Isle of Skye – Oggy where's yer troosers?* This refers to when Oggy's belt bost (broke) and his trousers fell down in the *Warren House Inn* (Postbridge) in Devon. The first pub we stop at for a drink is in the *Mermaid Hotel* (Mumbles). There are four interesting leaded windows in here featuring Walsingham, Raleigh, Drake and Sydney. The Welsh poet Dylan Thomas' work features heavily around the room and there's also a framed print of the production cast of one of his main works *Under Milk Wood*. Bed and breakfast is available with a single costing £18 and a double £32. Mumbles is a nice little place overlooking the sea so we decide to stop here a while and visit four more pubs. The next one is the *George*, a Beefeater pub with a large ceiling fan. Oggy says, "It looks like Glenn Miller's landed then."

The *Pilot Inn follows* this pub, with its all-wood interior and the bottom of a small boat stuck on the ceiling. Oggy tells the two barmen to smile a bit. Moving on we walk to the *Oyster Catcher*. Another pub where Glenn Miller must have landed and the other propeller is on the ceiling. Or is it a large fan? The last one in Mumbles is the *White Rose*. While the lads are drinking in here, Dawn and me nip over the road to Coral's bookmakers and put a £1 treble on three ossis (horses): Fragrant Dawn, Kittinger and Sneakapenny.

A short journey away by car is the *Plough and Harrow* (Murton) for a drink of Truman's Dark. Then it's off to the *Joiners Arms* (Bishopston) with its spiral staircase, followed by the *Valley Hotel* (Bishopston). About three miles away is where we stop for our next wazzin wash, the *Gower Inn* (Parkmill), run by licensees Jim and Angela Pritchard. This is a large, comfortable and relaxing place with a massive wooden barrel that's been cut out and has a seat inside; a unique thing to sit in. Continuing our drive along the A4118 we arrive at Port Einon and have a stroll along the beach. It's bloody freezing so our interest in a coastal view ends and it's off to the *Ship* (Port Einon). Inside, and on the wall is a large ship's wheel, which is off the *Tugboat Witte Zee* of Rotterdam. This was shipwrecked on Overton Mere on November 10th 1940. Dawn plays me at pool and I win. In Dawn's notes it reads *Bighead Hilly Billy wins a game of pool only by sheer luck*. But to be fair to myself, I was brilliant! Leo plays Oggy at darts and Drewy watches the football results on telly. Leeds end up losing 1-0 and Albion lose 2-0 to Bradford. At this, I thought I'd check the bet I had earlier. Fragrant Dawn wins 5-2, Kittinger wins 9-1 and I only need Sneakapenny for a fabulous treble. The thing should be put in a pie, as the donkey comes nowhere at 8-1. I can't stop thinking about this mule doing me out of £315 and I have another drink to drown my sorrows.

Moving on, we arrive at the *Worms Head Hotel* (Rhossili). It's a shame it's dark because this is the most beautifully situated hotel in Gower. It stands in a unique position high on the cliff edge overlooking Rhossili Bay. The name refers to the Worms Head, (which is derived from wurm – the Old English word for 'dragon'), a large rocky island jutting a mile out to sea. B&B is £16.50 per person. Next, we drive on to the *King Arthur Hotel* (Reynoldston). The gaffer Tony has been here seven years and hails from Coventry. I order a pasty but it arrives cold. Instead of complaining I chuck it down the bog. We head in the direction of Swansea stopping at the *Commercial Hotel* (Killay). Dawn decides to weigh herself in here and shouts to Oggy to take his foot off the scales. Oggy is nowhere near it and Dawn weighs in at 9 stone. We make the mistake of calling her Gert Bucket; this doesn't go down too well. Dawn has a wooty (sulk) on her and for the moment refuses to spake (speak) to us.

We're all clammed (hungry) now so it's into Swansea for excellent fish and chips. We then work our way northward and the *Railway Inn* (Tonna) is visited. This is followed by the *Harp Inn* (Merthyr Tydfil). Where Dawn disposes of all the drinks she's had today down the pon-hole (toilet). Next pub is the *Railway* (Abergavenny), then the *Bridge*

Inn (Llanfoist) and onto what should be our final pub of the day the *Lancaster Arms* (Pandy). Oggy insists we go in the *Rising Sun* down the road that we had visited back on September 25th 1988. He was hoping to see Ann the barmaid in there. Well, it turns out she's left and Oggy's not interested in stopping for an extra drink so we set off home. It's been a good tour today and another fabulous year of travels comes to an end.

The New Year begins, along with new challenges. It's January 1990. My scale model wall plaque of our 3,000th pub is now complete, along with its secret time capsule in the back of it. I've been and discussed the hand-over of this with Mr Ian Walden at the Black Country Museum and the date is arranged for Saturday 3rd February. Meanwhile we still have forty-eight pubs to visit so there's no time to waste. There are still a few pubs left to visit in the Cheltenham area. On our 6th tour to this town our 2,955th pub visit is the *Kemble Brewery*. We have the Archers bitter as the Archers Brewery in Swindon is celebrating its 'Thirst Decade' of brewing. The gaffer asks us a question. He said, "What Division 2 football team plays with 4 black players and 8 white players?"

"Hang on a minute gaffer, that means there's 12 players on the pitch." I replied.

"No, it doesn't. Have a think about it."

We're all stuck and give up guessing.

The gaffer then gives us the answer, which turns out to be a bit of a trick question. "It's your local team West Bromwich Albion, they have four black players and one of them is called Chris Whyte," he happily tells us. "Good un gaffer – like it."

Fancying himself as a stand-up comedian he went on.

"Can you spell hungry horse in four letters?"

"I haven't got a clue gaffer." I replied. "The answer is, M.T.G.G." (empty gee gee).

He's on a roll now and he comes out with another. "Name an

alcoholic drink with four letters starting with B and ending in a P?"

"You've got me again gaffer."

"It's BEER!"

Well, at least it's a jovial start to the New Year. He shouldn't give up his day job though!

The following Sunday on one of our numerous appearances in the Cheltenham area we go to Charlton Kings where we visit the *London Inn,* winner of the Cheltenham in Bloom competition in 1982, 3, 4 and 5. The landlord of this pub played football for Halesowen Town when Paddy Page (a friend of a pal of mine) was manager. Oggy gets a bad case of 'Hop Fever' and he sneezes twenty-two times beating his all time record by three. Not far out of town is the *Seven Springs* (Coberley). We're told that this is reputedly the source of the River Thames. At last, Cheltenham is finished. The following week we visit a pub called the *Cheese Rollers* (Shurdington), named after a strange annual event that takes place about three miles away at Cooper's Hill. Sue and Malcolm Mitchell are the proprietors and they briefly explain to me what it's all about. Every Spring Bank Holiday, villagers gather at the top of Cooper's Hill. At the command of a top-hatted Master of Ceremonies, the yampy buggers hurtle downhill in pursuit of an 8lb cheese that is rolled down the very steep hill and they try and catch it. Nobody ever does as it travels at 70 m.p.h. So it's the first across the finishing line. The winner receives a real Double Gloucester cheese as a prize. What a saft way to bost your legs! I'll keep my legs where they are meant to be; under a pub table!

It's our last beer run before a massive milestone in the BATS history takes place; our 3,000th pub. First, we must visit a few more, so tonight Sunday 28th January it's off to the Forest of Dean. We complete all the pubs in Cinderford before finishing in our final pub of the night the *Dog and Muffler* (Joyford). Over the years many licensees have given me quite a few black and white sketches of pubs, either on small business cards or postcards by a man called Alan Roulstone. This pub is no exception as the landlord gives me two more by this excellent artist. This is a comfortable old pub and we all finish off with two pints of Old Samuel Smith's brewery bitter. Leo turns Kermit green for the fust (first) time in wiks (weeks) and he's Bill and Dick outside the pub near to an eighteenth-century cider press. Meanwhile, Oggy carries on filling his belly with pickled eggs at 18p each and he's now become egg-bound and shell-shocked. In other words he's ommered (hammered). A sign on the wall says 'a teetotaller is one who suffers from thirst instead of enjoying it'. Incidentally, teetotal has nothing to do with drinking tea. It means a total abstinence from alcohol. With 'Tee' being the first letter in total.

Finally the day has arrived. It's Saturday 3rd February 1990. No one is driving today so we catch a taxi to the Black Country Museum, arriving at 1.30 p.m. The normal entry price is £3.50 each, but as we are the special guests today this is waived. Mr Ian Walden (museum director) is there to greet us along with the reporter and photographer from the local *Black Country Bugle* newspaper. Our pints of Mild are waiting for us too. Our **3,000th** pub, the Bottle and Glass has arrived at last. The hand-over of the metal model wall plaque is first on the agenda before we get yapping about our past exploits. The plaque is screwed onto the wall in the bar room of the museum pub and it is engraved with the names of all four remaining BATS: Joe Hill, Peter Hill, John Drew and Robert Jones (alias Leo). We have now officially become a little bit of Black Country history.

It makes a change for us to relax in just one pub instead of moving on to another, then another. Mr Walden gets us our next pint and he's chuffed to bits at the plaque we have presented to him and the fact we have raised £1,600 for local hospitals with a further £500 almost raised for the Smethwick Neurosurgery Hospital. With all the official business over, we all say a big thanks to Mr Walden and thank the *Bugle* for turning up to cover this milestone. We then raise our glasses to toast 3,000 pubs, "CHEERS!" Right... now for the serious stuff and it's time we hit the Mild for six (pints apiece).

Oggy tells us a story about PLUTO. No, not the Disney dog; the Pipe-Line Under The Ocean. None of us have ever heard of this. Oggy says he's proud of his connection with this historic pipeline and goes on to tell us all about it. "Well, back in 1979-80, Horace Keen who owned a scrapyard in Greets Green, West Bromwich, wanted a few lads to travel down with his son Graham to the Isle of Dogs, in London's East End, to another scrapyard owned by a Mrs O'Neill. She owned racehorses too."

This is one we ay heard of before, I thought. He continued. "So five of us worked down theer, cutting up this pipeline into twelve foot lengths and bringing them back to Keeny's tat yard for Wayne and Lowey to strip these lengths down for the scrap metal that was inside the black pitch casing of the pipe."

"What's so historic about that then," said a curious Drewy.

"The PLUTO pipeline was used to fuel the Normandy beaches after D-day in 1944, it was laid across the English Channel from the Isle of Wight and the Germans never knew how we were getting the fuel to our troops."

"Get out of it Oggy, yoem mekking it up!" laughed a gob smacked Leo.

"I ay, it's true honest, yoe ask Wayne," replied Oggy.

"Here Oggy, yoe need refuelling. Have another drink and shut up," I said, "Let's talk about pubs! Okay, who's still up for the challenge of touring the coastline of Great Britain and a drink in every county?" I asked.

They all agree to journey on. I explain the dedication and hardship it will take to complete such an adventure but they are all up for it and can't wait to start on our expeditions. If the future is to be anything like the past six years, it's going to be a hell of an achievement and one hell of a piss-up! The memories will hopefully stay with us forever and I still can't think of a better hobby than this.

"What's next then Hilly?" I am asked.

"3,001 of course!" It seemed obvious to me.